DAVID LEIBOW M.D.

HOW TO REAP THE REWARDS OF
ADULTHOOD
AND FIND REAL HAPPINESS

LOVE, PAIN
AND THE WHOLE
DAMN THING

VIKING

VIKING
Published by the Penguin Group
Penguin Books Canada Ltd, 10 Alcorn Avenue, Toronto, Ontario,
Canada M4V 3B2
Penguin Books Ltd, 27 Wrights Lane, London W8 5TZ, England
Viking Penguin, a division of Penguin Books USA Inc., 375 Hudson
Street, New York, New York 10014, U.S.A.
Penguin Books Australia Ltd, Ringwood, Victoria, Australia
Penguin Books (NZ) Ltd, 182–190 Wairau Road, Auckland 10, New
Zealand

Penguin Books Ltd, Registered Offices: Harmondsworth, Middlesex,
England

First published 1995
10 9 8 7 6 5 4 3 2 1

Printed and bound in Canada on acid free paper ∞

Canadian Cataloguing in Publication Data

Leibow, David, 1950–
    Love, pain and the whole damn thing

Includes bibliographical references and index.
ISBN 0-670-85949-4

1. Adulthood—Psychological aspects. I. Title.

BF724.5.L45 1995   155.6   C94-932641-0

For Sandra

One of the signs of passing youth
is the birth of a sense of fellowship
with other human beings as we take
our place among them.
                    Virginia Woolf

— —— —

To put it generally, all the valuable
qualities that youth and age divide
between them are united in the prime
of life, while all their excesses or
defects are replaced by moderation
and fitness.
                    Rhetoric II 14
                    Aristotle

ACKNOWLEDGEMENTS

I would like to acknowledge, in roughly chronological order, the contributions of a number of people.

By this criterion, as well as by many others, my parents, Kevey and Barbara Leibow, deserve to come first. Not only did they always believe in me and never fail to tell me so, but they always treated me like an adult even when I didn't feel like one.

My teachers and colleagues at the New York State Psychiatric Institute/Columbia-Presbyterian Medical Center, and the Columbia Center for Psychoanalytic Training and Research, and especially my patients in New York and in Toronto, taught me everything I know about psychiatry and inspired me with their intellect and hard work.

Tom Bernstein encouraged me on an earlier book that, although never published, earned his praise and support anyway, and gave me the incentive to keep trying. Dr. Norman Rosenthal inspired me with his own creative efforts and reminded me to write about what I know. Deepak Ramachandran, Drs. Phyllis and Michael Cedars, and Dr. Stephen Leibow gave me helpful suggestions and encouragement, especially on the more technical portions of the manuscript.

Irene Cox acted as my unofficial agent and took an active interest in my progress all along the way. Jackie Kaiser, my excellent editor at Penguin Canada, acquired the manuscript and vastly improved it. The value of her suggestions was inestimable, which makes her as an editor, estimable. Cynthia Good, the publisher of Penguin Canada, and her outstanding group of editors, designers, publicists, marketing and sales people helped transform my vision into reality.

My two wonderful daughters, Emily and Nicole—who have already given more to me than I can ever possibly give to them—made my life a joy and continue to give it meaning.

My wife Sandy—an attorney by profession but a writer by calling—never stinted in her forbearance and support during the three years of evenings, weekends and vacations that it took me to produce this book. She took up the slack when I was occupied with writing and editing, encouraged me when I was discouraged, gave me honest and useful criticism when I asked for it, and generally made my daily life so incredibly full that anything further will be mere gravy.

When I want to know what adult is, when I want to know what extraordinary is, when I want to know what happiness is, I need only think of her.

CONTENTS

LOVE, PAIN
AND THE WHOLE
DAMN THING

CHAPTER ONE

THE PURSUIT OF HAPPINESS

> Grown up, and that is a terribly hard thing to
> do. It is much easier to skip it and go from one
> childhood to another.
>
> *F. Scott Fitzgerald*

Adulthood is born of crisis. It is a crisis created by the collision of dreams and reality—the dreams that we've carried in the deepest recesses of our memory, and the reality of life as it is and as it can be. Depending on how we resolve this crisis, we can move forward to become adults, or fall back and remain in a state of limbo—neither adult nor adolescent.

Most of us grow up with a fantasy about what will make us happy and what happiness will feel like when we achieve it. It is a fantasy that has its origin in the oneness we feel with our mothers when we're very small, but it grows throughout childhood, nourished by the intensity of our needs and the intensity of our emotions. In childhood, it is both a fact and a memory. It is the fact of how happy we were on the day of our birthday or on Christmas Eve, and it is the reparative fantasy that consoled us when we were bitterly disappointed. It is a memory of the way we felt as infants when we were loved—or believed we were loved—absolutely and unconditionally by our parents, and it is the dream of love that consoled us when we were neglected and alone.

This sublime feeling, this memory of bliss, is composed not only of our parents' real or imagined love for us, but of our love for ourselves as well. It is a feeling that may never have existed, but only been dreamed of, yet it lodges in our mind like a fact and a memory and becomes a benchmark for all further experiences of happiness. It becomes our idea of ultimate happiness.

As we get older our dream of happiness begins to take on concrete form. We imagine that we'll be loved and admired and respected. We imagine that we'll have a beautiful house with a beautiful garden. We imagine that we'll do work that is challenging and fulfilling, work that we do better than anyone else, and work that is important. We might dream of having children, certainly of having friends and admirers. But we always dream of love—true love, deep love, love that transcends everything and that makes everything good and complete, love that recaptures and embodies the fantasy of happiness we've nurtured since before our memories began.

Though our fantasy of love may not be confirmed by what we see daily all around us, it is confirmed by what we read in romantic novels and especially by what we see in the movies. From the imaginations of romantic novelists and Hollywood screenwriters we learn that we can find true love and happiness and that dreams do come true. And, in truth, we can, and they sometimes do.

So we try to make our dream come true. We study and train. We build careers. We have adventures. We fortify our fantasy with new images from page and screen. We build friendships. We fall in love. We fall out of love. We continue to grow. And, from time to time, we have a small taste of the happiness we're seeking. Just a glimmer, perhaps, a brief moment, but enough to give us hope and to keep us striving.

Until one day we realize that, although we may be able to achieve a lot of what we thought would make us happy, we will still never be as happy as we dreamed we would be in our childhood fantasy. We will never recapture the state of bliss that we felt—or imagine we felt—when we were very, very young. It is this painful realization—the collision of fantasy and reality—that precipitates the crisis of pre-adulthood.

There are a few people, perhaps, who fulfil their childhood fantasies completely, and there are certainly a few who have success beyond their wildest dreams. But even these lucky few can't possibly achieve complete and unblemished happiness, and if that is their criterion for contentment, then their disappointment will be all the more bitter.

We have two choices when we confront this crisis of pre-adulthood: We can cling to our childhood fantasy and try even harder to achieve ultimate happiness, or we can modify our fantasy and try very hard to achieve real happiness instead. If we cling to our infantile fantasy of happiness, we will never completely grow up, but if we modify our notion of happiness so that it can be achieved in reality, we will become adults—and genuinely happy as well.

What is this fantasy of ultimate happiness and where does it lead? It is a feeling of oneness, of bliss, of utter love, of power, of euphoria, of limitless opportunity, of complete fulfilment, of ecstasy and of passion. We may feel it transiently when we paint a picture or write a story or compose a song, when we're listening to wonderful music, when we get a new job or a promotion or a raise, when we're driving or running in the sunshine, when we're dreaming or daydreaming, when we're making love, when we're beside the ocean, when we're a little high and dining with friends, when we win a tennis match or a lottery, when we discover the cure for an illness or a new subatomic particle or design a new microchip, when we sing a hymn or hum a song or when we perform a sacred or an heroic act. Most of all, we feel it when we fall in love.

But, try as we may, this feeling of ultimate happiness doesn't last. It can't last because we need variety in order to remain stimulated, and because constant stimulation itself can become boring. Life moves on, new experiences crowd in, and we soon taste the bitterness of disappointment once again.

Some people try to recapture the feeling of euphoria by thrill-seeking. They use drugs or alcohol, make lots of money or spend lots of money, have romantic affairs, become promiscuous, gamble, race cars, commit crimes. Some try to recapture the feeling by becoming workaholic or by seeking fame and power. Some try religion and some become cynics. Eventually, it's not euphoria they seek through thrill-seeking or work or fame, but relief from the everydayness of everyday life. Artists and manics can sometimes hold onto this feeling of euphoria for several weeks or months at a time, but even they can't bottle it for everyday use. And when they fall back to reality, as they always do, reality seems empty, flat and unfulfilling, and they land with a thud.

Children whose parents encouraged their infantile grandiosity by coddling and flattering them usually have considerable difficulty modifying their dreams in accordance with reality. But children whose parents forced them to escape into reparative fantasies of greatness by depriving and criticizing them, or by expressing chronic discontent with their own lives, always find it difficult to do so. They find it almost impossible to accept limits on their expectations, not because they've known great happiness, but because they haven't.

The crisis that gives birth to adulthood is the realization that we will never be able to achieve or sustain ultimate happiness. It is a painful realization, but a liberating one. Because once we accept the fact that we won't be able to achieve ultimate happiness, we're in a position to accept the fact that we can achieve real happiness. And once we're able to accept real happiness— the joys and challenges that real life provides—we're able to accept becoming adult. We may not feel bliss, or be able to maintain it when we do, but we can feel love and belonging, passion and pleasure, gratitude and fulfilment. We may not necessarily be able to achieve all our ambitions, but we can achieve some of them—and get satisfaction from those that we do. And we can continue to dream. We can continue to have fantasies and try to fulfil them. We just can't make those fantasies the basis of our current happiness.

Resolving our pre-adult crisis involves living our lives with joy and hope, pursuing our goals with enthusiasm and energy, resisting despair and cynicism, and continuing to work and grow. If we accept life in its entirety—love, pain and the whole damn thing—then we'll be able to achieve real happiness and learn to become adults too.

— —— —

Learning to become an adult is a lot like learning to ride a bicycle. In order to become a cyclist you have to be physically and mentally ready, and you have to be in the grip of an almost unbearable desire to break free of the pedestrian life. (It's the enthusiasm that helps you to overcome the fear.) Then, all it takes is a bicycle, someone willing to run along beside you, and a bit of perseverance.

At first you struggle. You wobble down the sidewalk in a confusion of disconnected actions—cycling, braking, steering, balancing, remembering to breathe, looking for an emergency patch of grass—with your father or mother, or perhaps an older brother or sister, puffing in your wake. Then all of a sudden, in one miraculous flash of insight, you get it. You acquire an intuitive understanding of the principle of centrifugal force, and a half dozen disconnected actions merge instantly into one smooth motion. The bicycle stays upright. Your helper lets go of the seat, jogs to a stop and recedes behind you. Then, for the first time in your life—balanced on a ribbon of hot rubber, flowing through an ocean of cool air—you are free. You've made it. You're a cyclist.

Learning to become an adult follows a similar course. Having mastered a critical number of adult behaviours, you begin to sense you are on the verge of a momentous change. The images you have of yourself performing each of these adult behaviours are still disconnected in your mind, yet you feel ready and eager for the change to begin. So, in a process of assembly that takes place with astonishing rapidity, these fragmentary, adult self-images are gathered up like the pieces of a jigsaw puzzle to form a new, coherent self-portrait. Preparing to be an adult may take many years—in some cases until the age of forty or later—but actually *feeling* adult, when it finally happens, takes less than a day. In a crystalline moment of self-awareness you go from feeling like a kid to feeling like an adult. Then, just as when you learned to ride a bicycle, the unpleasant feelings of turbulence and uncertainty you felt beforehand give way to exhilarating feelings of pleasure and competence.

The act of becoming an adult, however, like the act of becoming a cyclist, is not just the acquisition of an exciting new skill. It is the discovery of a whole new state of mind. And along with this new state of mind come new freedoms, new responsibilities, new horizons and new adventures.

Love, Pain and the Whole Damn Thing is designed as a guide for those who are working towards becoming adults and those who are going through the motions of acting adult but who still don't feel adult. It examines why being an adult—and feeling like an adult—makes life easier, and it explains what we have to do in order to become one.

In chemical reactions that produce new compounds, the old bonds between atoms have to be broken before the new bonds can be formed. This change won't take place, however, without the application of a strong force—energy—to get it started. Hydrogen and oxygen won't combine to form a molecule of water just by being pumped into the same jar. There has to be a spark.

As it is with the creation of a new molecule, so it is with the creation of a new adult. The proper elements certainly have to be present in the right proportions. But to make it happen, there must be a spark.

The purpose of *Love, Pain and the Whole Damn Thing* is to identify the elements that have to be present before you can become an adult.

The spark? That's up to you.

CHAPTER TWO

FEELING ADULT

Your lordship, though not clean past your
youth, hath yet some smack of age in you, some
relish of the saltness of time.
            Henry IV Part II
            Act I, Scene 2, 99–102
            William Shakespeare

The Easy Way to Go Through Life

We all want to become adults, yet we all have some fear of it.
We covet the pleasures and privileges of adulthood, yet we fear
the responsibilities and risks. So we inch forward through our
twenties and thirties nibbling at adulthood, but not quite digging
in.

We refuse to accept ultimate responsibility for anything. We
insist that there must be someone else who knows more than we
do, who's better prepared, more experienced and more willing
to be accountable than we are. We sit in our office, at our work-
bench or in our kitchen, and we think to ourselves: I'd better
check this out with somebody else first—my boss, my colleagues, my wife, my husband, my friends, my siblings, my
parents—anyone but me. And we try to reassure ourselves
that—thank God!—we're not the ones who have to make the
final decision. If we had a sign on our desk it would say, "The
buck stops *there*."

Yet deep down we know this passive stance is neither right

nor good. We know that we can't be adult unless we do take ultimate responsibility. And we *want* to be adult because, at some level, we know that being adult is not just inevitable, but easier and a lot more fun than continuing to be a scared wannabe.

But how do we overcome our fear? The adults we're most familiar with are our parents, and we don't necessarily want to turn out like them. And if we were to become our own court of last resort, then to whom would we appeal when we make a mistake? Who would be our safety net when we fall? Who would let us off the hook when we screw up?

So here we are at twenty-five, or thirty-five, or maybe even forty-five years old, still feeling like a kid because of our fear of growing up. And still faking it so that nobody else will know how insecure we feel about ourselves. We go through the motions of being adult—acting in a dignified manner, controlling our emotions, trying to be independent, and pretending to feel confident—so we won't blow our cover and get found out. And we keep waiting for someone to point at us and say, "You don't know what you're talking about!" or "I thought you said you were an expert on this!" or "Perhaps there's someone else here who can help me"—something that strips away our adult façade.

The problem is that we want it both ways. We want to be considered professional, yet retain our amateur standing at the same time. We want to enjoy the perks and prerogatives of adulthood, yet retain access to the excuses and freedoms of childhood.

Becoming adult is a struggle. It's a good news/bad news situation.

The bad news is: You can't be an adult and a child at the same time. You can't have the benefits of adulthood without the obligations. You can't have the rights without the responsibilities. And you can't have the pleasures without the pains.

The good news is: You *can* be an adult if you're prepared to stop being a child. You can have the benefits if you take on the obligations. You can have the rights if you assume the responsibilities. And you can have the pleasures if you learn to accept and deal with the pains.

Either way you're going to get older. You're going to have to try to solve problems, overcome misfortunes, endure losses, handle failures and successes, choose between right and wrong, and generally make your own way in the world. There's an easy way to do it, and a hard way. Being an adult—and feeling like one—is the easy way.

The Moment of Recognition

The moment of recognition—when we first see ourselves as adult—takes place only after many years of preparation. It may take place dramatically, in a flash of excitement and joy; quietly, in a moment of reflection and insight; or subtly, in a transient feeling that's scarcely detected and quickly forgotten. And though everything outside stays the same, everything inside changes. Though nothing in the world is really different, nothing looks quite as it did. In a gentle, pensive, bitter-sweet, but definite way, everything gets suddenly harder—and much, much easier too.

As an example, let's look at the case of Stewart, a thirty-five-year-old married man with three daughters, who came to see me because of problems in his marriage.

Stewart complained that his wife, Liz, was always nagging him to take more responsibility around the house, to help more with domestic chores, and to spend more time with their children.

As Stewart first began to describe his situation, it sounded as though Liz might have been making unreasonable demands on him. He told me that, in addition to working long hours at a very demanding job, he would perform whatever tasks Liz gave him to do when he got home. If she asked him to read the kids a bedtime story, he read the kids a bedtime story. If she asked him to empty the dishwasher, he emptied the dishwasher. Whatever she asked him to do, he did.

On further examination, however, the true nature of Stewart's co-operation soon became apparent. Whatever Liz asked him to do, he did—but in his own sweet time. Whatever she didn't ask him to do, he didn't do. Instead of taking the initiative when he saw that something around the house needed doing, he waited to be told about it and then did it grudgingly. Nevertheless, despite his campaign of domestic disobedience, Stewart considered himself not merely a liberated man, but a feminist.

We must, of course, respectfully disagree with Stewart. He is no more a feminist than a hen-pecked husband. He is, if anything, a passive-aggressive hair-splitter, who follows the letter of the law while flouting its spirit and then likes to complain that he's being oppressed. He does only the minimum asked of him, and even that he does in a foot-dragging fashion designed to drive other people—especially his wife—crazy. He isn't averse to taking the credit for being a liberated man, he just isn't keen on taking the responsibility.

Stewart's passive-aggressive behaviour was the direct result of a stunted self-image. He saw himself, not as an adult, but as a put-upon kid. It was Liz whom he saw as the true adult in the family. The buck stopped with her. She was the responsible parent. She looked after the house. She was the boss. He was only an employee, who, for reasons of his own, was on a work-to-rule campaign.

When Stewart was growing up, his father had been excessively strict and domineering. Stewart responded to this tyranny by doing just enough of what his father asked him in order to avoid open warfare, but not enough to give his father real satisfaction. He waged an underground rebellion.

Before marrying Liz, Stewart had lived on his own for three years. Soon after they got married, he began to re-enact with Liz the same rebellious role he'd enacted with his father. By playing the part of the hard-done-by adolescent, he forced her to play the role of the unreasonable oppressor—the role once played by his father.

But if Stewart knew that reprising this role would lead to so much conflict with his wife, why would he do it? The reason is that he didn't know he was reprising this role. He consciously believed he was responding appropriately to what he considered to be her unreasonable demands. He was unconscious of the fact that he was behaving like a rebellious kid towards Liz and that she reminded him of his father.

Once Stewart became conscious of this dynamic through his therapy, however, he did try to change his behaviour. He began, consciously, to shed the role of adolescent rebel in his relationship with Liz; he began, unconsciously, to identify with his father's real but unrecognized strengths, instead of reflexively rebelling against his familiar tyrannical weaknesses.

The changes weren't easy for Stewart to make—they took considerable effort. His laziness and rebelliousness were deeply ingrained. Like all bad habits, they popped up regularly despite his best intentions. But Stewart persevered. He was ashamed of his immaturity, and he tried hard to overcome it. And, over a period of many months, he did. He began to react to the clearly perceived present instead of the dimly remembered past. Whenever he was just about to shirk his responsibilities and dump them on Liz, for example, or whenever he was tempted to argue with her about the suggestions she was making, he would stop for a moment and remind himself that he wasn't her fourth child, but another leader of the family on whom they all depended. For the first time in his life, Stewart was able to see himself as he really was—not as his father's rebellious adolescent son, but as his wife's adult husband.

As a result of this new self-image, Stewart found it much easier to assume his share of the family responsibilities without being asked. And because Liz, in turn, had to issue fewer reminders and requests, things between them started to go much more smoothly.

Once he felt like an adult, Stewart was able to undertake with ease and satisfaction domestic duties that, in the past, he had undertaken only with great difficulty and reluctance. Because he understood his rebelliousness, he was able to transcend it. He no longer felt compelled to respond to household tasks as though they were being thrust upon him by a strict parent. He could see them now as duties that were perfectly commensurate with his role as husband and father. He performed them not out of reluctant submission to authority, but out of adult pride, and as a result, made his life a whole lot easier.

What Does Becoming an Adult Feel Like?

The realization that you've become an adult produces a thorough change in your mental life. It is at once intellectual, psychological and social.

You re-evaluate your past from the vantage point of your new adult self-image. Events that appeared to you in one light when you were going through them as a child or adolescent may now appear to you in a different light—in their true light—when you review them as an adult.

Perhaps your high school sweetheart dumped you just before the prom because you weren't cool enough, and ever since then, you've felt slightly goofy and embarrassed. But now that you feel adult, and being uncool is no longer such an issue for you, you can look back at that rejection without having to feel so inadequate and ashamed.

Or perhaps you felt doomed to become an underachiever because your sixth-grade teacher told you that you were too lazy ever to amount to anything. So even when you managed to do well in high school and college and in your various jobs since then, you continued to feel like an impostor. But now, reviewing that period from an adult perspective, you realize that you weren't lazy all the time as a kid: When you were doing things that interested you—and that included a lot of things— you enjoyed working hard and poured yourself into them. You're able to shed the image you have of yourself as an underachiever, and you can stop feeling like an impostor.

When you realize that you're an adult, you begin to think and feel differently, not just about yourself, but about the world as well. Some people who've undergone the transition to adulthood describe feeling as if they've taken on psychological ballast, as if they have more psychic weight and take up more psychic space. Political commentators like to say of a politician with this weighty quality that he or she has "gravitas" or is "presidential." The rest of us say of someone with this quality that he or she has substance or depth.

Being a person of substance gives you the feeling that you have a legitimate place in the world, that, as a person, you count—which means on one hand that you have to be taken into account by the world, and on the other hand that the world has to be taken into account by you.

Once you realize that you're an adult, there is also a change in self-acceptance and in the comfort you feel with yourself. Before the shift takes place, you may feel that you're acting like an adult, but you don't necessarily feel that you *are* an adult. After the shift takes place, you not only feel that you are an adult, but—in the sense of pretending to be something you're not—you stop feeling that you're acting like anything else but yourself.

The Change in Self-image

The change in self-image that takes place when you begin to see yourself as an adult resembles the feeling you get when you hold up side by side two photos of yourself—one taken five or ten years earlier, and one taken that same day. It's the kind of feeling you might experience when you get a new passport and compare it to your old one.

As you look at each of these two photos—the old and the new—you see similarities and differences. There is change, obviously, but there is continuity as well. You may not like the way you looked in the old photo, but the image is at least comfortable and familiar. You may not like all the changes you see in the new photo, but the image is at least up to date and accurate. During the transition period, just after you obtain your new photo, you may visualize yourself in your mind's eye sometimes in the old way and sometimes in the new. But when you visualize yourself in the old way, the image that forms in your mind no longer feels right to you: It doesn't incorporate the changes you know you've undergone. Yet when you visualize yourself in the new way, the image you form still doesn't feel familiar, though you know it shows you the way you really are.

As it is with getting a new passport photo, so it is with seeing yourself as an adult. During the transition period—which can last for several years—you see yourself sometimes as a pre-adult and sometimes as an adult. You may see yourself as a pre-adult

when you're feeling anxious or overwhelmed, and as an adult
when you're feeling calm and confident. You may see yourself
as a pre-adult when you're visiting your parents or being reprimanded by a cop for speeding, and as an adult when you're
making love or conducting a meeting or supervising your staff
or children.

Eventually, of course, you come to see yourself as an adult
almost all the time. When you do see yourself as a child or adolescent or pre-adult, you do so voluntarily, or at least consciously, because you want to recapture some part of the past, not
involuntarily because you can't cope with the present. You
regress for pleasure, and for art, to rejuvenate your spirit, and
perhaps even to learn more about who you are and where you
came from. But you don't stay there. Because once you've
made the transition to adulthood, once you've gotten into the
habit of seeing yourself as an adult, you can't go back to seeing
yourself routinely as anything else.

Simone began to see herself as an adult at the age of twen-
ty-seven, when she was given people to supervise at work.
She didn't feel adult for good, however, until she had a
baby at the age of thirty-one and had to take total responsibility for him.

Despite having graduated from engineering school and
having worked for NASA for seven years, Alexandra
didn't feel like an adult until her mother died when
Alexandra was thirty.

Kurt began to see himself as an adult when he graduated
from law school and got a job working in the government.
But he didn't feel really adult until he started a serious
relationship with the woman he ended up marrying.

Hanna, a thirty-two-year-old teacher married to a forty-
one-year-old film producer, felt like an adult when she was
teaching her tenth graders, but like a pre-adult when she
was socializing with her husband's colleagues. They were
such a cocky and self-assured bunch that, without trying to,

they made her feel pretty insignificant. However, one day during a dinner party she was giving, she overheard a few of them name-dropping and gossiping about people in the business who were even more cocky and self-assured than they were, and she had a sudden realization that made her feel differently both about them and about herself. She realized that her husband's colleagues, and all the other people who intimidated her, were no different from her or from anyone else, and that she had no reason at all to feel inferior to them. Because of this insight she felt like an adult all the time and much more confident when she was with her husband's colleagues.

If you've already accumulated a number of critical experiences that you associate with being adult, then the addition of any more such experiences will strain your pre-adult self-image. You won't be able to comfortably integrate the experiences of having a baby, losing a parent, getting married or feeling unintimidated until you start seeing yourself as an adult.

When this moment of self-awareness happens, and you know with certainty that you've become an adult, the experience is different from all the other inklings of it that you've had before. The experience has a clarity and rightness to it that permits no other interpretation but that you've crossed the line into adulthood once and for all, and that you are now permanently an adult.

Resistance to Change

Large-scale and fairly sudden shifts in perception and understanding, like the change in self-image that accompanies the transition to adulthood, are well recognized in many disciplines. In religion, for example, this kind of phenomenon is called an epiphany—a manifestation of the divine presence that leads to a sudden and convincing affirmation of faith. In science, this type of profound change is called a paradigm shift—a term that was coined by the sociologist of science, Thomas Kuhn, to describe a revolution in the way scientists perceive and investigate nature.

In both cases—the epiphany and the paradigm shift—something out of the ordinary takes place that changes irrevocably the way we see the world. Unlike the normal, incremental accretion of knowledge that results from our everyday way of thinking, the increase in knowledge that results from an epiphany or a paradigm shift is abnormal and massive. The change is sudden, radical and unprecedented. An insight of this magnitude is more than just a giant quantitative leap in knowledge; it is a thoroughgoing qualitative departure from the past.

The discoveries of Copernicus, Galileo, Darwin and Einstein all produced shifts in the prevailing scientific paradigm. And as we know from the popular depictions of these intellectual revolutions, they were not always greeted with enthusiasm by the scientific and social establishments of their day. If the revolution is radical enough to threaten the sacred beliefs of the larger society, the new knowledge and its proponents may be repudiated and suppressed.

But resistance to looking at the world in radically new ways doesn't result just from political prejudice, it results from intellectual prejudice and from limitations in the way our minds work as well. As Kuhn points out, the resistance to a shift in paradigm is partly the result of a naturally existing mental inertia that makes it nearly impossible to break the ingrained habits of perception. That's why it takes a visionary—someone who actually "sees" the world differently—to break the grip of an old paradigm, and establish a new one that accounts for all the data. When that happens, there is a total change in the accepted view of things—the consensual reality. The sun stops revolving around the earth, and the earth starts revolving around the sun.

Freud discovered a more important source of resistance to new ideas: They scare us. They threaten our psychic equilibrium. We don't resist unsettling ideas just because they're socially taboo, we resist them because they're personally threatening. And we don't just consciously suppress them, we unconsciously *repress* them. The psyche puts the kibosh on threatening ideas before we're even aware of them. Mind you, they don't stay repressed—they're entirely too juicy for that. They push their way into consciousness through fantasies, dreams, symptoms, and disguised actions.

The change in self-image that we undergo when we stop seeing ourselves as pre-adults and begin to see ourselves as adults is a psychic revolution too. And it provokes just as much resistance. One form of resistance is intellectual—the mental inertia (best described by Kuhn) that makes it difficult even for scientists to see things differently. The other, more important, form of resistance is psychological—the various mental defence mechanisms (best described by Freud) that cause us to ward off and repress disturbing thoughts and feelings.

These two forces keep us from seeing ourselves as adults until an unexpected reaction, a comment, a reflection in the mirror or some other novel and incongruous experience, forces us to shift our perspective and makes it possible for us—indeed necessary for us—to change our self-image.

This leads me to my final point. Somewhere along the line, if only briefly, we have to actually *think* about the fact that we've stopped seeing ourselves as pre-adults and started seeing ourselves as adults. We have to become conscious of the fact that we've changed our self-image. The events leading up to this change don't have to be conscious; the recognition of this change does. In order to be able to construct a coherent self-portrait, we have to consciously *know* that we've become adult.

Why is consciousness a necessary step in seeing ourselves as adult? The answer depends partly on theoretical ideas and partly on clinical experience. The tradition of analytically based psychotherapy is "to make the unconscious conscious." If repressed knowledge emerges into consciousness, it means that the internal resistance to it has been weakened. Once it has been let out of quarantine, the embargoed material is finally free to mingle with the rest of our memories and perceptions and to find its proper place in our understanding.

There certainly are cases where complex synthetic mental activity seems to have taken place outside conscious awareness. The German chemist August Kekulé, for example, is said to have discovered the ring structure of the benzene molecule while dreaming of snakes biting each other's tails. Nevertheless, before any use could be made of this dreamlike creativity, it first had to see the light of day. Had Kekulé's model of the benzene molecule remained in the cryptic form in which it originally appeared to him in his dream, even he might have ignored it. Before his dream image could have any meaning, he first had to express it in conventional chemical nomenclature—a deliberate conscious process.

Perhaps all new discoveries are synthesized in the unconscious part of the mind first, and are then shipped to the conscious part of the mind to be assembled and labelled. If that's true, then conscious recognition of the fact that we see ourselves as adults may only be the late manifestation of a process that's been brewing in the basement of our unconscious for a long, long time.

But the main reason for the delay in seeing ourselves as adults is that it's too threatening—which is why it doesn't happen as soon as we're physically mature or when we first leave home. Facing adulthood precipitates a crisis. It forces us to make an unprecedented accommodation with reality. And before we can make such an accommodation—before we can consciously admit that we're really adult—we first have to feel confident that we'll be able to handle it. We have to believe that we're ready to deal with the responsibilities and freedoms of living adult lives.

CHAPTER THREE

THE THREE PRIMARY TRAITS
OF ADULTHOOD

> We have not passed that subtle line between
> childhood and adulthood until we move from
> the passive voice to the active voice—that is,
> until we have stopped saying "It got lost," and
> say, "I lost it."
>
> *Sydney J. Harris*

What is an adult? What traits do adults possess that make us
think of them as such? Do they display admirable qualities such
as stability, virtue, generosity, wisdom, responsibility, reliabili-
ty, a degree of selflessness, unflappability, fairness, understanding and honesty? Or do we think of them as adult because they
seem self-possessed, strong, integrated, autonomous, coura-
geous, authoritative and competent—in short, their own per-
sons? Do they intimidate us? Are they powerful, frightening,
authoritarian and tyrannical? Or is it simply that they've lived
long enough to have achieved a certain stature and to demonstrate the physical evidence of having weathered a few storms?

The first requirement for being considered an adult is having
reached a certain age. Since that age will vary according to culture and historical epoch, let's be arbitrary about this and say
that adulthood is the age at which you achieve physical maturity—the age at which there is no further growth in height. This
endpoint, initiated by puberty but not usually reached until the

early twenties, is attained when the growth plates at the ends of the long bones seal shut. (For the medically inclined, this is called closure of the epiphyses.)

Physical maturity is certainly necessary for feeling adult, but it isn't sufficient. And since psychological and social maturity both take considerably longer to develop than does physical maturity, most people stop getting taller long before they start feeling adult.

There are three other traits, besides physical maturity, that everyone needs to possess in order to feel psychologically and socially mature. First is the ability to take responsibility for yourself. Second is the ability to take responsibility for other people. And third is the ability to function competently in certain specific spheres of activity. These three traits are at the very core of what we mean when we say that someone is an adult, and all three have to be present before we're able to say it.

There are twelve secondary traits of adulthood but, unlike the three primary traits discussed in this chapter, they are not mandatory for being adult.

TAKING RESPONSIBILITY FOR YOURSELF

The ability to take responsibility for yourself involves two developmental achievements that are fundamental to any meaningful concept of what it is to be adult. The first developmental achievement is the attainment of self-sufficiency. The second is the attainment of self-government. For the sake of clarity, I'll call the attainment of self-sufficiency *independence* and the attainment of self-government *autonomy*.

Independence is more familiar and easier to understand than autonomy. When we say that someone has achieved independence we mean he's able to look after himself—that he's able to get his physical and emotional needs met without having to rely excessively on anyone else. But what do we mean by the term autonomy? What does it mean to say that someone has achieved the capacity to be self-governing? When we say that a state is autonomous we mean that it has its own government, makes its own laws and polices itself. When we say that a person is autonomous we mean nearly the same thing. We mean that he thinks for himself, makes his own decisions and accepts responsibility for his own actions. A person who has achieved autonomy has developed free will.

Let's examine these two components of the capacity to take responsibility for yourself one at a time.

Independence

Total independence is an impossibility. No one can achieve complete self-sufficiency, and no one should even want to try. It is our dependence on one another that makes us social beings and leads us to become civilized. We depend on one another for our material needs, our bodily comforts, our emotional sustenance, our entertainment, our enlightenment and our inspiration. We divide up our tasks and our talents, our products and privileges. All we can achieve in our individual lives is relative independence.

But how much independence do we need in order to become adult? The quick answer is that we need enough independence to be able to survive no matter whom we lose from our lives. In general terms, it will mean that we're dependent on other people, but that, if necessary, we could live without, or replace, any one of them. And in specific terms, it will mean that we can look after ourselves without any help from our parents (or later our spouse).

To become independent we need to be able to provide for our own physical and emotional needs by earning a living, obtaining food, clothing, shelter and health care, and by forming relationships with other people for our mutual benefit, companionship and love. Nothing less, and nothing more, is required.

Autonomy

To become autonomous a great deal more is required. Autonomy, as I'm using the term here, is a more complex concept than the concept of independence, and it is also a more subtle one. Autonomy means the capacity to govern yourself, to be truly your own boss. Autonomy, therefore, implies the acquisition and exercise of free will. It means having a mind of your own. Autonomy is the engine of moral, political, psychological and personal choice. It's what makes you accountable for your own actions. It's what allows you to be responsible not just for yourself, but to yourself as well. Autonomy is the *sine qua non* of adulthood: Without it you're just an aging kid.

Whereas independence has to do with the relationship between a person and one or more other people, autonomy has to do with the relationship between a person and his or her own self—with his or her own soul. If you are independent, you are independent from somebody or something else. But if you are autonomous, you do not require somebody or something else as a reference point at all.

The achievement of independence often seems to require a struggle with external authority—rebellion. The achievement of autonomy does not. It requires a struggle with internal ambivalence instead. The struggle to achieve independence and the struggle to achieve autonomy might both result in the same final action, but in each case, the motive for acting, and the process by which the decision to act was reached, would be quite different. To be independent, you'd have to take into account how your action would be seen by other people. To be autonomous, you'd have to take into account only how your action would be seen by your own conscience.

As an example, suppose Jane has grown up in a family that is deeply religious. They go to church every Sunday and say grace before every meal. At age five Jane accompanies her parents to church every Sunday and says grace before every meal without deciding for herself whether she wishes to be religious. She is too young to be either independent of her parents or autonomous in her own thinking.

At age sixteen, however, Jane decides that going to church every Sunday isn't cool. She refuses to go. She isn't sure what she believes, but she does know that she's tired of doing things just because her parents do them. At age sixteen Jane is trying to become independent of her parents, and she is doing so by rebelling against their values. She is not autonomous in her thinking, however, because she hasn't yet made up her own mind about her religious beliefs.

At age twenty-five, Jane has made a home for herself in a different city from her parents. She hasn't attended church in many years, and her parents have all but given up mentioning it to her. One Sunday, however, Jane decides to go to church. She doesn't mention it to her parents right away; she wants to decide how she feels about it first. As she listens to the prayers and the sermon and the choir, she begins to feel differently about the place of religion in her life. She decides—for herself—that she wants to cultivate the spiritual side of her life and that she will begin to attend church when she feels like it.

At this point Jane is operating autonomously. Her decision about her religious practice, though quite conventional, is entirely her own. She is neither rebelling against her parents, nor submitting to them. She might equally have decided not to make religion a part of her life. It wouldn't have mattered. What mattered was that she made up her own mind.

If you develop autonomy—if you acquire the capacity to make up your own mind—you might end up being independent of other people's points of view, but that would not have been your goal. Independence in this case would be a coincidence. That's why you can't tell whether individuals are autonomous merely by knowing what they think. You would have to know how they arrived at what they think. An autonomous person might have views that are quite conventional, whereas a non-autonomous person might have views that are quite unconventional—ideas he or she picked up from family, friends or even the media.

Of course, no one is totally autonomous, and certainly no one is autonomous all the time. There are many occasions, in fact, when we don't think particularly deeply about important issues, and just go along with the sentiments prevailing around us. Under special circumstances, such as when we're listening to stirring music or watching a storm or making love, we can even find it deeply pleasurable to voluntarily surrender our autonomy to the powerful, oceanic and awe-inspiring feelings that are welling up inside us. And there are many occasions when we're unable to exercise complete freedom of the will simply because we aren't fully conscious of our options. This ignorance can be the result of limited knowledge or of neurotic repression, but either way it curtails our capacity to be autonomous.

The point is, though, that if we put our minds to it, we could arrive at our own conclusions on the important issues that affect us, and, most of the time, this is exactly what we do. That's autonomy.

SELF-ACCEPTANCE

There can be no autonomy without self-acceptance.

Parents, therapists, educators, prison reformers and public policy makers sometimes operate as if they believed that human beings could be endlessly improved. They have boundless faith in the power of education, therapy, legislation, litigation and social engineering to eradicate the unpleasant parts of human nature. They subscribe to the doctrine of infinite perfectibility. Would that it were so.

Some things can be changed, and it's often worthwhile to try to change them. But many things can't be changed, and it's best to learn to accept and to deal with them. Complicating matters further, the "good" and "bad" elements of human nature are hopelessly entangled. If we try to dissect out the bad strands, we run the risk of removing some of the good ones as well. There are people who are obsessively perfectionist but wonderfully focused, for example, and people who are annoyingly self-centred but spectacularly imaginative. Erase the bad and you may end up damaging the good.

Moreover, change takes time. Most of the things we can change can't be changed overnight, and even when we think we've succeeded in changing them, they return to confound us.

In order to be autonomous, we have to be able to sort out for ourselves what we can change and what we can't. We have to keep in mind not only that change takes time, but that it's often incomplete. Therefore, achieving self-acceptance means having to unlearn the doctrine of infinite perfectibility. And that usually means learning to disagree with a lot of well-meaning, but coercive, experts.

FOLLOWING YOUR DREAM

The most powerful force in establishing a feeling of autonomy is following your own dream. The happiest people in the world, and the most autonomous, are those who are doing what they love. If you're lucky, you find this thing you love to do in childhood. Sometimes it's a talent that can't be denied, but more often it's a dream that you want to make come true.

Here is how the highly regarded author V.S. Naipaul realized his dream of becoming a writer:

> [My father] made the vocation of writer seem the noblest in the world; and I decided to be that noble thing.
>
> I had no gift. At least, I was aware of none. I had no precocious way with words, no talent for fantasy or story-telling. But I began to build my life around the writing ambition. The gift I thought was going to come later, when I grew up. Purely from wishing to be a writer, I thought of myself as a writer.... There were one or two boys at [school] who wrote better than I. There was at least one boy...who was far better read and had a more elegant mind. The literary superiority of this boy didn't make me doubt my vocation. I just thought it odd—after all, it was I who was going to be the writer.[1]

This was his payoff when he wrote his first novel many years later:

> Then for three weeks at a stretch I worked on my novel. I wrote with joy. And as I wrote, my conviction grew. My childhood dream of writing had been a dream of fame and escape and an imagined elegant style of life. Nothing in my father's example or conversation had prepared me for the difficulties of narrative prose.... But, equally, nothing had prepared me for the liberation and absorption, [and the] joy.[2]

The reason that pursuing your dreams reinforces autonomy is that doing so invariably involves resisting the inner temptation (and the pressure from other people) to do the tried and true, the possible and the practical. Keeping the flame alive within yourself takes passion, self-knowledge and strength. If you pursue your own most cherished aims despite your own doubts (and the doubts of others), then you have firmly established the basis for autonomy.

Most of us, unfortunately, get waylaid en route to pursuing our dreams. We are told that we don't have the talent or the discipline, that the chances of success are very low, that our dream isn't practical or profitable, or that we're too young or too old to try it. Any of these considerations may have some merit. And all of them are offered by people who only want the best for us, and who may even be right.

All important decisions involve trying to balance competing goods. Artistic self-expression is good, but so is making enough money to be able to support yourself. Having intellectual stimulation from solitary scholarship is good, but so is having contact with other people. Helping other people is good, but so is helping your family and yourself. Too often these choices are presented as though they were irreconcilable. The trick is to find out what good qualities and behaviours are truly important to you—which involves some capacity to anticipate what your needs will be in the future—and then to find a way of reconciling them with the demands of reality.

The cliché case of irreconcilable differences is the Al Jolson story. Al's father wanted him to be a cantor and sing in the synagogue, but Al wanted to be a jazz singer. As we know, Al went on to become the famous actor-singer who made the first talking movie—thus proving that he was right and his father was wrong. Of course, if Al had ended up singing jingles in Ishtar, instead of schmaltzy songs on the stage and screen, we might have come to a different conclusion about who was right, and we might have wondered about the advisability of always following your dream.

There are a million of these stories, all revolving around a generational conflict—the kid wants to pursue her dreams, and the parents want her to enter the family business or some other safe job. There are two facts to note about these Hollywood tales: (1) the kid had a true and valid passion, not merely a desire to rebel, and (2) in order to heighten the drama, the parents have to be depicted as old-fashioned, narrow-minded or frightened of the world. In most real families (unfortunately not all), parents are generally supportive of their children's dreams, or at least benignly indifferent, and the children are respectful of their parents' wisdom, or at least not reflexively dismissive.

Nevertheless, you can't be autonomous, or happy, doing only what you *think* other people think is right for you; you have to do what you think is right for you. You do have to be realistic, of course—there's no point in trying to be a pilot if you have bad vision—but there is almost always a way to make most reasonable dreams come true. If you fail in the pursuit of your own dreams, you may feel disappointed but you won't feel disillusioned. If you succeed in the pursuit of other people's dreams, you may feel successful but you won't feel fulfilled.

MORAL AUTONOMY

Of all forms of autonomy, moral autonomy is the most important. This is a fact recognized both in law and by custom. An adult is expected to know the difference between right and wrong and to live by that knowledge. She is expected to know the consequences of her actions and to take full moral responsibility for them.

When a person makes the transition to adulthood, the basis on which she makes decisions about right and wrong changes. It goes from mere rule following to moral reasoning. Instead of just obeying the law, the newly minted adult identifies with the nuanced and abstract principles underlying the law—not just with existing laws and mores, but with universal human values; not merely with *realpolitik*, but with real politics; and not only with the *status quo*, but with the noblest of human aspirations.

She doesn't behave morally out of a fear of punishment for breaking the rules. She behaves morally out of a sacred trust that weaves her into the social fabric. She takes as her conscience not just the authority of her own parents, but the abstract authority of humankind's highest ideals. Liberated from mere obedience to parental authority, the morally autonomous adult becomes, in a psychic sense, her own parent. Her adult conscience becomes the embodiment of principles of civilized conduct—as she understands them—rather than a mere repository of local rules and regulations.

What does all this mean? For one thing, moral autonomy permits the adult a greater acceptance of her own sexuality. Adult morality is sexually liberating because it is less automatically tied to social convention. For another thing, moral autonomy permits an adult to stand against the mainstream in following the dictates of her own conscience (not to be confused with mere rebelliousness).

Adults can't easily subordinate their morality to that of a charismatic leader or tyrant because to do so would be tantamount to re-assuming a childlike self-image (which is precisely what people in the thrall of a demagogue often want to do). Yet they can identify with a great and noble cause. They have an instinctive allegiance to their own moral code (not necessarily identical with society's moral code) and will vigorously defend it, but they have an instinctive aversion to the imposition of someone else's moral code (fanaticism) and will vigorously oppose it.

But given the complexity of the world we live in, and the number of different moral viewpoints that exist out there, how strong should our moral conviction be? And given the number of transgressions we're likely to make anyway, how do we know whether we have any moral conviction at all? In trying to answer these questions, it is important not to get too hung up on the obvious fact that many moral issues aren't simply black or white, and that, in trying to decide the moral course of action, there are sometimes shades of grey, competing goods or a hierarchy of principles involved. Because the truth is that, most of the time, our moral decision making involves questions that aren't particularly complex or subtle at all. In fact, most of the time they're pretty mundane and straightforward. For example, we rarely have to decide such difficult questions as whether to pull the plug on a comatose relative or blow the whistle on a corrupt employer. But we frequently have to decide whether to cheat on our expense reports or have an extra beer before driving home. We may never have to decide whether to divorce an unfaithful spouse, but we will almost certainly have to decide at some point whether to be unfaithful ourselves.

Of course, there is little point in creating a definition of adulthood that is contrary to human nature; the temptation to cheat is universal, and we all succumb to it once in a while. But there is a point in creating a definition of adulthood that includes a strong sense of moral autonomy and conviction, because without moral autonomy and conviction there can be no other autonomy, and without autonomy we would be doomed to a life of subservience to our parents or other people. We are not looking for moral perfection, only moral strength.

What distinguishes the moral from the immoral person is this: The moral person commits trivial transgressions, feels guilty about them and doesn't ultimately try to justify or deny them; the immoral person commits grave transgressions, doesn't feel particularly guilty about them and tries as long as possible to deny or justify them. A moral person may occasionally charge a personal lunch to her company's credit card, but she will do it rarely, feel uncomfortable about it and reimburse her company if the expense is challenged. A less-than-moral person will seldom pay for her own lunch, take pride in ripping off her employer and act outraged and refuse to pay if her expenses are challenged.

Adults understand they aren't perfect. Because they know they have to live with some degree of moral ambiguity and sense of personal guilt, they try to bear it with dignity and without self-pity. It is this consciousness of guilt that makes adults unsanctimonious and forgiving on the one hand, yet prepared to atone and make restitution for their serious transgressions on the other. In fact, in order to restore a sense of their own personal worthiness and to honour the social compact with which they identify, adults feel compelled to make amends for their serious wrongdoings.

For pre-adults the situation is easier. Because they know they're rarely going to be put in a morally challenging position, they have the luxury of espousing a moral code that is rigid and unambiguous. Yet when they do transgress, they're much quicker to make excuses for themselves. Here's an example of someone who rejected a critical opportunity to display moral autonomy:

Patrick was the manager of a mutual fund that bought and sold bonds. He was very bright and successful, and the fund made lots of money for its clients—ordinary people like you and me. He liked finance, enjoyed trying to out-perform the market, loved making money and mingling with the rich and powerful, took his responsibilities seri-ously and got a tremendous kick out of wheeling and deal-ing. He couldn't imagine a more fulfilling life.

One day Patrick got a telephone call from Michelle, a bond trader with a large block of junk bonds for sale. These bonds offered a high rate of interest because they'd been issued by a company that already had lots of debt and was therefore somewhat financially precarious. Exercising his fiduciary responsibility, Patrick reviewed the balance sheet of the company and decided not to purchase its bonds for his portfolio.

But Michelle needed to sell her junk bonds, so she decided to bribe Patrick—legally—by offering to let him in personally on a deal that she said would make him a lot of money. He invested $100,000 in her scheme, and six months later, as promised, his investment had grown to $150,000.

After Patrick had cashed out of his investment on her advice, Michelle returned to Patrick with the same junk bonds he'd turned down six months earlier—not for his personal portfolio this time, but for the portfolio he man-aged. And this time, Patrick decided that he would pur-chase tens of millions of dollars of these bonds for his fund, reasoning that Michelle's financial acumen had shown itself to be pretty exceptional.

Did he do anything wrong? Yes, he did. The problem here was not just that Patrick relinquished his indepen-dence by making himself beholden to Michelle, nor that he had taken a subtle, though legal, bribe. No doubt he told himself that he could still exercise his fiduciary responsi-bility despite his arrangement with Michelle, though that, of course, would have been a rationalization. The real problem here was that Patrick didn't continue to use his own judgment in assessing the safety of Michelle's bonds. He sacrificed his autonomy and relied on her judgment instead.

Patrick's betrayal of his responsibility to his clients, and to his own conscience, would have been bad enough. But, to add insult to injury, the company defaulted on its interest payments to the bondholders, and Patrick got sued for breaching his fiduciary responsibility.

And here was where the truly egregious bit of folly came in. When Patrick was called into court to testify, he tried to justify his unethical actions by producing an outrageous, though common, excuse. "There was so much pressure on me to get good results," he whined. "Michelle was so persuasive that I couldn't say no. And my wife had developed such expensive tastes that I was afraid to disappoint her. I just cracked. I didn't know right from wrong any more!"

In other words, Patrick tried to cop an upscale insanity plea—a plea of reduced capacity and diminished free will. But the capacity for autonomous thought, which is the basis of accountability in the legal system and of morality in general, is *the* central trait of adultness. And in the eyes of the court he was an adult. It should come as no surprise, therefore, that Patrick's expedient display of victimhood evoked not pity but contempt, and that the judge found him liable for damages.

SELF-DISCIPLINE AND STRUCTURE

There can be no autonomy without self-discipline. In fact it's hard to have a life of any kind without self-discipline. And there is no magical way to get it.

The problem of lack of self-discipline is extremely common. Psychotherapists get called regularly by people seeking treatment for underachievement. The situation is invariably the same: The caller is someone who dropped out of school before completing his degree or was at the bottom of his class. He now works as a salesman on commission or perhaps as a freelance writer, but can't seem to get his career off the ground. Because he's unsuccessful and has no money, he can't find a girlfriend. So naturally, as a consequence, he's depressed and feels in a rut.

But he has a dream! He knows that if he can just get himself motivated he can make a fortune. He'll start his own business, invent a gizmo or write a screenplay. Then he'll be his own boss. He'll be that greatest-of-all-things—an entrepreneur.

Unfortunately, he can't get himself motivated. He hasn't started his own business (no capital), invented a gizmo (he has the idea in his head, though) or written a screenplay (no time). In fact, he is having trouble going to bed on time, getting up in the morning, making cold calls on customers, closing sales and dealing with his sales manager (who is five years younger and doesn't treat him with enough respect). It also doesn't help that he is cranky, short-tempered and procrastinating.

In addition to learning how to become more motivated, he would also like to lose weight, quit smoking and cut down on his marijuana use.

He says that he's been told he's very bright and he could do anything he really set his mind to. He believes that the only possible explanation for his stunning lack of success must be some kind of mental disorder—a work phobia perhaps, or maybe a fear of success. His father, after all, was very critical of him when he tried to do things as a kid and didn't give him much encouragement (though his mother, luckily, was a saint who let him do whatever he wanted).

This man's condition may be extremely common, but it isn't psychiatric. It's educational. His real problem is that, when he was growing up, he wasn't given enough structure that he could internalize later as self-discipline.

We all go through fallow periods from time to time; it's easy to get stuck in a rut, and not all that easy to muster the self-discipline to get out of it. That's why it's important to get some structure, and for most people, that structure comes from a job. If structure is necessary even for people with an above-average amount of self-discipline, then for people with a below-average amount of self-discipline it is essential. And they shouldn't be ashamed to try to get it. After all, it's a whole lot easier and more efficient to add structure to your life than to try to reinvent your personality.

It takes only a few minor adjustments to get your life back on track—adjustments like going to bed on time, getting up early, doing first things first, setting priorities, making appointments, following through on commitments and cutting out alcohol and drugs (especially marijuana, which is the great killer of drive). All these actions are more useful than trying to figure out why you supposedly have a fear of success (a neurosis that's about as common as getting hit by a meteorite), and they're all things that your parents could have told you about, and probably did.

Bronwyn was a woman in her forties who complained that she was having trouble trying to quit cigarettes and alcohol. She worked as a freelance food writer and lived impecuniously with her fifty-year-old boyfriend of many years, a barely productive freelance journalist. They lived in a one-bedroom apartment with few frills, except for the free meals she could wangle out of the various magazines she reviewed restaurants for. Her boyfriend was an even more committed smoker and drinker than she was.

It seemed to me that Bronwyn's willpower was not yet a sturdy enough base on which to build any immediate plan of action. She also didn't seem to be terribly autonomous. In fact, if anything, she was excessively adaptable—more or less going along with her boyfriend on most important matters whether or not she agreed with him, and without much thought. I had a suspicion—a suspicion I shared with her—that had she been living with a man who was a non-smoker, moderate drinker and more productive worker, that she too would have been all those things.

In most cases, people who lack self-discipline should first try to acquire not self-discipline, but structure. I stopped short of recommending the termination of Bronwyn's co-dependent relationship with her boyfriend because I felt that such an intrusive piece of advice would interfere with her autonomy too much. However, I did recommend Alcoholics Anonymous to help her stop drinking and a nine-to-five job to help her increase her productivity.

Initially, Bronwyn refused to go to AA; like many people she objected to its religiosity and constraint on free will. But when she was unable to remain abstinent on her own, she relented and began to attend regular meetings.

After a year of being sober herself, Bronwyn gave her

boyfriend an ultimatum either to get into an alcohol treatment program himself or to get out of her life. Under pressure, he stopped drinking for one or two months. But he refused to get into treatment and, before long, was back to drinking again. After several months of wavering, Bronwyn finally ended her relationship with him and moved in with her sister. And once she'd left him, just the absence of his negative influence allowed her to make further changes in her life. She stopped smoking, got a good job and moved into her own pleasant apartment.

At first glance, autonomy and structure might seem to be mutually incompatible. We usually associate autonomy with freedom and structure with constraint. But autonomy and structure are not only compatible, they are mutually enhancing. Indeed, autonomous people can seek the structure of an organization to help them fulfil their own aspirations. They recognize the benefits of structure—the set work hours, the explicit goals, the companionship of others sharing a common purpose, the rewards for good work—and they harness those benefits to their own ambition. Scholars, for example, work within the structure of a university. Writers work to a deadline or to fulfil the obligations of their contract and to earn their advance. And many artists claim they're at their most creative when they give themselves some formal constraint to discipline and focus their energies.

TAKING RESPONSIBILITY FOR OTHERS

We now turn our attention to the second primary trait of adulthood—the willingness to acknowledge and assume responsibility for others. Though responsibility for others sometimes entails self-sacrifice, it actually flows from responsibility to the self because it presupposes the exercise of free will. Before a person can *choose* to be responsible for others, she first has to be autonomous, otherwise she is merely following duty or instinct. And while pre-adults either have responsibility thrust upon them, or take it in only limited areas of their lives, adults take responsibility for themselves and others voluntarily, and do so across the board.

Responsibility changes the person who assumes it. When one person assumes critical responsibility for another person—especially life and death responsibility of the kind a parent assumes for a child, a doctor assumes for a patient, a general assumes for an army, or any adult assumes for a sick partner, parent or friend—the person taking on this weighty responsibility becomes stronger and more mature in the process of discharging it. Thomas J. Watson, Jr., the man who took over as CEO of IBM from his father in 1956 and then ran it until 1971, describes the transformative effect of his wartime responsibilities this way:

> If it hadn't been for World War II, I might never have become my own man. After 1939 my favorite recreation, flying, suddenly became serious business. I joined the Air Force as a pilot and learned to be responsible for an airplane full of men. The military took me far outside my father's influence, and by 1943 I had made it to lieutenant colonel. Though I never got promoted beyond that, I came back from the war confident, for the first time, that I might be capable of running IBM.[3]

The responsibility Watson took for the welfare of his flight crew during the war not only gave him a feeling of confidence he'd never had before, but permitted him to conceive of taking on further responsibilities—namely, leading IBM into the computer age. Taking responsibility for others fosters the transition to adulthood by making the tasks of adulthood seem progressively easier and less intimidating.

> Aaron was in his mid-twenties when he came to see me because of marital problems. His wife, Amanda, was pregnant with their first child, and she was enraged at him for reasons having as much to do with her obsessiveness as with his immaturity. At his first appointment, Aaron asked me if I had children because, he said, he would want my guidance and needed to be sure that I spoke from experience.
>   Amanda was quite a few years older than Aaron, and her marriage to him was her second. She'd met Aaron at a

party shortly after his graduation from engineering school and, initially, had a positive effect on him. He was quite bright, but he had poor work habits. A chronic under-achiever, Aaron had disappointed his teachers all the way through school and was in the process of floundering at his first job. After they started dating, however, Amanda helped Aaron to pull himself up by his bootstraps. She encouraged and cajoled him into developing more disci-pline and perseverance, and his performance at work showed dramatic improvement.

In short order, they got married, but before long they started to fight. Amanda noted that any of the benefits of his new-found energy and drive seemed to be confined to the job site. His participation at home was lacklustre. She worried that she would end up having to push him through his life, and with a new baby coming, she was getting fed up with it.

Aaron had grown up as one of the younger children in a large privileged family outside Ottawa. He had always been the fair-haired boy—precocious, articulate, clever, quick—but he was easily bowled over by adult men, beginning with his successful father. Men intimidated him.

Things had come so easily to Aaron that he was not much in the habit of having to work at them. He under-achieved at school, but could always get by. He'd made a few stabs at trying to be his own person: He went away to college, travelled alone through Europe for nine months, and did a stint in the Navy. But basically he felt like a clever kid—until he met Amanda. Placing himself in her hands, he began to assume the trappings of adulthood—first buckling down at work, then marriage and soon fatherhood. He hoped that by acting like an adult, he would quickly become an adult. To his wife's chagrin (and his own), he didn't. The problem was that Aaron still didn't *feel* adult.

Shortly after Aaron started therapy, Amanda gave birth to a baby boy. As the demands of child rearing got added to the demands of work, they fought more and more often. There were constant threats of separation on both sides. Only the baby kept them together.

To all outward appearances, Aaron looked to be a very responsible father and husband—and, in fact, he was—but inwardly, he felt he was just going through the motions. He felt ground down. He felt as though he were working merely to live up to an image of adulthood that he admired, but could never achieve. His sense of responsibility for his family was not voluntary; it was assumed in response to a desire to try to be grown up. He felt joyless and over-burdened.

As often happens in therapy, his desire to learn to become a grownup was played out in his relationship with me. Though his own judgment was usually excellent, he felt compelled to ask my advice on all sorts of matters, from child rearing to office politics. He knew as well as I the right way to behave, yet, having no faith in his own adultness, he still believed he needed to check with a "real" adult.

When I pointed it out to him, Aaron was mildly shocked to recognize that, despite having acquired all the accoutrements of adulthood, he still didn't really *feel* adult. As we explored the causes of his arrested psychic development over many months, he began to feel less and less burdened by his various duties. His actions became more autonomous. Instead of merely going through the motions of fulfilling his family responsibilities because that was what he was supposed to do, he began to perform his duties voluntarily because that was what he wanted to do. Now and again, he even began to enjoy them.

The interesting thing to me was that Aaron underwent an almost instantaneous change in mood as soon as he recognized that he didn't see himself as an adult. Though his actual behaviour didn't change until later, his *feeling* about himself improved right away. You might have predicted the opposite—that he would have felt ashamed or deflated on discovering that he didn't feel adult—but he felt relieved instead.

This is a common paradox in psychotherapy—the person hears "bad" news yet feels better. The reason he feels better is that he now understands his behaviour better, and therefore feels he has more control over it. There is nothing more discouraging than feeling that your fate is not in your own hands—especially if you're not happy with the way things are turning out.

When Aaron realized that he wasn't seeing himself as an adult—but as a kid who had to do what he was told—he understood why he felt put upon and why his responsibilities seemed burdensome. And because this obsolete image of himself was now conscious, he could challenge it. He could make the assertion—based on his new self-awareness—that he was not, in fact, a kid any more, but an adult.

"More and more, I think my own thoughts," he told me a short time later. "As a result, I feel like I'm in the driver's seat. I used to avert my eyes from my own life, as if I thought, by ignoring them, my problems would go away. But of course they didn't, and I was constantly worrying about them anyway, and getting down on myself. Now I'm pro-active. I meet issues head on. And I feel much more in control of my life."

Aaron's new adult self-image transformed him. He felt liberated, renewed and eager to meet the challenges of adult life.

COMPETENCE

The third primary trait of adulthood—the acquisition of a sense of competence—is one of the golden threads that joins childhood to adulthood. The reason that Aaron was able to feel adult was because he was a hard and intelligent worker, a serious husband and a devoted father. He possessed the traits and accomplishments worthy of an adult. Had he not, in fact, been competent, no amount of wishing to be an adult would have made him one.

Of course Aaron had all these traits before he actually saw himself as an adult. This illustrates an important point: Although the psychological transition to adulthood is generally rapid and discontinuous with the period preceding it—perhaps taking no more than a day—the acquisition of adult traits is gradual and continuous—sometimes taking as many as two decades. A skill or quality acquired in early childhood may form the seed of a trait that eventually blooms in adulthood.

Physical Competence

One facet of the overall sense of competence that helps define adultness is physical competence. The child's feeling of control over his body becomes the basis of his feelings of efficacy and emotional strength later on.

Adults who lack a feeling of physical competence, and even of physical attractiveness, usually lacked it as children too. They report feeling awkward, unco-ordinated, unathletic and ashamed of their bodies from an early age. They were often embarrassed or ridiculed for being overweight or short, or for undergoing puberty earlier or later than their peers. They were picked last for teams and games, but first for risky stunts or degrading dares. And they were rarely anyone's first choice for friendship.

The key to feeling physically competent is not inborn athletic ability, although that certainly helps a great deal. The key to feeling physically competent is the attainment of that wonderful feeling of oneness with your physical being and of physical mastery over yourself that is acquired by the exuberant practice of athletic skills.

It has always been recognized that boys need to develop comfort with their physicality in order to feel masculine. It has been less well recognized that the same comfort is required by girls in order to feel feminine. We know that boys who never achieve physical competence may always doubt their masculinity and that this doubt can interfere with their later sexual competence. But we have been less well aware that the negative consequence of childhood physical ineptitude among girls is more or less the same one suffered by boys—namely, the impairment of an adult feeling of physical competence. Females translate this negative feeling about themselves into insecurities about attractiveness, work competence and sexuality, just as males do.

This point was brought home to me in a rather interesting way. I happened to be treating two women—one aged thirty-three, the other fifty-four—who had both attended the same private girls' school, albeit twenty years apart. The school had been modelled on the values and traditions of the élite British boarding schools of an earlier period. It was authoritarian, rigid, highly conformist, hierarchical and intensely conscious of wealth and class. Both women had felt like outsiders when they were students there, and this feeling had persisted right up until the time they came for therapy.

They had very different personalities and backgrounds, and at first it was not entirely clear what had caused them to feel like outsiders. In time, however, the reason emerged, and it was the same for both of them: They felt like outsiders—and were treated like inferior beings—because they weren't good athletes. Whereas the acceptable girls were robust and aggressive and threw themselves with reckless abandon into field hockey, lacrosse and basketball, my two patients were slow, awkward, unco-ordinated and timid and floundered in obscurity on the sidelines.

The two women carried these feelings of awkwardness wherever they went, and far into their adult lives. They continued to feel unattractive, socially inept, and uncomfortable with both men and women. Indeed, somewhere in their forgotten pasts—making a virtue of necessity—each began to actively foster her outsider status. By the time they entered therapy, they were not only lamenting their fate, but deliberately arranging it as well, and had developed an entrenched love-hate relationship with the rest of the world.

Once they realized why they felt alienated, and once they stopped trying to feel persecuted, they actually started to feel better about themselves. One started to do aerobics and the other made herself physically active in her garden. They stopped feeling the way they had as children—awkward, unathletic and socially inept—and began to feel more like adults—physically competent and socially adept.

Given the connection between childhood physical competence and adult physical competence, the logical implication is that we ought to be encouraging our children to develop their physical skills sufficiently to achieve this essential sense of body competence. It is nothing more than the ancient Greek ideal of a sound mind in a healthy body.

Moral Competence

By moral competence, I mean moral conviction and moral courage—the willingness to act on and accept the consequences of your convictions, to stand up for yourself and others, and to take risks for a worthy cause. If a person has attained moral competence, it means not only that she has developed her own moral code, but that she's prepared to live by that code—that morality is one of the forces that determines how she chooses to act. To the morally competent person, morality isn't just a brake on her actions, it's a spur to them.

The two pre-adult forerunners of adult moral competence are physical bravery and the willingness to risk ostracism in the face of opposition—physical and social bravery. Therefore, moral competence requires both physical competence and moral autonomy. People who acquire physical and social bravery during middle and late childhood usually find it easier to attain moral competence in early adulthood. Unfortunately, childhood is also the toughest time in which to be brave. Children are not only more physically and verbally aggressive towards each other at this stage, they are also more intolerant of deviations from the norm, have thinner skins, have a greater need to belong and have less well developed skill at resolving conflicts than they'll have later in life.

Many children find it hard to handle the rough and tumble of schoolyard politics and, as a result, enter adolescence or pre-adulthood feeling weak and cowardly. They often try to conceal these feelings from other people by affecting an air of superiority and ironic detachment, but they can't conceal these feelings from themselves, and they don't succeed in acquiring enough moral competence to feel comfortably adult later on.

So what can you do if, like many people, you reach pre-adulthood without feeling physically or socially brave? Sometimes you can overcome these residual childhood feelings by getting into good enough physical shape that you feel confident of your ability to defend yourself. And sometimes you can compensate for these feelings by developing other competitive skills or by having other competitive achievements. But usually these feelings cannot be totally overcome. They have to be accepted as part of the past and put into some kind of perspective. You should keep in mind that most childhood defeats or retreats are not due to cowardice; they're due to reasonable fear and appropriate judgment. After all, every child is intimidated or humiliated by someone, and every child feels like a weakling or a coward at least once.

Ironically, the traits that are devalued as wimpy in the schoolyard—courtesy, easy-goingness, the ability to defuse a showdown, the ability to help other people save face, the ability to reach a compromise, sensitivity, respect, knowing when to give in—are the very traits that are valued in adult life. Children who are naturally inclined towards these adult social skills may feel ashamed of them, however, because they see them not as strengths but as weaknesses. If they carry this shame into adulthood, it may hamper their ability to employ these skills when they're needed. It's easier for children who are ordinarily brave; they feel less ashamed of these social skills when they finally acquire them and less conflicted about using them when they're really needed.

Fortunately, the acquisition of moral courage does not require heroism; it requires only ordinary bravery. And an act of ordinary bravery may be the very event that initiates the transition to adulthood.

Natalie was nineteen in 1985 when she began her first job as a bank teller. Having just graduated from high school, she was full of idealism and was grateful for the opportunity to work. She worked hard and quickly established a reputation for enthusiasm, diligence and friendliness. Before long, however, the assistant branch manager began making improper sexual advances towards her. For three years he made Natalie's life increasingly miserable. He made lewd suggestions about what he wanted her to do to him. He demanded that she give him a wake-up call every morning. He commented on how sexy her clothing was. And he "inadvertently" brushed up against her while she was working.

Natalie didn't know what to do. One of the other tellers told her just to ignore the assistant manager, but that only made him more aggressive. She tried rebuffing him, but that only made him more threatening. He told Natalie that he would accuse her of having made sexual advances towards him if she reported his behaviour to the branch manager, and he threatened to give her a bad evaluation if she decided to quit.

Natalie became more and more depressed. She developed chronic, severe abdominal cramps and regularly called in sick. One day, after she'd been enduring his harassment for over three years, the assistant manager stepped over the boundary of decency one too many times—he whispered an insulting remark about her sex life to the branch manager as Natalie was walking by. They were both smirking when Natalie stormed into the branch manager's office and demanded to know what they were laughing at. The assistant manager who'd been harassing her tried to mollify her, but Natalie ignored him and told the branch manager that if he didn't fire the assistant manager immediately, she was going to bring a complaint against both of them.

"You know darn well what's been going on here," she told the branch manager. "But you just stood by and watched it happen. I'd quit myself, but I'm not going to give you the satisfaction."

By the end of that day, the assistant manager had been fired, and the manager had offered her an apology. For the first time in three years, Natalie left work feeling clean and comfortable with herself. And for the first time ever, she left work feeling like an adult.

People who are morally competent don't need to assert their rights at every opportunity. They feel strong enough to know when it's appropriate not to assert their rights. And they feel brave enough to know when backing down is no humiliation. They don't confront every person who's rude to them or slights them or hassles them in the street.

There is a problem, however, when the sense of public safety and civility has been eroded to such an extent that people have to turn the other cheek over and over again in order to avoid becoming embroiled in trivial or potentially dangerous confrontations. The problem is that an accumulation of such subthreshold indignities gradually erodes the sense of bravery and self-worth that underpins moral courage. And moral courage that has been shamed may become distorted and perverse. It

may take the form of moralistic hostility towards easily identifi-
able scapegoats: excessive punitiveness towards criminals,
intolerance of "threatening" races or ethnic groups and contempt for those people—from welfare mothers to the home-
less—who can't succeed in a competitive world.

Social Competence

Social competence is the ability to get along with other people—those who are familiar to you and those who are strangers.
It is the ability to overcome the discomfort you feel working and
playing with other people. And it is the ability to make other
people feel comfortable with you. Social competence allows
you to accomplish your aims that involve other people, but it is
not just a means to an end. Social competence is an end in itself.
Acquisition of social competence represents the highest development of a universal human skill—companionableness—and
the enjoyment of a unique human gift—companionship.

Some people are naturally more comfortable socially, and
some people are naturally less comfortable. People who are less
comfortable, especially people who are very shy or very homesick, may have to work harder in order to achieve an adult feeling of social competence. But everyone can do it.

SHYNESS

There are very few of us who have never felt shy. Yet there are
very few traits that undermine the feeling of being an adult
more than shyness does. This is especially true if the shyness
has been painful, debilitating and lifelong. Shy children find
social interaction frightening, intimidating, embarrassing and
anxiety-producing. As a result they feel awkward, inept and
unattractive. They expect to be excluded, humiliated, disliked,
ignored or outright rejected in any social setting, so they hang
back, hoping someone else will take the initiative, and if that
doesn't happen, they pout.

Children whose shyness is severe may begin to develop a
phobia of all social interactions taking place outside a narrow
circle. They will avoid gatherings of other children, which they
find too frightening, and confine themselves to social encoun-
ters only with adults. When they become adults themselves,

they often prefer the company of books and movies to the company of other people. Their reclusiveness, however, creates a vicious circle: lack of practice in social settings erodes whatever social skills they possess, which leads to further social awkwardness, shyness, avoidance and so on.

Eventually these super-shy children pre-empt the rejection they expect from other people by rejecting others first. They become defensive, angry, bitter and lonely. When they grow up, they have a chip on their shoulder. They don't consider getting together with other people pleasure (particularly if the occasion is informal or there's no set agenda), they consider it work, and within a short period of time they're exhausted by the effort.

Not surprisingly, shy people rely heavily upon their families and their few friends for the little social stimulation they can tolerate. Yet this dependency doesn't make them grateful, it makes them resentful. And it keeps them feeling weak, incompetent, and childish as well. The families of these stay-at-home people get used to prodding, cajoling, steering and haranguing them, in the hope of getting them socially engaged. Very shy people don't know how to make conversation. They refuse to make small talk or to talk about themselves for fear of being boring or appearing shallow, so they tend to force conversations in an intellectual or political direction, which allows them both to appear serious and to hide themselves at the same time. Although some shy people can be coaxed to open up if they're given considerable encouragement and support, most shy people prefer discussions about ideas to discussions about feelings (as though the two were really separable). And when they do talk about feelings, they often talk about them only as ideas.

Some shy people try to overcome their shyness by using drugs, alcohol or sex. Others join a church group or club or, in the extreme case, a cult. And some get their dependent needs met in relationships that allow them to bypass the give and take of normal human interaction altogether—they either become medical hypochondriacs and fall under the perpetual care of physicians, or they become psychological hypochondriacs and fall into an interminable psychotherapy.

Shy people tend to gravitate towards occupations that have a defined and circumscribed mode of interacting with other people—jobs such as editing, teaching, acting, engineering, accounting, medicine and social work—where their shyness can be concealed beneath a veneer of professionalism.

The best way to overcome shyness, however, is not by restricting yourself, but by repeatedly forcing yourself to interact with other people in a social setting. Social adeptness is a skill like any other. There are people who are gifted at it, people who are slow learners and people who are average. With practice, however, everyone, regardless of aptitude, can learn to be competent at it. The trick is to observe the social behaviour of competent people and then to experiment with the same behaviours yourself, until they begin to feel natural.

People with social phobias—those few who are absolutely paralyzed by the prospect of having to appear before other people—may require some form of treatment in order to bring their anxiety down to a level that will permit them to practise socializing. But even social phobics can acquire enough comfort with other people to allow them to be comfortable with themselves.

SHAME

Like shyness, shame is a form of social discomfort—but far more painful. And unlike shyness, which rarely has a cause, shame always has a cause—something that looks or smells bad or that leaves a bad taste. Shame is the mirror image of disgust: It's the shrinking feeling we get when someone looks at us with disapproval. Because shame derives from distaste for bodily functions, it attaches itself to violations of privacy and to the acts of looking and being seen. When we're ashamed, we want to avert our gaze, hang our head and disappear. We don't want to be looked at—and if we are looked at, we can only blush. Shame is such a potent feeling that it makes us want to hide even from ourselves. That's why shame is so easily repressed and so hard to uncover.

As children, we feel ashamed when we soil ourselves with feces or urine or dirt, or when our insides—our private thoughts, feelings and desires—are exposed to the outside world. As adults, we feel ashamed when we fail to live up to our own standards and ideals or when we do something that makes us look unworthy, shabby or dishonourable. Though guilt and shame are related, they're slightly different: Guilt is the feeling we have when we do something wrong; shame is the feeling we have when we do something beneath us.

Shame begins in childhood and returns us to childhood every time we experience it. We need only picture our parents looking at us with disappointment and disgust in their eyes to remember how we felt. And since anything that reminds us of our childhood shame can bring that feeling back, we're in constant danger of feeling like a chastened child. Shame makes us secretive and defensive, undermines our confidence and prevents us from feeling adult.

Sam was a forty-nine-year-old commodities trader who came to see me because of an ongoing conflict with Larry, his college-age son. The most recent incident centred on Larry's tuition: Sam had embarrassed Larry by sending it to the school late, and Larry had punished Sam by avoiding him on his vacation.

When I asked Sam why he'd been late with Larry's tuition, he gave me such a convoluted and long-winded explanation that I had to give up trying to follow it.

"If this is how you deal with Larry," I told him, "it's no wonder he's angry at you. You're impossible to pin down."

"You're right," he said, trying to appear helpful while pre-empting any further comment, "but I don't think the tuition situation was necessarily the best example.

"Let me offer a better example," he said. And then, through a series of skilful quibbles, he proceeded to refute everything he'd just agreed to.

Sam repeated this pattern of defensive obfuscation every time I put him on the spot. And every time I pointed it out to him, he repeated it once again.

"You're so afraid of looking bad," I finally told him after many such episodes, "that it makes me think you're ashamed of something."

"Like what?" he asked, suddenly alert.

"Like something from childhood you feel extremely embarrassed about," I answered.

Sam blushed deep crimson and for many minutes was

uncharacteristically silent. Then, without his usual bombast, he told me how ashamed he'd felt at eight years old when he inexplicably started to wet the bed again.

"I couldn't figure it out," he said with evident pain. "I had been dry for four or five years. My parents were beside themselves. They kept saying, 'Sam, what's the matter with you? You're not a baby any more. You should be ashamed of yourself.'

"And I was. They thought I was doing it deliberately to get attention. They made me wash the sheets as a punishment and, during the summer, they made me hang them out on the line. I couldn't even go to camp.

"I stopped wetting the bed after about six or seven months, but I never forgot how my parents reacted to it: 'Oh no!' my mother would say in a disappointed voice when she came up to my bedroom. 'Not again, Sam! I thought last night was going to be the last time.' The next night I'd lie in my wet bed, shivering, afraid to get up and change the sheets because I might wake her up.

"After that, whenever they got angry at me or I did something to disappoint them, that feeling would come right back to me and I'd be the same smelly little kid I was when I was eight."

We continued to explore the implications of Sam's enuresis for many months afterwards. But from the moment of that first cathartic insight, Sam made an effort to change. For example, when he realized that his withholding and obfuscation had started as a way to frustrate and get revenge on his parents, he tried to be less passive-aggressive and more straightforward with his current family and friends. And when he realized that his repressed shame had made him defensive and childish, he tried to be more confident and fatherly.

As a result of his efforts, Sam started to get along better with Larry. And for the first time in his life, he felt like an adult instead of a kid.

Because unresolved shame makes us feel childish and defensive and prevents us from feeling adult, we have to root out its sources and try to come to grips with it. If our shame is caused by youthful acts that were genuinely unworthy, we have to atone for them, if possible, and try to put them behind us. But if our shame is caused by youthful acts that were essentially trivial, we have to figure out why we've blown them out of proportion and return them to their proper size. With or without the benefit of therapy, getting to the root of our childhood shame takes courage and effort. But the payoff is great. Because once we overcome our residual feelings of childhood shame and achieve self-acceptance, we can be more confident and feel more adult.

HOMESICKNESS

All healthy children are biologically programmed to form attachments to their parents (or parent surrogates), and to experience fear when they're separated from them (especially their primary caretaker). These twin instincts—the drive to form attachments to parents and the anxiety triggered by separation from them—are of enormous survival value, both for the individual child and for the species as a whole, and they persist at least as long as the child requires adult protection.

When very young children are separated from their parents, they demonstrate all the behavioural manifestations of fear, anger and despair. They cry, they scream, they cling, they resist comforting, they hold onto their dolls and stuffed animals, they avoid strangers, they resist going to sleep, they lose control of their bodily functions, they rock, they run around or they remain fixed to one spot.[4] When older children are separated from their parents, they demonstrate all the same behavioural manifestations of fear, anger and despair as the younger children, but in more subtle and complex forms. Taken together, these muted manifestations of separation anxiety are what we denote by the term homesickness.

Homesickness, then, is normal. It is a mature derivative of childhood separation anxiety, and it indicates that the person experiencing it has a strong attachment to his parents. But there's a hitch: Homesickness can also be an occasion for profound embarrassment. Children who lag behind their peers in overcoming homesickness often feel weak, pathetic, inferior and inadequate in comparison, and they can carry those feelings well into their thirties or even beyond.

The truth is that *anyone* can feel homesick—and at any age. All it takes is the right mix of loneliness and fear. But to the young person who experiences homesickness when he sleeps over at a friend's house, or when he goes away to camp or college, or when he travels to Europe with a friend, this ubiquitous feeling can seem unique and shameful. Homesickness can sap your courage, undermine your confidence, and force you back into an ambivalent dependence on your parents.

Some young people try to conceal their homesickness. They adopt a hostile "I don't need you" attitude towards their parents, and get recklessly involved with the outside world. Ironically, by depriving themselves of the very nurturing and security that would have helped them overcome it, they make their homesickness worse. They may even become so isolated and depressed that they rush into "desperation attachments"—masochistic or promiscuous relationships with people who are unsuitable or even dangerous, but who give the illusion of being nurturing.

Homesickness that has been driven underground by shame can resurface in obscure and perverse forms. It can erupt as a vague and hard-to-diagnose psychosomatic illness, for example, that lingers on and on and "forces" the young person to return home in order to convalesce, or, more familiarly, it can lead to underachievement and failure in school or at work. Either way, those who feel ashamed of their homesickness as children carry the stigma of social inadequacy, at least in their own minds, throughout their lives. It interferes with their psychological and interpersonal development and robs them of the precious feeling of being normal. Yet, if they try to conquer their homesickness by leaving home before they're really ready to (even if it's later than the norm), they may do further damage to their already precarious sense of social competence and make becoming an adult all the more perilous.

Barbara was twenty-three when she came to see me because of depression. She felt like a failure, she explained, because she had not been able to achieve her childhood dream of becoming a concert musician.

When I first saw Barbara, the thing that struck me about her was that, although she was twenty-three, she looked fifteen. She dressed like a student and walked with her head down, avoiding eye contact as if she were unbearably humble.

As a child Barbara had been a good athlete but an indifferent student. She felt so ashamed of her poor scholastic performance that she did whatever she could to stay out of school. Her usual ploy was to feign illness. On a dark winter morning her worst fear was to be told by her mother that her temperature was only 98.6.

At six Barbara was given a clarinet (her father admired Benny Goodman) and music lessons with the first chair of the local symphony orchestra. She showed immediate promise and progressed with amazing rapidity. Having found something at which she could excel, Barbara stopped studying almost completely and devoted herself to learning her instrument instead. She never needed prompting to practise by herself, but she was too shy to perform in front of other people.

At fifteen she was told that she would have to go to Manhattan to find the kind of instruction she would need to propel her into the top rank of woodwind soloists. So, overcoming considerable separation anxiety, Barbara dutifully moved to Manhattan.

Her new teacher was a true sadist. He denigrated her playing and compared her unfavourably to his other students. She felt overwhelmed by the competition and humiliation and was constantly homesick for her family. Before long, in order to gain relief from the pressure to perform and to provide herself with a "legitimate" reason to return home, Barbara developed a muscle tension problem that interfered with her playing. Her mouth would go into spasms after only a few minutes of blowing through the mouthpiece. Soon she couldn't maintain her embouchure well enough to produce a good tone at all.

Barbara sought advice from other players. She consulted doctors who specialized in the medical problems of musicians. But she was only able to play for shorter and shorter periods of time, and always in greater and greater pain.

By the time she returned home in shame at the age of seventeen, her friends had all gone ahead of her by two grades. Too embarrassed to return to school, Barbara earned a very modest living working for her former music teacher instead. She was quite miserable and dejected, yet she never abandoned the hope that she would one day overcome her tension problem and return to performing.

At twenty Barbara married an accountant who had been taking saxophone lessons from her boss; she felt she had been given a new lease on life. However, as the years passed, her playing difficulties only worsened, and she found herself getting more and more depressed.

She was desperate. Having exhausted all other options, she finally decided to seek psychiatric treatment.

At first the therapy was quite laborious. Because of her shame about dropping out of high school and not succeeding as a musician, she assumed that I would look down on her. She was very defensive, treating any mild comment as a criticism.

Eventually, however, she began to open up. She told me that her parents had been subtly critical. They offered no praise that wasn't tempered by gentle suggestions for improvement. Under a brittle veneer of self-effacement, her parents were fiercely competitive with other families. They devalued anyone outside the family who did things differently from them and praised Barbara for doing things their way. They were hypochondriacal and obsessed with illness, so illness became the only legitimate excuse Barbara had for opting out of their oppressive competition.

That was why Barbara developed her muscle tension problem. Being "sick" was the only way she could seek help for her homesickness and let herself off the competitive treadmill without feeling she had disappointed her parents. Of course, her parents were disappointed anyway, which was exactly the point. They had usurped her pleasure by pushing her to become a musical star, so she had unconsciously thwarted them by becoming a musical failure. She had hurt herself to spite her parents but, in so doing, had made herself depressed.

Homesickness is the most obvious manifestation of separation anxiety, but it isn't the only one. Some people experience separation anxiety even when there's no actual separation from family or loved ones, but merely a temporary or symbolic loss of contact with the outside world. Some people, for example, get separation anxiety when they have to start a work assignment, do their homework or go to sleep—any activity that is solitary and keeps them from interacting with other people. Though the actual separation may only be for several hours, the time can seem endless.

The prospect of aloneness makes some people restless. Nancy, for example, always had to look for ways to distract herself when she was alone in her room, studying or doing her homework. She would read, watch television, masturbate, prepare something to eat, clean her room or talk on the telephone—anything to avoid feeling isolated.

As often happens, unfortunately, the behaviours that Nancy had used initially to distract herself from feeling lonely eventually broke free of their association with her separation anxiety and ended up becoming bad habits in themselves. She then had two problems to deal with—separation anxiety and bad work habits.

What's the solution then? How do people who still get homesick past the "normal" time regain their self-esteem? How do they become adults—responsible for themselves and others—if they still find it so hard to cope with their own loneliness? The answer is rather straightforward: They break the bad habits that sprang up to cope with the separation anxiety, and they create a network of friends to cushion the loneliness of being away from home. Stripping away the bad habits, the distraction and the procrastination is key to overcoming homesickness because it builds self-esteem. And when people are feeling good about themselves, they tend to feel less needy.

Because homesickness is so universal, overcoming homesickness is an important developmental step along the pathway to adulthood. It is a big enough accomplishment that it helps us to feel socially competent and, ultimately, to feel adult.

Sexual Competence

Many adults have sexual dysfunctions. They either can't perform sexually at all or can do so only under very specialized circumstances, which, for moral or logistical reasons, they may have considerable difficulty contriving to arrange. They may have difficulty becoming aroused or achieving orgasm, or they may be able to do so only when the sex is accompanied by pain or domination or some kind of fetish. If this sexual dysfunction arises *after* the shift to adulthood has taken place, then it will damage self-esteem but not destroy the adult self-image. But if the sexual dysfunction develops *before* the shift to adulthood has taken place, then the formation of an adult self-image may be delayed or distorted.

As with all such injuries to self-esteem, compensatory measures are quickly mobilized in order to help heal the wound of sexual dysfunction. A man who lacks a feeling of sexual competence around which to build his sense of masculinity, for example, may compensate by over-emphasizing "noble" traits like sensitivity, stoicism, self-sacrifice and the backing of lost causes. Similarly, a woman who feels sexually inadequate may see herself as defective and undesirable and may compensate by being seductive but aloof, or by being cute but asexual.

If sexual incompetence doesn't actually delay the feeling of adultness in a particular individual, then it may at least distort it. It may lead a person to avoid romantic relationships altogether—a renunciation that usually leads to bitterness, envy and despair—or it may lead to the compensatory over-emphasizing of "intellectual" or self-abnegatory traits.

One big cause of sexual dysfunction is the widespread belief that to be a good lover you need the physical endowment of a porn star, the flexibility of a gymnast, the technical facility of Masters and Johnson, the endurance of a marathon runner and the libidinal drive of a dog in heat. This is a tall order. It causes some people to give up sexual relations prematurely or to make only a half-hearted stab at them, and it causes others to over-value sex, or to make it into a competition.

Ron was a twenty-five-year-old lawyer. He was a young partner at a prestigious law firm on Bay Street. He had attended Queen's University and University of Toronto Law School and clerked for a Supreme Court judge. He was tall, handsome, reasonably affluent and athletic. Naturally, women loved him. He asked out dozens of desirable women, behaved like a perfect gentleman—and never called them again. He just couldn't get excited about any of them.

One day, however, Ron met a beautiful model at a party and began talking to her. To his surprise, she consented to go out with him. On their first date they went to an avant-garde play (very arty and hip), had supper in Yorkville, and then went back to his apartment. She turned out to be incredibly bright and funny, and he fell in love with her right away. She obviously liked him, but when they made love for the first time he was unable to maintain an erection. He felt humiliated and she felt unattractive.

They continued to date, but each time they got into bed the problem returned. Feeling frustrated and frightened, Ron finally decided to seek therapy.

Initially, the reason for Ron's impotence had been that he was intimidated by his girlfriend's beauty and reputation. Her face appeared regularly on the covers of magazines, men stared at her in the street and her name had been romantically linked with millionaire playboys, rock stars and movie moguls. When Ron went to bed with her the first time, all those other men seemed to be right in there with them, and he just couldn't perform.

Ron was an only child. His father, a successful lawyer himself, was in his mid-forties when Ron was born. Ron's mother, who got pregnant right after university, never worked outside the home. They both doted on Ron, but his mother in particular made him her dreamboat. She involved herself in every aspect of his life and treated him like a prince.

In order to avoid being smothered by her, Ron became disobedient. He did whatever he wanted whenever he wanted. If she wanted Ron to do one thing, he just had to do something else. He refused to give her the satisfaction she sought from him.

The one thing he did do right was school. But even there he was an iconoclast. He had to be different. If everyone else dressed one way, he dressed another. He always looked stylish—indeed style and appearances were very important to him—but never predictable.

He was a marked contrast to his father, who was a paragon of establishment propriety and form. Indeed, differentiating himself from his father was one of Ron's main (unconscious) missions. He felt that he couldn't compete with his father by being the same, so he carved out his own niche—not too distant from his father's, but with its own special panache and élan. He got into the habit of avoiding head-to-head competition. He always looked instead for an offbeat venue where he could be the star.

When Ron finally got into bed with his girlfriend, however, he could no longer avoid going head to head with his imaginary competitors, so instead, he copped out altogether. He didn't even try to perform. And because he felt pressured to satisfy her, he deprived her of satisfaction, just as he'd done with his mother.

Of course, when Ron entered therapy, he didn't understand why he couldn't perform with his girlfriend; he just knew that he couldn't. He worked hard at therapy, however, and because his impotence had not yet become self-perpetuating or independent of its original cause, it went away quite easily once he gained a rudimentary understanding of what had brought it on.

Occupational Competence

The sphere of competence that is most crucial for the acquisition of an adult sense of self is occupational competence. By occupation, of course, I am referring not only to conventional jobs or careers, but also to the central activity that fulfils a person's ambitions. For many people, that will be their jobs, but for others it may be child rearing, the pursuit of artistic or athletic excellence, or some other form of self-expression. I am not referring to the period of formal education, that, unless undertaken later in life, tends to postpone the feeling of being adult.

When Freud was asked what a normal person should be able to do in order to be considered mentally healthy, he is reputed to have said, *"Lieben und Arbeiten"*—love and work. Although I've separated competence in these two spheres for the sake of clarity, they are not really dichotomous. Love takes work, and work takes love. One reason that pre-adults find work intimidating is that they are afraid to love it. They don't allow themselves to become enthusiastic about it, even if the work they've chosen is the fulfilment of their childhood dream. They wrestle with their work when they ought to be dancing with it.

> Maureen, a young journalism student, told me that she was very depressed about getting a C+ on a story she'd done. Her instructor told her that her writing was good, but that her reporting was inadequate because she hadn't used enough sources. Maureen told me that she hated having to track down sources for a story, and that she felt awkward about having to interview them. It seemed like too much of an effort to her.
>
> I suggested that she was holding herself back from getting enthusiastic about her chosen craft. She was hedging her enthusiasm in order to avoid the risk of a disappointment should she fail. If she were more enthusiastic, I told her, she would feel less intimidated.
>
> Once Maureen allowed herself to love her work, she no longer found it so hard or so intimidating. She became less concerned about marks and more concerned about achieving professional competence. As a result, her enthusiasm grew and her performance continued to improve.

It's easier to work hard when you're an adult than when you're a pre-adult. Not only is hard work consistent with your new adult self-image, but you also now have the courage to enjoy your work.

It's important, however, to find work you can enjoy. You may know what you want to do from the time you're a small child, or you may not know what you want to do and have to try several things before you find the work that's right for you. But sometimes, the work you're looking for has been latent in your unconscious all the time, and you stumble upon it as if by destiny.

For example, Barbara, the clarinetist who was depressed about being unable to perform in public, got pregnant while she was still in therapy. Her pregnancy was difficult, but her husband was wonderfully supportive. When she gave birth to her son, Joshua, her husband stayed home for several weeks to help her. And after he returned to work, he relieved her in the evenings and on the weekends.

Barbara was a terrific mother—a bit of a worrier at the beginning perhaps—but very empathic with Josh and very sensible. She displayed a confidence and pride that I had never seen in her before. She stood up to her parents when they criticized her child rearing (which they did constantly), and she began to walk with her head held high. She grew from a shy, self-effacing, angry twenty-three-year-old "teenager" into a poised, friendly and self-assured woman of twenty-five.

For the first time in her life, Barbara felt competent. She had always wanted to have a child and, because of the pain of her own upbringing, had given parenting a lot of thought. She was very good at it and got a lot of pleasure from it. Because she now saw clearly the ways in which her parents' constant criticism had undermined her self-confidence, she was able to be less critical of herself.

She felt like an adult. And this too made her more confident. As result, neither her parents' criticism nor her own self-doubt could seriously erode her feeling of competence. Having assumed responsibility for another person, she became truly her own person. She was autonomous. She didn't need my approval in order to live her life, and she didn't need her parents' approval (which, in any event, she was unlikely to receive). She knew that she could do just as good a job raising Joshua as anyone else. In fact, she believed she could do a *better* job raising Joshua than

THE THREE PRIMARY TRAITS OF ADULTHOOD 59

anyone else. She had earned this conviction about her own competence, and that's what made her feel adult.

Barbara still felt sad that her dream of becoming a concert musician had not been fulfilled, but she accepted the fact that, for the time being, it would have to be placed on the back burner. She also understood that her childhood dream might never be fulfilled, and that she might have to mourn its loss and find a more attainable dream with which to replace it.

In the meantime, however, Barbara honed her skills as a clarinet teacher, quit her old job and started seeing students in her own home.

Occupational competence is so integral to the concept of adulthood that it deserves to be kept as free as possible from contamination by problems in other spheres, whether psychological, physical or social. Adults do not miss work for frivolous reasons—not for minor illness, not over romantic woes, not due to irritation at co-workers, and not because of a "rough night." Where work is concerned, adults cannot afford to be neurotic or self-indulgent.

There are many reasons why work should be kept sacrosanct: economic necessity, maintenance of self-esteem, distraction from your woes and the opportunity to form relationships. Work not only helps you to sever your pre-adult dependency on your parents or the state, but it also strengthens your tie to society at large. But the main reason you can't afford to bring your neuroses into work is that it's just too darn tempting not to work. We all have strong passive tendencies, and, from time to time, we all have to struggle with them. Think about how hard it is to go back to work after a vacation, for example. Or better still, think about how depressed you sometimes feel on a Sunday night.

Of course, giving in to passivity at the *right* time—at bedtime, for instance, or when you board an airplane or undergo surgery—isn't just acceptable, it's sensible. But giving in to passivity at the *wrong* time—at work, for instance, or in a crisis—isn't just unacceptable, it's un-adult. Shirking responsibilities—work foremost among them—makes you feel not only

guilty and slothful, but also tempted to rationalize your delinquency and more inclined to shirk your responsibilities again in
the future.

Passivity is so tempting, in fact, that some people on disability never fully recover from their injuries because of it. Despite
concrete evidence that their injuries have healed, they continue
to experience both pain and impaired function. They've got
used to getting paid without the hassle of having to work, and
they're willing to continue feeling sick just to be able to stay on
the dole.

Are they malingering? Not always. Often, because their
motives are truly unconscious, these people really do feel sick.
Since disability pensions are usually a fraction of what the person could have made by working, there is very little financial
benefit. The real benefit is the gratification of passive wishes.
But having given in to their passive tendencies and taken the
"easy" money from the insurance company, they feel an enormous sense of shame. And, in order to disavow this unconscious sense of shame and to justify continuing to receive their
disability payments, they remain disabled. That's why workers
who return to work quickly tend to recover faster and more
completely than those who don't—they have less time to get
used to being passive and rationalizing their shame about being
passive.

Over the years I've treated several people who've ended up permanently disabled despite being free of any serious handicap.
They start out with a "legitimate" illness, but once they start
collecting disability, the illness never goes away.

> Marcel was suspended from his job as the president of a
> film production company when the company's independent
> auditors discovered that he'd been back-dating contracts
> with the distributors to inflate revenues for the prior quar-
> ter. Because of the disgrace, Marcel became suicidally
> depressed and applied for disability. His disability policy
> was fairly generous, though not as generous as his salary
> would have been, but, more importantly, it contained a
> clause that allowed him to continue collecting from the

insurance company unless he got another job in his own industry. The problem was that he couldn't get a job in the film industry because of the scandal, and he didn't want to take a job in another industry because he didn't find the work interesting or glamorous enough. He ended up not working at all and becoming chronically depressed.

Several years later, when the scandal had been forgotten, one of Marcel's former colleagues offered him a job selling television pilots to the networks. By this time, however, this poor man had developed a phobia of working and, after some soul searching, turned the job down. I can't help but think that, were it not for his disability pension, this man would be back to work, feeling stressed perhaps, but happy, instead of stuck at home, free of stress, but depressed.

Once an escape hatch has been opened from work, it will be used over and over again. As long as you use it, you will never achieve occupational competence and never feel like an adult.

CHAPTER FOUR

THE TWELVE SECONDARY TRAITS OF ADULTHOOD

> The mark of a mature man is the ability to give
> love and receive it joyously without guilt.
> *Leo Baeck*

In the last section I described the three primary traits of adulthood: the ability to take responsibility for yourself, the ability to take responsibility for others and the ability to function competently in certain specific spheres of activity. These three primary traits constitute the core of what we think of as adult, but they do not exhaust our understanding of the concept any more than the law of supply and demand exhausts our understanding of economics, or the rules of baseball tell us why we enjoy watching a well-executed double play.

There are twelve other important traits of adulthood that merit our attention also. Although they aren't mandatory, these twelve secondary traits of adulthood are in some ways more sophisticated and interesting than the primary traits. For that reason, they loom large in our minds when we are trying to decide whether or not we're adult.

LOVE

Adult love is about one thing: commitment. Commitment to a spouse or partner, and commitment to a child or children.

The important thing about commitment is that it requires you to make a choice. You can't make a commitment to your partner and continue to date other people; you can't make a commitment to your children and continue to put your own needs first.

Commitment and choice are scary. Most people like to keep their options open. They resist having to give anything up. They fear that if they specialize in one line of work, for example, they'll miss out on opportunities to pursue another line of work. And they fear that if they make a commitment to one person, they'll miss out on an opportunity to get involved with someone else more desirable. This strategy may work well in pre-adulthood when you're trying to gain broad experience, but it doesn't work as well in adulthood when you're trying to pursue things as deeply and fully as you can. It's impossible to become master of one trade while trying to be jack of all others. And it's impossible to achieve a deep and satisfying love relationship with one person while trying to pursue several more.

Many pre-adults panic when they try to choose their partner. They're romantic enough to believe that marriage, or its equivalent, is for keeps, and they're afraid of making a mistake. They procrastinate and equivocate. They try one person, then another. They search for the perfect partner—that one-in-a-million person who will sweep them off their feet, sweep the images of all other lovers from their minds and sweep away all further doubts and comparisons. Needless to say, they usually search in vain.

Because finding a suitable partner and establishing a permanent relationship is generally considered to be proof of a person's maturity, those who haven't done so often feel immature or inadequate. They may even make an arbitrary choice just to prove they're capable of making a commitment. But rushing into a long-term relationship like marriage in order to prove that you're grown up, is a big gamble. Making a commitment may lessen your shame, and it may or may not put an end to any obsessing you've been doing about whether your partner is right for you, but it won't improve the likelihood of making the right choice or of achieving long-term happiness.

So how do you make the right choice? How do you decide if you've found the right partner, especially when you're not head-over-heels in love with the person—and even if you are?

Listed below are ten general principles that can help you to decide whether you've found a soul mate.

Principle 1: Don't hold out for perfection.

No one is perfect. No one person is going to fulfil all your needs. There really is no "one-and-only love." This doesn't mean that you should accept anyone you're not repelled by and who happens to like you—far from it. You should choose someone to whom you're attracted and with whom you're *simpatico*. You should choose someone who will love you and make you happy. But sometimes the best is the enemy of the good. If you're searching for the perfect mate, you might just pass up a very, very good one.

Principle 2: The most sexually exciting person is not always the most suitable person for a commitment.

If a person stimulates your sexual interest a lot more than usual, it ought to raise a yellow flag. It may indicate there's a neurotic component to your sexual excitement that will blow the relationship apart later on. The extraordinary attraction may be based on the fact that your partner is vain, flirtatious, aloof or challenging—all traits that turn people on but are hard to live with over the long haul. Not only are these traits irritating in themselves, but they're indicative of an unrecognized neediness in the person that will be hard for you to satisfy and may lead him or her to seek attention elsewhere.

People who are very intense, zany, scintillating, quick-witted, enthusiastic or entertaining can be an incredible turn-on too. They seem to know every trashy book, ironic joke, slang expression, Broadway show tune, great movie and nostalgic TV program that you know, and they can complete every one of your thoughts before you've even finished thinking it. But people who are very "up" can also become very "down." And when their mood takes a plunge, they can enter states of apathy, bitterness, coldness, rage or despair worthy of a character out of Dostoyevsky. When they're not inundating you with affection, they're tearing a strip off you. When they're not pumping you up, they're wearing you down.

It *is* necessary to be attracted to your partner, otherwise you may end up resenting him or her, but it's not necessary to be extraordinarily attracted to the person in order to have a sexually satisfying relationship.

> Linda was a thirty-one-year-old advertising account executive who kept getting sexually involved with her mentors at work. Unfortunately, they were all married men. At first she attributed this doomed attraction to the fact that these men were movers and shakers who could teach her about her business. The only hitch in this analysis was that she wasn't attracted to all the male leaders in her business, but only to some of them. What all these attractive men had in common was that they were very seductive. And Linda was very seductive in return. They gave off sexual vibes that they were up for a fling, and so did she.
>
> Of course, because these men were capable of cheating on their wives and needed the ego gratification of attracting other women in order to feel satisfied, they were precisely the wrong type of men for Linda, or for any woman, to get involved with. Linda's problem was that she had got hooked on the high of this kind of illicit and clandestine affair and, as a result, wasn't attracted to men who weren't seductive. Before Linda could become attracted to men who weren't overtly seductive, she first had to wean herself off the excitement of men who were.

Principle 3: Love gets gentler with time.

Falling in love and being in love are not identical. Falling in love is more intense, all-consuming and passionate; being in love is quieter, gentler and more nurturing. Falling in love is exciting; being in love is satisfying. Falling in love is transient; being in love is long-lasting.

Many people seem to get hooked on the high of falling in love. After the high has worn off—as it always does—they lose interest in their partner and begin searching for the next high. They have a series of short, incandescent affairs that promise fulfilment but don't deliver. Perhaps that's why people, like movie stars and moguls, who are used to getting a high from their celebrity, have more than the usual trouble remaining in love. They crave the high of falling in love, but get bored with the tranquillity of being in love.

True love gets gentler, mellower, deeper and more fulfilling with time. It doesn't get more exciting.

Principle 4: Character is a person's most important characteristic.

Under the term character I include a person's personality, integrity, interpersonal skills and emotional health. Character is rarely the reason two people fall in love, but it is usually the reason they're able to stay in love and help each other to grow and be happy. People fall in love because they're attracted to each other, have fun together and find each other interesting. They stay in love because they respect each other, help each other and fulfil each other's needs.

Falling in love is determined by the heart. Deciding to make a commitment is determined by the head. You have to decide whether your prospective partner is someone you can live with for a very long time, quite possibly for the rest of your life. Clearly someone who is warm, generous, gentle, kind, honest, faithful, energetic, good-natured, charming, hard-working, intelligent and open-minded will be easier to live with than someone who is chilly, selfish, aggressive, insensitive, apathetic, crafty, conniving, flirtatious, temperamental, rude, lazy, dull and rigid.

Principle 5: Love brings out the best in you.

A sure sign that your relationship is bad is that it frequently brings out the worst in you: pettiness, jealousy, vanity, competitiveness, hostility, antagonism or fantasies of conquest and revenge. A good relationship should bring out the best in you, most of the time. It should make you want to be your best because you love and respect your partner and want her to love and respect you, and because you feel valued and understood and want her to feel that way too.

When someone you like likes you, it is very flattering. It makes you feel very good about yourself and enhances your feelings of strength and confidence. But those feelings will turn out to be very fleeting if you can't be yourself when you're with that person. There is a world of difference between being on your best behaviour because you fear rejection, and being your true best because you feel valued and understood. If you know that your partner loves the real you, then you'll feel safe enough to be generous and loving to her in return.

Principle 6: The most satisfying long-term relationships are based on equality.

No relationship can be fulfilling over the long term unless both partners are equal and treat each other as equals. There can be a division of roles and tasks, but there must be a clear understanding that both people have an equal right to establish the *modus vivendi* of the relationship. If one person has the upper hand, both partners suffer; the "inferior" one suffers because he can't fulfil his desires or put his agenda on the table, and the "superior" one suffers because she isn't having a relationship with someone who's her equal.

Only someone who's your equal can truly appreciate you. Someone with fewer attainments and less character may not even be able to recognize those subtle and deep elements of your character that make you special. When you're in love, you may over-value your partner and credit him with more character than he actually has. One way to test your lover's character is to determine whether he's about as in love with you as you are with him. If he is, then it implies at least enough character to recognize why you're lovable.

Principle 7: Fidelity is essential.

There's another problem with inequality: Relationships that are unequal often contain within them a malignant seed of discontent. And the discontent can lead to infidelity. The "inferior" person feels discontented because he's unloved and the "superior" one feels discontented because she has no soul mate. This can predispose both partners to look outside the relationship for what they're missing.

Most of the time, however, infidelity is sparked by boredom and the desire to be adored. Getting someone else to find you desirable is an ego trip. People who get bored easily, who need continual and fresh adoration and who easily give in to their impulses are more likely than average to have trouble remaining faithful to their mates. So if you're considering someone who continually flirts with other people, enjoys making you jealous, keeps secrets from you and has already cheated on her mate in order to be with you—watch out! Chances are that, sooner or later, your love won't be enough.

Principle 8: Getting out of a bad relationship increases the probability of getting into a good one.

Ending a relationship with an inappropriate, unloving or abusive partner will increase your self-esteem and help strengthen your resistance to being treated badly in the future. Many people resist doing this, however, for fear of being alone. They tell themselves they'll never find anybody as wonderful, attractive, charming, successful and smart as the person who's been mistreating them, or that this person can eventually be won over or "fixed." But a relationship with a reluctant lover is doomed; if the mistreated person gets rejected first, he'll feel even more worthless and abused, but if he succeeds in extracting a commitment, he'll end up being stuck in an unloving and destructive relationship. In cases like this, it is far better to be the dumper than the dumpee. Breaking up is good to do.

Principle 9: Reality counts.

We'd like to believe that true love conquers all. And it does, but not for long. Sooner or later we have to return to earth and live in the real world. In the real world, poverty, unemployment, poor education, low ambition, large discrepancies in age and background, poor health, substance abuse, mental illness, a history of violence and antisocial tendencies all tend to undermine a relationship. When we're young and idealistic, we tell ourselves that we're indestructible, and we resist the entreaties of our friends and families when they tell us to be careful. There are millions of couples in solid permanent relationships who have overcome such difficulties, of course, but it is one thing to cope with them when you have no choice, and another thing to cope with them before making a commitment, when you still do have choice. Sometimes avoiding people with these problems is wiser than tying yourself to them.

Principle 10: The whole is greater than the sum of the parts.

Love involves sacrifice. There is no fulfilment in a loving relationship unless both partners are fulfilled. It is better to give up a little bit of your own happiness in order to ensure that your partner is happy. That's why making a good choice is essential. If you and your partner are too far apart, especially in the essential things—like values, outlook, temperament, background, education, goals and morals—then your sacrifice or your partner's will have to be too big.

When two people who are very suited to each other fall in love, they often feel as if they've known each other all their lives. They tend to be more alike than different in the ways that matter, though they may complement each other in the ways that matter less. If you and your partner are soul mates, if you love each other and care for each other, then the total happiness between you will be far greater than any happiness you could achieve alone.

SEX

Licit Sex

It is often assumed that sex is less important to adults than it is to pre-adults. We tend to believe that sex is more fun in our teens and twenties, when every activity is a new discovery, our bodies are coursing with hormones, we aren't restricted to just one partner, and each relationship is accompanied by the exquisite turmoil of new love. And it can definitely be a lot of fun.

But the best kept secret of adulthood is that grownup sex is potentially more satisfying than youthful sex because it's not as often accompanied by debilitating guilt. Most adults feel morally entitled to have sex in a way that most pre-adults do not. The achievement of adult status carries with it the right—not merely the legal right but the psychological right—to enjoy sex. As a result, adult sex is generally more relaxed than pre-adult sex.

Lucinda, a woman in her early thirties who'd never been able to have intercourse before without experiencing vaginal pain and spasm, told me that she was finally able to have intercourse with her new boyfriend only after giving herself a stern lecture. Lucinda told herself that nobody had the right any more to tell her that having sex with him was dangerous or wrong. She realized that she had always imagined her mother standing over her during intercourse, chastising her for running the risk of getting pregnant. But once she reminded herself that she had taken the proper precautions and that she was no longer accountable to her mother, or to anyone else other than herself for that matter, she was able to relax and enjoy the experience of making love without feeling either guilty or inhibited. Though it took a few tries before Lucinda was able to tolerate complete penetration during intercourse, her boyfriend was wonderfully supportive and patient, and she was eventually able to enjoy sex without anxiety or discomfort.

During the maturation process, adults construct their own conscience. In doing so, they take into account not only their morals and values (as they now independently conceive them), but also their needs and desires (as they have come to know them). Because their conscience is more in sync with their wishes than it was when they were children, they are less likely to run afoul of it. Adults are their own authorities. They determine what they consider right and wrong for themselves and are less dependent on external authority to regulate their conduct.

This doesn't mean that adults are antisocial. In fact, generally speaking, the morality of adults is usually quite harmonious with the values of society. The difference is that, in adulthood, the harmonization of internal conscience and external authority is more abstract and more nuanced than it is earlier in life. And adult morality is more autonomous. Whereas pre-adults are more inclined to obey or disobey society's rules, adults are more inclined to set their own rules (which are often similar to society's rules) and to live comfortably in accordance with them.

A rather mundane but commonplace example of this harmonization process was described to me by a woman in her late twenties who had an inhibition about having oral sex performed upon her.

Jennifer was afraid that her partner would find her genitals smelly and disgusting. She tried to avoid having oral sex performed on her, or at least to keep it brief, but her feelings of awkwardness and embarrassment interfered with her overall enjoyment of sex and with her desire to have sex altogether. In therapy, she traced her fear back to a discussion she'd had with a girlfriend when she was just a teenager. Her friend had told her that oral sex was unsanitary and that men were turned off by it and did it only to please women. Once she thought about this fear from an adult perspective, however, she realized that it no longer made sense to her, that it was inconsistent with her own experience. By re-examining her own sexual rules and restrictions, and making them more consistent with her experience and desires, she was able to become less inhibited about oral-genital stimulation and more comfortable about sex in general.

For many adults sex takes place within a permanent, monogamous relationship such as marriage. Monogamy is more the norm in adult life than it is in pre-adult life. And marital (however defined) sex (of whatever sort) is almost always more acceptable to the conscience than extramarital sex.

Monogamous sex is a great deal more intimate and, therefore, at least in theory, more deep and intense. In an established relationship there is more trust and less awkward unfamiliarity than in a new one. The most powerful descriptions of erotic experience that I have heard in my practice are those of happily married men making love to their wives.

Before he married Georgina, Brent always had to be the initiator during love-making. He felt weak and effeminate if his partner took the lead or even if she got on top of him. But after he got married, Brent was able to let Georgina take the lead without feeling threatened by it.

On one occasion, Georgina forced Brent to be entirely passive while she did all the work. At first he was tempted to resist, but because he trusted Georgina and felt sexually secure with her, he was able to lie back and let her give him pleasure. She controlled the depth and tempo of their love-making, and because he had no control over it, Brent found the experience incredibly liberating and erotic.

Happily married people can combine intense passion and focus with emotional nakedness and love, lyrical tenderness with wild abandon, take-charge cockiness with self-effacing humour, and even lousy performance with good self-worth. Great sex requires a letting go and a vulnerability that, in most cases, only maturity and the security of monogamy can provide.

Inez had dated many men during her twenties and early thirties. She was sexually active with many of these men, but rarely enjoyed sex until she met the man who subsequently became her husband. The reason for her lack of sexual enjoyment was rather simple: She was unable to tell any of her lovers that she couldn't have an orgasm during vaginal intercourse. Because she was afraid that her lovers would think her sexually inadequate if she told them about this, she was forced to lie there silently as they plugged away on top of her, trying to bring them both to simultaneous orgasms. But as she began to develop a feeling of trust and security with her future husband, she was able to be more and more open about her sexual needs and preferences. She told him that, although she enjoyed intercourse, it would not bring her to orgasm and that he need not make a huge effort to try doing so.

Her new openness about sex took a great deal of pressure off both Inez and her fiancé. They were able to relax and focus on their mutual pleasure, not tense up and focus on their individual performances.

Illicit Sex

Before I proceed so far down this road that the reader starts to think I've lost touch with reality, let me deal with the fact that extramarital sex—sex with a stranger, novel sex, offbeat sex— can be incredibly intense and exciting, sometimes more so than the familiar monogamous sort.

What these varieties of sexual experience have in common,

of course, is that they are forbidden fruit. They are especially exciting precisely because they are—psychologically at least— illicit; they challenge the authority of conscience. Immature sex isn't sexier than mature sex because it's guilt-free; immature sex is sexier because it's guilt-ridden. That makes it seem riskier and more dangerous. It's outlaw sex—fugitive, evanescent and uninhibited. You feel as if you've stolen fire from the gods.

But it can't last. It's great as a snack, but too rich to be taken as a steady diet. Indeed if you tried to make unconventional sex the norm, as some self-styled sexual pioneers have advocated, it would cease to be more exciting than the regular sort. It would *be* the regular sort.

Illicit sex isn't more intense than licit sex because the physical experience is dramatically better. It's more intense because it's more narcissistically gratifying. It makes you feel special. That's why most people have extramarital affairs—not for the sex, but for the ego gratification. It makes them feel more desirable. After all, if someone who is normally off limits will let you perform your sexual depredations upon him or her, and vice versa, then it must mean you're one hell of a sexy devil.

For pre-adults, sex almost always has this ego-boosting effect. When they succeed in making their fantasies into reality, they can't believe their good fortune. There is a tremendous feeling of power and amazement, which adults, because they're more experienced, are less likely to feel. But once this disbelief wears off, once the conquest has been made, the bloom is off the rose. We don't count ourselves quite so lucky to possess the objects of our desire once we possess them.

Illicit sex, like pre-adult sex, is seldom based in reality. Not only is the affair kept in quarantine—away from the humdrum concerns of everyday life—it often has the quality and form of drama. Consciously or not, the participants imagine themselves to be actors in a romantic movie or book. Because they're play-acting, their actions seem so much more gripping and significant than do the activities of everyday life. Like lovers in romances, they are outside the real world and exempt from its demands; their souls are tuned to a higher frequency audible only to themselves.

A married man who was having affairs with two different women jokingly told me that his life seemed like an episode from a TV soap opera. He was more right than he realized. His escapades had a cinematic, make-believe quality to them, as if they were being performed for an audience. He and his lovers sometimes even re-enacted scenes from their favourite movies.

Illicit lovers often believe they're being very brave and daring. But, ironically, the reverse is true. Because play-acted love is segregated from the demands of everyday life, it is usually much less risky than love that requires a full-time commitment.

Since illicit love has a dramatic quality, you might think it takes more imagination than the licit variety. Exactly the opposite is the case. Cheating is a failure of imagination. If you need to have an illicit relationship, it means that you've been unable to sustain a mental image of your partner as someone desirable. It represents a failure of the capacity to fantasize without the benefit of a Hollywood script and a prop—the prop being the person with whom you're having your affair. By cheating you're saying that you need to substitute a *real* person—a person who can't be your mate—for a *mental* image—the image of your partner as an object of desire. Philandering takes less imagination than fidelity.

During the pre-adult period, before you've consolidated a secure sense of yourself, all sexual relationships will have a large element of affirmation through acceptance. Your worth is affirmed by your lover's love. Hence the emotional roller coaster of young love.

In the adult period, when you have a more secure sense of yourself and when you have one established mate, being loved by your lover is less intoxicating. Unfortunately, some people can't feel sexually aroused without that intoxication. They try to introduce uncertainty into their love lives by seeking a new lover or imagining that their mate is unfaithful.

People who employ jealousy as a means of sustaining erotic interest play a little mental game in which they imagine they've been betrayed. They need to see their mate as someone lusted after by others. This creates an exciting illusion in which their mate is exalted and they are demeaned. Then when they "win back" their mate's affection they feel their own worth has been reaffirmed.

Because the quest for sexual intoxication can be never-ending, it is a trap that prevents people from achieving happiness and keeps them from enjoying the one they love.

Adults Have a Secure Sexual Identity

In adulthood, sexual identity is more secure. You know with greater certainty and comfort whether you are heterosexual, homosexual or bisexual.

Having a firm grasp of your own sexuality allows you the freedom to play. You can permit yourself greater scope. If you are a man, you can gratify your feminine desires without losing your sense of masculinity. If you are a woman you can gratify your masculine impulses without losing your sense of femininity. In both cases you can allow yourself deep feelings of dependence, love and fusion without feeling weak and without feeling that your separateness will be swallowed up in the process. Adult sex, because it rests upon a more secure foundation, can be more intimate, more passionate and more whimsical.

Furthermore, because your sexual identity is more secure in adulthood than it was in adolescence, and because, as an adult, you don't require as much ongoing reassurance that you're normal, you're better able to accept people whose sexuality is different from your own without feeling threatened. You can accept that other people may have a greater or lesser sexual appetite than you do, may have more or less experience, may be more or less giving and empathic, or have narrower or wider sexual interests. Adults who are sexually secure are also able to be genuinely less sexist and less homophobic than pre-adults.

Sometimes Sex Is Just Sex

Of course, not all sex is love-making; sometimes it's just sex. Adults can accept straightforward recreational sex without feeling demeaned by it and, more interestingly, without having to fall in love.

Many women will tell you that divorcing sex from love is something that men find much easier to do. But both sexes have trouble separating sex from love—especially when the sex is illicit. Here are two brief examples that illustrate how sex leads to love, or at least, the illusion of love:

Max, a forty-year-old law partner, with a wife and three children, started an affair with one of the associate lawyers at his firm. To be sure, he'd had marital problems before his affair, but what he did once the affair was underway just made matters worse. Instead of limiting the damage to a sexual dalliance with his associate (which would have been bad enough), Max fell in love with her, confessed his affair to his wife and moved out of his home.

Not by coincidence, both his wife and his lover were volatile, sexy, intelligent women, and soon he was having the same problems with the one that he'd had with the other. Eventually his associate dumped him, and Max returned, hat in hand, to his wife.

Anita, a physiotherapist in her early thirties, went to see a massage therapist for relief of back pain. The massage therapist was devastatingly handsome and very sensitive, and pretty soon he was massaging her ego as well as her back. He listened to her problems, advised her on her diet and before long began having sex with her.

Although he was actually manipulative and fatuous, Anita found him incredibly clever and intuitive.

Unfortunately, Anita was already engaged to a college professor whom she still greatly admired. Yet here is how she chose to resolve her dilemma: She fell in love with her massage therapist (whom she even claimed to find more interesting to talk to than her fiancé!) and broke off her engagement.

Anita finally came to her senses several months later when her affair fell apart and she saw the therapist for the shallow cad that he was. But by then, it was too late for her to pick up the pieces of her shattered relationship with her fiancé, so she rationalized to herself that he probably wouldn't have been right for her anyway.

Both these cases illustrate the fact that most people—men as well as women—can't engage in sexual activity without tossing a bone to their conscience. They appease their consciences by falling in love with the person they're having sex with. This isn't a self-indulgent little affair, they tell themselves. This is *love*! And to convince themselves of the sincerity of their love (which they unconsciously doubt) they fall in love in spades.

Normally we associate the ability to combine love and sex with mental health, and the inability to combine them with neurosis. Let me explain: It *is* true that detachment is the hallmark of the neurotic who can't get aroused when tender feelings and sexual feelings are brought too closely together. The detached person thinks that sex is dirty and is afraid he will soil his lover with it. Therefore, the detached person has only two choices: he can have sex with someone he doesn't love, or love someone with whom he has very little or passionless sex.

That's one way of coping with guilt about sex. The other way to cope with sexual guilt—the opposite of detachment—is to romanticize sex. This kind of person dignifies physical arousal, no matter how shallow, by converting every sexual feeling into a romantic feeling. He's not too *de*tached; he's too *a*ttached.

That was the tack taken by the lawyer and the physiotherapist in our two examples—they "fell in love" because they felt guilty about cheating on their mates. They needed to blur the distinction between sexual attraction and love by elevating mere titillation into an affair of the heart.

The wisdom to be able to distinguish between sexual attraction and real love is evidence of maturity. An adult *can* get sexually aroused by someone he loves (he doesn't need to be detached), yet he *doesn't* need to love everyone who turns him on (he doesn't need to be attached). I'm not advocating meaningless sex or the separation of sex from affection, and I'm certainly not advocating infidelity. I'm making the point that just because you have sexual feelings for someone doesn't mean you have to fall in love with that person. There are times when sex and love should be separated.

Intercourse

Something else about adult sexuality: It's less narcissistic. It involves intercourse (in both senses of the word) with someone *outside* yourself. Adults have a sexual partner, not merely a human object with whom they arouse themselves auto-erotically. Adult sex involves concern for the other person's pleasure, a willingness to be flexible and compromising, the adoption of an outer-directed sexual stance, responsibility for contraception and concern for safety.

This doesn't mean that adults never masturbate. Adults continue to do lots of things that younger people do. The point is that they interact in responsible ways with the world. That's a general principle of adultness: Adult activity is increasingly outer-directed. Because the process of preparation for life has been largely accomplished, more energy can now be channelled into the living of it.

A Brief Disclaimer on the Subject of Sex

Having said all this stuff about sex, a disclaimer is in order. As a psychiatrist, I am constantly reminded about how potent, unpredictable and varied sex really is—and I don't just mean kinky sex, I mean normal sex. Sex is not something that can be neatly managed or fully explained. Its power continues to confound and amaze us all. Sex can be the opponent of our reason or the source of our strength and the wellspring of our love and creativity. We love sex just as much when we're old as when we're young. But when we're mature sex becomes less of a fetish: We seek it, we enjoy it, we just don't make a religion of it.

PLEASURE

Pleasure and Puritanism

As sex goes, so goes pleasure. Like sex, other forms of pleasure—self-expression, the exercise of power, even lazing about—are less guilt-ridden in adulthood than in childhood and adolescence because they've been earned through achievement.

One of the painful lessons a child has to learn is that certain pleasures are contingent on the performance of socially sanctioned actions. Pleasures don't come merely by wishing for them; they have to be earned. This may be a painful lesson, but it is also the beginning of happiness. The person who is willing to perform the requisite actions is able to bring the possibility of happiness under her control.

If a school-age child wants to receive academic recognition, she has to get good grades. This is largely under her control because she is able to study in order to get those good grades. If a teenager wants to buy clothes or CDs, she can save her money or get a part-time job. Even if her parents don't give her the money, she can still earn the things that give her pleasure.

It is true that some pleasures are unearned. You can enjoy the simple things of life—a sunny day or a beautiful song—without performing a positive deed. However, if you want more than the simple pleasures, you have to be prepared to work for them.

It is also true that rewards are not always commensurate with deeds. Some people are rewarded inordinately for their contributions, and some are rewarded inadequately. Some pleasures, like getting a bargain by threatening to shop elsewhere, are coerced; some pleasures, like playing hooky from work, are stolen. They're all the more sweet for being unearned. However, even in the face of occasional evidence to the contrary, the principle of just deserts remains secure. Were it not so, then stolen pleasures would be indistinguishable from earned pleasures, and they'd lose their special charm.

Adults are entitled to enjoy certain pleasures and prerogatives because they've agreed to accept the responsibilities that accompany them. These pleasures include the exercise of power, the right to enter into responsible relationships, including marital and commercial contracts, the freedom to choose a vocation and life-style, and the chance to gratify desires and ambitions and pursue adventures that might be off limits to people who are still dependent on their parents. Pre-adults may partake of these pleasures too, of course, but when they do so they often feel guilty and defensive about it. Since they can't pay for their adult pleasures with adult achievements, and since they are unable to take on the responsibilities that are attached to these pleasures, they are forced to pay for them with guilt and atonement instead.

Many pre-adults fear adulthood because they fear the adult responsibilities that are associated with it. But they need not fear it. Adulthood is rewarding far beyond the imagination of someone who hasn't yet reached maturity.

How can this be, though, if adulthood carries with it responsibilities, cares, duties, woes, sacrifices and obligations from which younger people are mostly exempt? The reason is that in adulthood these responsibilities, cares, duties, woes, sacrifices and obligations *feel* lighter. Pre-adulthood may be more carefree (though often more emotionally turbulent) than adulthood, but it is also more easily weighed down by demands when they arise.

During this earlier phase, as responsibilities begin to accumulate, the pre-adult feels increasingly burdened. She discovers, for example, that she has to go to work no matter how she feels. She has to spend time with her young child when she'd rather be alone. At work she has to be polite to people she's dying to tell off, and so forth. All these obligations seem more burdensome to her, because they feel as though they've been imposed from *outside*, like the chores assigned by her parents, rather than initiated from *inside*, like the activities prompted by her own desires.

Once she undergoes the transition to adulthood, these activities begin to feel less burdensome. Her reason for doing them changes. Instead of being done out of obedience to external authority or to ameliorate guilt—to please her mother or her boss, for example—they are done out of her own internal desire, because doing them gives her a sense of well-being and pride. Therefore, as she makes the shift to adulthood, she automatically experiences a net gain in pleasure. Responsibilities that once seemed heavy suddenly feel much lighter.

SERIOUSNESS
Time Marches On

During the shift to adulthood there is a change in attitude from "facetiousness" to "seriousness." By seriousness I don't mean frowning sobriety or no-nonsense sombreness; I mean the realization that life is for keeps—that time waits for no one. Adults have as much fun as pre-adults, or perhaps more, and they can certainly maintain and expand their sense of humour, but they also take life more seriously.

Before the shift to adulthood, we imagine that we can continually reinvent ourselves or turn over a new leaf. Life seems to stretch out before us like an endless, green plain, full of promise and opportunity. We are still *in statu nascendi*—a state of being born. We will always have another chance.

But after the shift, when we've become psychologically adult, we realize not only that life is finite, but that *our* life is finite. It won't go on forever. The once distant horizon of our vast, green plain begins to come into view. We accept in a more real, less intellectualized way the inevitability of deterioration and death, the fragility of human life and of the life of the world, and the impermanence of health and happiness. We discover that action and inaction have consequences that are sometimes irreversible. Doors *do* close forever. Opportunities *can* be lost. There is *not* always another chance. Things done badly *can't* necessarily be undone. And all our losses will *not* be recouped.

Facetiousness

The realization that time marches on is deeply unsettling. Those who are emotionally unprepared—like most pre-adults—tend to shy away from facing it. This avoidance is reflected in their attitude towards life. They may become cynical about life—the "angry young man" syndrome—or they may become (or remain) facetious about it.

Facetiousness is a defence against a frightening reality. To the facetious person, life is so scary, it's a joke.

There is a wonderful example of the defensive use of facetiousness in the movie *Sometimes a Great Notion,* based on the novel by Ken Kesey. The movie stars Paul Newman as a ruggedly independent lumberjack. He and a fellow lumberjack are felling trees near a river when one of the trees they're cutting falls the wrong way and pins Newman's friend beneath it in the shallow water near the bank. At first Newman's friend is able to keep his head above the water, but, as the log inexorably settles, it threatens to pull him beneath the surface.

Newman struggles to free the man but is unsuccessful. He tells his friend that he'll have to give him mouth-to-mouth respiration under the water until help arrives. But the image of Newman giving him mouth-to-mouth respiration and the imminent prospect of his own death strike his friend as unbearably funny. He makes mock-romantic gestures towards Newman, as if Newman were using the opportunity to kiss him instead of trying to save his life. Newman warns his friend not to fool around, but the fool can't resist the tickle of his own giddy humour and continues to wise crack while his situation deteriorates.

The huge log continues to slowly sink, and Newman's friend is dragged below the surface of the cold murky water. Newman inhales a lungful of air and plunges beneath the water to blow it into his friend's mouth. At first his friend co-operates, but then he starts to giggle. A jet of bubbles rises to the surface, and the man begins to struggle. Newman refuses to give up. He resurfaces for another breath of air and plunges again beneath the water to replenish his friend's dwindling supply of oxygen. But again the logger starts to giggle. And unable to take in the air Newman is trying to give him, he drowns in a paroxysm of laughter. He expires, literally, of facetiousness.

Facetiousness isn't usually fatal, of course, but seriousness, as I'm using the word here, does take courage. And this kind of courage takes life experience. The pre-adult hasn't yet overcome enough of life's obstacles to acquire that courage. He still has a paralyzing fear of failure, rejection, shame, embarrassment, disappointment and loss of face. He copes with his fear by playing the wit and the satirist and by avoiding commitment, effort and sincerity. Because he is threatened by all genuine feelings, any expression of sentiment that does manage to escape his suppression has to be undone, or at least spiked with irony, self-effacement, self-confession, self-criticism or self-spoofing. Like the facetious logger in *Sometimes a Great Notion*, the facetious pre-adult can't resist any joke or clever turn of speech—no matter how inappropriate or damaging it might be.

Bennett, a man who was in marital therapy with his wife, Wendy, recounted an argument they'd had during the preceding week. During the argument Bennett had been on the verge of responding to Wendy's criticism in his usual fashion, when something in her voice had suddenly made him realize the gravity of their situation and caused him to pull up short. He decided to try a different tack. Instead of defending himself and attacking her, as he would normally have done, Bennett acknowledged Wendy's complaint and offered to try changing his behaviour.

Since this struck me as a breakthrough in their relationship, I tried to underscore it by pointing out to them that Bennett's apology had prevented their argument from escalating, and that Wendy, in turn, had responded in kind. After I did so, however, Bennett confessed that his gesture had been calculated only to get Wendy off his back. And on hearing this "confession," Wendy burst into tears of despair.

Even before this incident, their marriage had been hanging by a thread. Why would Bennett jeopardize it further by making his gratuitous "confession"? He was only admitting the obvious anyway. *All* apologies are designed to defuse conflict. Why, in the guise of honesty, did he undermine the headway they'd made in handling their argument?

Bennett was not cynical about marriage in general, or about his own marriage in particular—quite the reverse. He was concerned about his marriage and deeply afraid of losing his wife, whom he loved. But the same feelings of concern and fear that had prompted him to take a more constructive tack in the argument with her also made him feel embarrassed. He couldn't handle the seriousness of the situation or the sincerity of his own feelings, so he made a mockery of them by "confessing" that his apology was merely tactical.

Fortunately, Bennett was able to acknowledge the perversity of his pseudo-confession and to reassure Wendy that he really did care for her. Had he failed to do so, however, had he stuck to his facetious "honesty" for fear of taking his own feelings seriously, he might have permanently severed the slender thread that held the marriage together.

The Young and the Charming

Becoming adult is especially arduous for those who, as children, are very bright, or are precociously verbal, witty, charming, insightful, beautiful or clever. They have access to the tools of facetiousness early and may be able to ward off their day of reckoning until it's too late. They substitute "people skills" for actual skills or rely on charm instead of accomplishment. They grow up to be articulate, flippant, clever, seductive, manipulative, amusing, glib, youthful and disarming adults who are spared the consequences of their own actions—but only up to a point. Eventually, like everyone else, they have to perform. At that point, they either rise to the occasion or fall by the wayside.

These delightful people may take a pleasantly meandering course in their psychotherapies as well as in their lives. They never quite get around to grappling with important therapeutic issues on their own steam. They engage in pseudo-therapy. Instead of focusing on the events in their own lives that really matter, they talk about academically interesting or abstract issues that they think will intrigue their therapist. At other times they'll be unprepared or their mind will go blank. So even though they're stuck in a dead-end job or an unsatisfactory relationship, they'll claim to have nothing to talk about. Just as they hope to leave it up to their parents to take care of their happiness, they hope to leave it up to their therapist to take care of their therapy.

David, a young man who bore the surname of a nationally prominent publishing family but was too distant to share their wealth, dreamed that he would one day be anointed to run the family business. Even though he had done poorly in university and was able to land only a low-level job in one of the family's subsidiary businesses, his fantasy endured.

David decided he wanted to be a writer but never took the responsibility of putting pen to paper. It was as if he imagined that life would go on indefinitely and never pass him by. He was "forever young" and funnily enough, like many of these perpetual pre-adults, he actually looked young. He was thirty-five but looked twenty-five. (Sometimes the day of reckoning comes for these "forever young" people only when they finally begin to look their true age.)

Naturally David was very concerned about appearances. He didn't want to appear serious even to himself. If something didn't come to him naturally, he shied away from doing it altogether. He wanted to appear smart without actually having to be smart. He didn't want to raise expectations by succeeding or in any other way put pressure on himself to perform.

David was always preparing for life but never quite engaging it. He lived in the future where the promise of better things—sexier women, more money, fame and power—were always right around the corner. Like a gambler who doesn't know his luck's run out, David believed he could reshuffle the deck, over and over again, until he finally dealt himself a winning hand.

David was afraid that growing up meant not having fun, so he remained a clever kid instead. At thirty-five he was still working at an entry-level job in publishing but claimed he wasn't in the least depressed about it. To admit that he was depressed would have undermined his conviction that he was still a "student" of life, still in training for adulthood. David couldn't afford to get serious.

When we become adults, we renounce facetiousness and get serious. But what happens to our facetiousness? Does it disappear? Is there a danger that we'll become too serious? Are we at risk of becoming humourless drones, devoid of irreverence, wit, satire and the ability to laugh in the face of suffering? Of course not. When we get old enough to have sexual intercourse, we don't stop kissing. When we get serious about life, we don't lose our sense of humour. If anything, it gets better. Facetiousness just ceases to be the primary mode of expression, and humour isn't used only as a defence against fear.

Compromise

The ability to reconcile opposing aims, like seriousness and fun, is one of the marvels of the human mind. In the human psyche nothing is lost or wasted, and in the conflict of aims, there are no decisive victories. The relationship between conflicting human desires and feelings—love vs. hate, attraction vs. repulsion—involves compromise. The resolution of competing psychological desires is not a zero sum game, with a clear winner and loser. One side in the conflict doesn't triumph over the other—they form an alliance. You don't end up with pure love or pure hate, pure desire or pure repulsion; you end up with a compromise synthesized from elements of both.

When you move from one life stage to the next, the later stage doesn't triumph over the earlier stage. The later stage merely contributes an ever larger share to the overall product. More mature behaviours, perceptions, attitudes and feelings supersede less mature ones; they don't replace them.

What's more, according to the psychologist Erik H. Erikson, there is a specific and universal conflict that takes centre stage at each new phase of development. Adolescents, he says, have to strike a balance between what he calls identity consolidation on the one hand and role confusion on the other. Young adults have to balance intimacy and isolation. And adults have to find a compromise between what he calls generativity and stagnation.

Although it may appear that one side of the conflict is definitely to be preferred to the other (that intimacy, for instance, is preferable to isolation), Erikson believes that the optimal condition would be a blend of the two. If a person couldn't stand to be alone, for example (i.e. if she couldn't tolerate being isolated), she'd be as limited as someone who couldn't form attachments (i.e. someone who couldn't be intimate). The relationship between the opposing poles of each developmental phase is not dichotomous, it's dialectic—a synthesis of the two.

The Pros and Cons of Maturity and Immaturity

Psychic maturation is the art of making better and better compromises. As we mature, we get better at balancing our desires with the dictates of our conscience, and our capabilities with the demands of reality. The compromises we forge produce more and more pleasure and less and less pain.

A good example of compromise formation is the resolution of the conflict between the desire to work and the desire to play. Here, however, we encounter something of a paradox. Adults have a greater capacity for work than pre-adults. They are less distractible, more efficient and have greater *sitzfleisch* (the capacity to keep their behind on the chair) than younger people. Furthermore, because adults have more established careers than pre-adults, they feel less need to prove themselves at work and are better able to achieve a balance between work and play. The work adults perform is commensurate, not with the need to enhance self-esteem by being seen as a hard worker, but with the needs of the task. Adults work reasonable hours (more if really required) and spend the rest of the time with their families and friends or pursuing other interests. They don't have to prove that they aren't lazy.

There are some benefits to immaturity too, however. The pre-adult's need to prove himself allows him to do just that—to sacrifice himself for his work in order to achieve recognition. And because most pre-adults have fewer dependants than most adults, they can devote longer hours to their work. The apprentice may be less efficient than his older colleagues, but he also has greater energy to burn and more time to spare.

The period from the mid-twenties to the mid-thirties is the time when doctors complete their specialty training, apprentice electricians become master electricians, lawyers earn their partnership offers, sales people become sales managers, scientists launch independent research careers, teachers become department heads, investment bankers begin to develop deal-making expertise, mechanics become master mechanics, professors earn tenure, and architects develop their distinctive styles. They all work prodigious hours but, in so doing, lay the groundwork for the mature phase of their trades and professions.

Once they arrive at the mature phase of their careers, trades people and professionals switch from trainee status to colleague status. The relationship between junior and senior colleagues becomes somewhat less hierarchical. Their method of learning changes also. They learn less from mentors and more from peers, specialty journals, professional and trade conferences, informal consultations and—most of all—from experience.

REALISM

Living in the Real World

Adults live in the real world—which means that they're realistic, not that they're incapable of idealism or fantasy, or that they blithely accept the *status quo*. Unlike those who are less mature, adults are capable of functioning in an imperfect situation, under conditions of limited information, *without* losing their idealism or their capacity to dream. They don't need to escape into cynicism, complacency, false naïveté or fantasy in order to cope with reality. It may be unfashionable to say this, but adults aren't easily "stressed out" and they aren't isolationist.

The Acceptance of Fallibility

Adults understand that people aren't perfect. They reject the doctrine that experts and other authorities are supposed to be infallible. They are willing to acknowledge mistakes and learn from them. And they know that doing so will diminish their self-esteem and prestige less than covering up will. Adults admire people who are willing to admit honest mistakes and accept the consequences, and they pity those who don't.

Nobody's perfect. Even Ty Cobb, the baseball player with the best lifetime batting average in the history of the major leagues, batted only .367. Yet many pre-adults refuse to accept anything less than perfection from their heroes. They're easily impressed and just as easily disillusioned. They admire figures of authority—politicians, physicians, sports heroes, teachers, business leaders and scientists—but envy their prestige and covet their power. In order to be reassured about their own inadequacy, they look for reasons to devalue them. And the doctrine of infallibility provides just the ticket because no one can live up to it.

There is a downside to the doctrine of infallibility, of course—you have to sacrifice realism. The only people who achieve perfection are those who never act. And only those who never have to make decisions and forge compromises never make mistakes. Adults are more realistic. They know that nothing worthwhile is free of risks, and that failure in the pursuit of a worthwhile goal is preferable to inaction.

An Awareness of Time

Realism involves an awareness of time. Adults are aware that time waits for no one, but they're also capable of being patient. They know that events and people (themselves included) go through phases and cycles. Sometimes people are motivated and productive, sometimes they're lazy and unproductive, sometimes the world seems sensible and calm, sometimes incomprehensible and chaotic. Wild children can grow up to be model citizens, and happy children can grow up to be unhappy adults. Adults realize that most things develop according to their own timetables. They're not dismayed that children are childish, that beginners are slow, and that most people learn only from bitter experience.

Mind you, it's easy to lose sight of the fact that human growth takes place slowly. For instance, it surprises me sometimes when a twenty-year-old doesn't already know that being rejected by someone doesn't mean she's a loser, that missing a deadline won't be indulged at work the way it was at home, or that having good manners and performing filial duties is not incompatible with being self-assertive and autonomous.

Mortality, History, Tolerance and Stewardship

The transition to adulthood is a milestone, and like most milestones it reminds us of our own mortality. But when we reach adulthood, the reminder is more powerful than at any other time—not because we're much older, but because we are no longer the future, we're the present.

When we read love poems by Shakespeare or Wordsworth, we know that both the poet and his lover are long since dead. And we know that we too shall soon be a fading memory. Because this is a fate we share with Shakespeare and Wordsworth, it links us with them and gives us a sense of history. But mortality is a fate we share most acutely with the people who are alive today with us, and it links us with them even more strongly, making us more tolerant of them, regardless of their differences or where they live. Finally, we know that there will be future generations who will be reading about us with the same poignancy and kinship that we feel towards those who've gone before us. And this knowledge reminds us of our stewardship of the planet and of our responsibility to keep it habitable for those who will come after us.

Good and Evil

In adulthood there is a recognition that the world contains evil as well as good. Adults accept that there are limits, that there is ignorance, prejudice and error. There are bad people, bad actions and bad ideas. Therefore, they don't act as if they were innocents. They don't expect naïvely that good will triumph over evil without effort and sacrifice. They don't play with fire unless they're prepared to get burned. They don't espouse dangerous dogmas in order to be fashionable or provocative. They believe in the rule of law and in social responsibility. They're civil and civilized.

Does this mean that pre-adults can't be civil and civilized? Of course not. But pre-adults have less at stake. They don't yet run things, so they can afford to fool around with ideas and actions that might be damaging to themselves or to other people. There are college students, for example, who seem to believe that it is acceptable for them to disrupt lectures by people with whom they disagree. Freedom of speech, they insist, must take second place to social justice—as they define it. But, clearly, they could not espouse such a view if they were responsible for running a university or for maintaining a liberal state. They can afford the luxury of trashing these liberties only because they know that those who are responsible for maintaining them will strive to do so.

Because their identities and beliefs are still in flux, pre-adults are more susceptible than adults to utopian and dystopian ideas. Adults are more aware that they can't escape civilization, and that, even when their ideas are iconoclastic and anti-establishment, they are helping to construct it.

Reason and Reasonableness

As a result of their knowledge of good and evil, adults value reason and reasonableness, and they're sceptical of rhetoric and fanaticism. They know that living in reality requires rational thought. They may trust their own intuition, because it's been born out by long experience, but they don't trust external authority without seeing the data that supports it. They don't promulgate rash, emotionally satisfying ideas, such as fascism, racism, sexism, homophobia and tribalism, that appeal to the evil in us and can produce great harm. They have too much respect for the power of "unreason" to advocate transcendent and persuasive doctrines that can unify, homogenize and embolden people and turn them into a mob. They eschew the demagogic and the superstitious, not because they see these forces as obsolete instruments of human self-expression, but because they see them as very seductive and very difficult to put back in the bottle once they've been let out.

The problem, in our media-blitzed age, is that it's often difficult to separate the rational from the irrational, and the reasonable from the unreasonable. All beliefs nowadays are made to appeal to reason, even those, like religion, that should be made to appeal to intuition and faith. And every fad is trumpeted as a breakthrough. The sellers of snake oil still roll into town to bilk the locals, but their spiel is now a multimedia production at the airport Hilton instead of a hard sell in the town square. The new gurus buy television time and sell tapes and videos, and they're as slick and glib and seductive as any drug dealer.

In order to slip by the healthy scepticism of rational people, fraudulent ideas are invariably cloaked in either the objective jargon of science, technology and medicine, or the humane poetry of philosophy, healing and spirituality. Once it's been camouflaged in the appropriate lingo, prejudice can then masquerade as fact, superstition as science, folklore as wisdom, authoritarianism as technology and narcissism as empowerment.

EQUALITY
Comfort With Yourself Is Contagious
(So Is Discomfort)

Not only do adults live in the real world, they know their place in it as well. They understand themselves, and they understand their relationship to other people. Because they feel comfortable with themselves, they feel more comfortable with other people. They see other working adults as their equals, regardless of their occupations, and they enjoy the confidence that true equality brings.

When a person has a sense of his own stature—when he feels his own strength and value because he's earned a place in the world—it's readily apparent to other people. He's comfortable with himself and that makes others comfortable with him. But the opposite is also true: When a person *lacks* a sense of his own stature, that too is easy for others to detect. He has a discomfort with himself that goes beyond ordinary reserve, and that discomfort is rapidly transmitted to those around him.

People whose sense of their own stature is still evolving will sometimes be overly deferential or overly familiar towards people whom they think have a higher status. They can't tolerate feeling inferior to these higher status people, but they can't tolerate feeling equal to them either, so they flip-flop between awe and envy. On one occasion they may be shy and tongue-tied, on the next bold and provocative. Because they aren't sure yet of who they are in the world, they don't know how to feel or behave. Sometimes they feel grand, other times they feel puny. Sometimes they act timid, other times they act pushy. Either way, they have trouble maintaining a consistent sense of equality with other people.

Adult Stature Confers Equality

Feeling equal to other people—no matter how exalted—is the most important result of feeling a sense of your adult stature. You feel equal to others in the sense of participating along with them in the management of the adult world. Clearly adults are unequal in many ways. They differ in natural endowment, economic advantage, even in luck. But all adults are equal in two ways that matter most. They are equal in the possession of inalienable rights and (if they earn it by participating responsibly in civic life) in being worthy of respect. That's why the salesman who has a sense of his own stature and does his job well is equal to the CEO for whom he works. They are equal to each other not in status, but in something far weightier and more difficult to accomplish—the achievement of adult stature.

How does this translate into behaviour? What's involved in treating another person as an equal? That depends on the context. For example, it isn't necessary, within the context of work, for the CEO and the salesman to be friends, to socialize together, to invite each other to parties or even to like each other. It is necessary for them to be polite, respectful, pleasant and mindful of their responsibilities to each other. It is no violation of equality for the CEO to give legitimate direction to the salesman within the mandate of her leadership responsibility. It is a violation of equality for the salesman to be insubordinate, because that would imply a feeling of inferiority on the one hand and a lack of respect for the legitimate authority of the CEO on the other. It would, of course, violate the principle of equality if the CEO were to use her power to coerce the salesman into an action, such as lying to a customer, that violated his dignity, but it would equally be a violation if the salesman were to use his subordinate status to wheedle unreasonable concessions from the CEO.

Hierarchy and equality are not inconsistent with each other, provided the ranking doesn't undermine the adult stature of any of the participants. The resolution of conflict between equals in the work sphere usually involves compromise, but in an all-out battle neither side asks for or gives special consideration.

In the context of personal relationships, however, equality demands different behaviours than in the context of work. Personal relationships—acquaintanceship, friendship, partnership and family—require more finesse, consideration, compromise and emotional involvement. If care isn't taken to exclude outside differences in status, power or wealth from inside a relationship, then these differences can undermine a feeling of equality between friends and partners. And within the context of personal relationships, the resolution of conflict almost always involves compromise and almost never involves a no-holds-barred battle. But as in the work sphere, equality in the personal sphere still precludes the abuse of power or the manipulative use of weakness.

Grownups who don't feel equal to other adults either have not yet consciously thought of themselves as adult or are confusing social or professional *status* with personal *stature*. If they still feel unequal, despite understanding that equality is a sense of personal validity based on adult stature, then they have not yet completed the process of forming an adult self-image. It is flatly impossible not to feel the equal of other adults, if you truly think of yourself as an adult. There are no exceptions.

But what if the other person were the prime minister of Canada, a famous scientist, a wealthy business person or the Queen of England? Would you feel equal to those people? The answer is yes, you would. You would feel equal to them *as people*. You might defer to them by virtue of their office, or achievements, or age, or brilliance. And you might not feel equal to them in status, power, wealth or level of responsibility. But as a person—as an adult making your contribution to the world in your own way—you would feel their equal. And that is the most important form of equality.

There are a small number of people who act ostentatiously inferior to other people. They are falsely humble. They act as if they thought everyone else really were the Queen and that they themselves were mere commoners. Like the unctuous clerk Uriah Heep in the Dickens novel *David Copperfield*, they act so self-effacing, it's actually arrogant. They are not truly humble, nor do they feel really inferior. They actually feel that they have *greater* worth than their position in the world would suggest, and they want to draw attention to this travesty by making an exaggerated show of humility. By exaggerating their show of deference, they intend to mock the notion of their inferiority and, by implication, of your superiority.

It's easy for most people to assert that they're equal to people above them in status; it's much harder for them to extend that same consideration to people below them in status. But to have any real meaning, the principle of equality must apply equally down the social ladder as well as up.

That's the beauty of feeling adult. When you make the transition to adulthood, you don't just gain enough stature to feel the equal of others, you gain enough stature to permit others to feel equal to you. You are increasingly able to feel comfortable with people both above and below you on the social ladder. You don't need to be either condescending or falsely humble.

An adult, in fact, *insists* on the equality of others. She holds them to the same standards of social conduct as she holds herself, and she fosters their transition to adulthood whenever possible. She is a leader. She is willing, when necessary, to focus on the needs of other people and to set aside her own agenda to promote theirs. As a parent, she is willing to devote the time and energy to educate, encourage and discipline her children. As a manager or supervisor, she is willing to teach and support her employees or apprentices and to delegate responsibility to them so that they can get ahead. She is a promoter of other people. She rewards merit and reinforces effort. She enjoys seeing other people get their just rewards. She is even willing, if they deserve it, to let other people surpass her.

It is axiomatic, therefore, that a person *can't* be a true leader until she, herself, has undergone the psychological shift to adulthood. She can be a lieutenant, perhaps, but not a general. If she takes the helm before becoming psychologically adult, like the potentate of a military dictatorship who wears the regalia of high rank but knows he hasn't earned it, she'll feel like an impostor. A true leader has a sense of comfort with herself that comes from a willingness to assume ultimate responsibility.

A true leader, in other words, has legitimate authority. And every adult is in some way a leader, if only in her own family or at her job. By definition then, an adult doesn't need to rebel against authority for the sake of establishing her own stature. Because she recognizes that there is such a thing as legitimate authority, she challenges authority only if it is illegitimate or unjust.

CITIZENSHIP
Adult Status Confers Full Citizenship

The term citizenship defines a relationship between the individual and the society that is initiated by the psychological shift to adulthood. In some sense the two terms—citizen and adult—are synonymous. Just as the onset of a mature relationship with the self is the inner expression of adulthood, the onset of a mature relationship with the world—citizenship—is the outer expression of adulthood. One requires the other, and each is enriched by the other.

The desire to identify with our culture and to play a part in preserving and enriching it, is a universal human impulse that's realized at the moment we start to feel adult. The notion of adultness has meaning only in a social context. We feel adult only to the extent that we fulfil our society's responsibilities and share in its privileges—responsibilities and privileges that we've been preparing for and accumulating during the earlier part of our lives.

Perhaps in some less complex era, when the voting age was twenty-one and twenty-one-year-olds were mature, the right to vote and the transition to psychological adulthood were precisely coincident. Nowadays people vote at eighteen but generally don't feel adult until they're about thirty, so the relationship between the two doesn't quite hold up. Just as the legal onset of adulthood has become temporally separated from the psychological onset of adulthood, so the legal onset of citizenship has become temporally separated from the psychological onset of citizenship as well. In fact, the actual relationship between the two is now reversed from what it once was: The acquisition of legal citizenship does *not* produce the feeling of being an adult, but the feeling of being adult *does* produce psychological citizenship.

The feeling of becoming an adult carries with it the feeling of having been granted membership in society. We feel a sense of belonging in the community of adults—a community that extends from our families to our culture to the entire species and ultimately to the entire universe.

Liberation from the Self

A trivial manifestation of the psychological transition towards citizenship, but one that a surprising number of people have reported to me, is an increased interest in reading non-fiction in general and "the great books" in particular. Whereas they once read contemporary fiction almost exclusively, they now read a greater number of books on science and contemporary social issues, biographies and the classics of literature and philosophy. The reason for this increased interest in history, religion, philosophy, justice and politics is not just pragmatism, but intellectual curiosity and a desire for meaning.

Once we become adults we seem to want to cast off some aspects of our narrow self-interest and turn our attention to the outside world. We know ourselves well enough to be able to be liberated from ourselves. We can turn some of our attention to things greater than ourselves, and we are happy to be able to do so. We discover that activities, tasks and perceptions that we previously experienced as meaningless suddenly become meaningful. Once we feel adult, we find that doing our jobs and performing our familial and social duties become zestful and fulfilling.

At the very least, they become less burdensome. The energy once spent in *becoming* can now be used in actually *being*.

Religious people base their morality and selflessness on a belief in the omniscience and supremacy of God. Non-believers need a bit more ingenuity. For many, the civil religion of citizenship—a belief in inalienable rights, in democracy, in humanism, in law or in the necessity of preserving civilization—is sufficient reason for leading a good life.

LEADERSHIP

One of the privileges and prerogatives of adult status is the right to assume positions of leadership. The desire to lead comes from three sources: (1) the desire for power, (2) the desire to make things work well and to contribute something of value, and (3) the desire to foster the growth of other people.

Not everyone wants power, but those who do gain the confidence and means, as adults, to seek it. However, the desire for power is not the only factor—or even the main factor—that motivates most adults to assume positions of leadership. More important to them is the desire to make things work well and to contribute something of value. Leadership—and power—is a means to that end.

Plato argued that the most capable people in a community would naturally want to assume positions of leadership, because it was in their rational self-interest to do so. If *they* didn't lead, he said, then those of lesser ability would lead, and the capable people would be forced to accept directives from the less capable and to live in a world that was less desirable than the one they could have constructed themselves.

Leadership is also the expression of a creative impulse—the desire to shape events and to leave an imprint on the world. Like all creative impulses, leadership gratifies the desire to extend our reach, to touch other people and to produce something that might outlive us.

The desire to foster the growth of other people really begins only in adulthood, and it's only at that point that it contributes to the motivation to lead. Before adulthood, we don't feel fulfilled or strong enough to happily tolerate the success of others.

Yet it's this capacity to tolerate and even to take joy from the achievements of others—even when there's the risk of being surpassed by children, students, apprentices and protégés—that is the hallmark of true leadership.

In order to feel respect for other people, and even to admire them, you need to believe that their stature doesn't diminish your stature. You have to believe that the world is big enough for the both of you. This secure sense of self comes from the feeling of fundamental equality that is implicit in the achievement of adult stature. Adults feel rich enough to be generous, yet deserving enough to not have an embarrassment of riches.

In order to bolster his self-esteem, a man empowered by the achievement of adult stature doesn't need to abuse his power over subordinates, children, women, dependants or people weaker than he is. Similarly, a woman who feels psychologically adult doesn't need to exploit those who are dependent on her in order to work out her own feelings of powerlessness. She doesn't feel the need to envy or deprecate men, nor to curry their favour. Mature men and women aren't afraid of their sexuality, but they don't use it for intimidation or manipulation.

WISDOM

Wisdom is a synthesizing function of the human mind. It melds experience, prediction, judgment, knowledge, intuition, ethics, empathy and creativity into understanding. And it distills pure enlightenment from raw data. Those who are unable to accurately perceive or interpret events that take place in their lives are unable to learn from experience and can never achieve wisdom. They continue to see things in the same narrow way, maintaining obsolete ideas and prejudices and repeating the same mistakes over and over.

Wisdom is both conservative and experimental, complex and simple, cautious and adventurous. It is a process as well as a product, a trait as well as a state. Wisdom is the thing that transcends all the other individual elements of adulthood and combines them in the right proportions. Wisdom depends for its own soundness on the soundness of each of the other elements of adulthood, but it is greater than the sum of these elements.

Wisdom can't be taught, but it can be learned by observation, evaluation and reflection, and by trial and error.

Wisdom helps us decide what's possible and what isn't, what we can change about people and the world, and what we can't. Wisdom helps us to establish priorities. It helps us decide what's important in life and what isn't. Wisdom helps us figure out what we need in order to survive, and what we need in order to be happy. It helps us decide what our role ought to be in the world, what actions we ought to make and what results our actions are likely to produce. Most importantly, wisdom helps us to understand and accept human nature.

Peggy was a twenty-six-year-old psychiatric nurse who was feeling increasingly isolated from her colleagues at work and was beginning to have doubts about her suitability for her job. She was on the crisis intervention team of a major psychiatric teaching hospital. The team was composed of a social worker, two psychiatrists and four psychiatric nurses, who took turns handling the psychiatric emergencies that showed up in the emergency room or called for help from the community. The team met daily to review all the active cases and to evaluate the new cases in great detail. Most of the direct management of the patients and their families, however, was left up to Peggy and the other nurses.

In the beginning, Peggy felt privileged to be a member of such an élite group of professionals and wanted to be accepted by the other members of the team. She had been specially picked for the job because of her skills, experience and excellent reputation. But after a very short period of time, she began to feel more and more unsure of herself, not just professionally, but personally as well. She became less and less confident when she was presenting her cases in formal meetings of the team, and more and more unwilling to open herself up to her colleagues when they were sitting around shooting the breeze.

Peggy's loss of confidence resulted from a very specific problem: In the course of working with her patients, Peggy discovered that she had many of the same thoughts, feelings and behaviours as her patients—behaviours that her colleagues viewed as evidence of serious neurosis. She was very ashamed of these thoughts, feelings and behaviours and was afraid that her colleagues would find out she was something other than the paragon of mental health she seemed.

For example, one of her fellow nurses in casual conversation interpreted a patient's lateness as evidence of repressed hostility. But Peggy was sometimes late for meetings. Was that evidence of hostility too? She wasn't sure.

On another occasion, a family refused to take a psychotic patient home from the emergency room, claiming that he was too disruptive for them to safely manage. Peggy secretly agreed with the family, but after the team's social worker interpreted the family's refusal as an attempt to deny their own problems by blaming the patient, Peggy kept her opinion to herself.

After many months of this, however, Peggy began to have a change of heart. She began to doubt the sour views of her burnt-out colleagues. She realized that they were cloaking their own frustrations and shortcoming in pejorative jargon to protect themselves from feeling inadequate or overwhelmed. She could empathize with why they needed to do it, but she didn't want to continue doing it herself.

When she reviewed her own rather effective functioning in the world, she came to the conclusion that most of the reactions she had, and most of the reactions her patients had, which were being labelled as abnormal, were, in fact, reasonably normal. She realized that most of the thoughts, feelings and actions she had that were being seen as suspect in her patients were actually universal. Everyone had them some of the time—even psychiatric doctors, nurses and social workers—because they were part of human nature.

For Peggy, this insight marked the beginning of a new wisdom. It allowed her to perform her job with greater zest and empathy for her patients. And it allowed her to feel less intimidated by her colleagues and more comfortable with her own opinions, feelings and behaviours.

Wisdom Helps Us to Benefit from Experience

Wisdom isn't just a byproduct of good living; wisdom helps us to live a good life. But there is another advantage to wisdom: It makes it easier for us to acquire *more* wisdom. Most people know that it's easier to acquire more complex knowledge after you've mastered the rudiments. It's easier to learn new strategies for playing chess, for instance, after you've played a few games and know the names of the pieces, how they move and which are more valuable. It's easier to play the violin after you've learned another musical instrument like the piano, and it's easier to learn almost anything after you've learned how to read. In short, the capacity to benefit from experience increases with the amount of experience already gained.

With increasing knowledge, you gain a more worldly perspective and more mature judgment. The more literate you become, for example, the more you'll appreciate great works of literature, and the more politically sophisticated you become, the more you'll appreciate great leadership and administrative excellence. These developments are not just a function of taste; they result from an increased knowledge of the complexity and subtlety of human nature, and an appreciation of those who can translate their understanding of human nature into useful artistic and political achievements. Self-knowledge and knowledge of other people both increase with experience. And increased knowledge of human nature is the essence of wisdom.

Wisdom Helps Us to Delay Gratification

As people get wiser they gain a greater capacity to delay gratification. They require less immediate satisfaction of their desires. Healthy people in their thirties and forties have less peremptory passions, less rage and more tolerance of anxiety and of desire than people in their teens and twenties. This is partly due to biology, but mostly it is due to wisdom. Adults know that changes take time to unfold, that results may not come immediately after the application of effort, and that many things that look doubtful in the short term work out satisfactorily in the long term. Adults are more patient with people who frustrate them, more persistent with tasks that don't yield quick results, more comfortable with uncertainty, and more willing to postpone pleasure until the necessary work has been done.

The capacity to delay gratification is a form of self-mastery that begins in childhood, increases with practice and is intimately connected with the capacity to achieve. Immature people have more difficulty in accomplishing things when they're hungry, tired, bored, restless, stimulated, worried, distracted and discouraged than mature people do.

The increasing capacity to delay gratification makes it easier to work, to assume responsibility, to deal with relationships, to make long-term plans and commitments and to pursue complex and subtle goals.

More important, as a result of the ability to delay gratification, your "self" gets more stable. Because you're less likely to be blown about, like a raft on the ocean, by your impulses and emotions, you can predict with greater certainty what you'll be like the day after next or how you'll behave in a novel situation. This stability permits you to get a fix on yourself. A stable self enhances self-esteem and allows you to extrapolate into the future. It gives consistency to your life. Contrary to popular belief, being stable does not make life boring; it makes life manageable. And it makes it easier to feel adult.

EMPATHY

The deepest source of knowledge about other people is empathy—the mental and emotional exercise of putting yourself in the other person's shoes to see what his experience feels like. Empathy isn't specific to adulthood, but this is when it blossoms. It actually begins quite early in childhood, and along with fear of authority, contributes to the formation of a conscience. We abstain from injuring other people not only because we fear reprisal, but also because we know—or can imagine—what it feels like to be similarly injured by someone else. Empathy requires not only imagination but the ability and willingness to extrapolate from our own experience.

There are two reasons why empathy reaches full flower only in adulthood: First, it takes considerable experience with people, as well as considerable self-knowledge, to be able to predict another person's reactions. An inexperienced person tends to project his own reaction onto the other person. But that isn't really empathy. Empathy is the capacity to intuit what the other person actually feels. That takes experience. Second, it's easier to empathize downwards than it is to empathize upwards. That is, you tend to feel more comfortable empathizing with the underdog than with the top dog, with someone below you in status and fortune than with someone above you. And you're more likely to be in a position to empathize downwards once you've achieved adult status.

Empathizing with people of lower status gives us that pleasant glow of superiority, of course, but that's not the only reason empathizing downwards is easier than empathizing upwards. There's a more important reason: Empathy requires two separate mental actions: (1) putting yourself inside the other person's skin (identification) and (2) pulling yourself outside of his skin and back into your own secure sense of self. Young people are better at putting themselves inside another person's skin than they are at getting themselves back out again. Children have nightmares after seeing *Snow White*, for example, in part because they're unable to let go of their identification with her at bedtime. Some young people, in fact, have great trouble *not* identifying with other people. Their identification, however, is often faulty. They aren't really identifying with the other person; they're projecting their own very intense feelings onto him. They may pity a person who's deaf, for example, even though that person isn't unhappy about his condition.

Pre-adults also generally have more trouble in getting inside another person's skin than adults do. They find that the other person's emotional pain is too close to home or too recently experienced to be tolerable. Lacking the confidence to identify with the other person's pain, pre-adults may need to repudiate it instead. That's part of the reason why adolescent boys, especially gangs of adolescent boys, treat adolescent girls as sexual objects instead of as people with feelings: They're afraid to identify with the girls' feelings of sexual vulnerability for fear of losing their own sexual nerve.

The risk of identifying too closely can be a special problem for a new parent, especially with her first child, or with a child who reminds her of herself. The parent tends to project her own childhood fears onto this child and then become overly protective of him.[1] Because these parents have lost track of what's them and what's the child, their over-identification with the child makes it more difficult to truly empathize with him. When they look at their child, they don't really see him, they see only themselves. And quite often, this "favoured" child becomes overly identified with his or her parent in return.

Under normal circumstances, the other parent's relationship with his partner and child, the birth of a sibling and the beginning of school, all help to break this magic spell between the overly identified parent and child, freeing them from their symbiotic relationship. But where the overly identified parent is especially needy because she was deprived by her own primary care-giver, or where the other parent is absent or aloof because he's working all the time or is afraid to express emotions, or where the child is overly sensitive to the needy parent's needs because he's the eldest or most empathic, this unhealthy bond may persist until the end of pre-adulthood.

This abnormal bond then makes it much more difficult for the pre-adult child to become an adult. His attempts to become autonomous are resisted both by his overly identified parent, who reacts as if she were being betrayed, and by his own psyche, which reacts as if he were undergoing a traumatic separation or being disloyal. The pre-adult who finds himself in this unfortunate predicament is often tormented by guilt and loss. Ironically, his only recourse may be to become more distant from this parent than he might otherwise have been. He may have to go through a prolonged period of anger towards her before he can be free.

In order to truly empathize with another person, you have to be able to do more than identify with him. You have to be able to be somewhat detached from him and objective about him as well. Here too adults have an advantage over pre-adults. Because of their greater emotional strength, adults are better able to achieve distance from another person's misery or triumph than pre-adults are.

Paradoxically, this strength makes adults better able to withstand emotional closeness too. They are able to tolerate being close to another person, because they have less fear of drowning in his feelings. Just as it's easier to display generosity, mercy and forbearance from a position of strength, it's easier to feel empathy from a position of emotional safety.

The capacity for emotional distancing also makes it easier to empathize with those who are more fortunate than we are. Without some emotional distance, identifying with people of higher social status is especially difficult because it leads to feelings of envy. When the immature person finds his feelings of envy too threatening, he will need to break off his identification with the person above him. The mature person takes other people's successes less personally and is better able to tolerate his own feelings of envy without being threatened by them; he can sustain his identification with the person above him and not push it away prematurely.

Immature people often resent the successes of other people—especially the successes of those close enough to them in status to be seen as genuine rivals—and they gloat when other people fail. Mature people are able to appreciate the successes of other people and feel compassion for them when they fail.

If you don't have great emotional strength, it's at least helpful to be able to tolerate strong feelings. In general, women are more apt to be able to do this than men are, which is why women are more likely to be able to experience empathy for other people than men are. Empathy is usually thought to be a "female" trait. Perhaps that's why empathy has traditionally been considered an unimportant feature of adultness.

Yet empathy is extremely important. It is one of the main adhesives that binds individuals together in social groupings larger than the family. Neither tolerance and respect for the social contract, nor the pure utilitarian calculation of self-interest, is emotionally compelling enough to produce understanding between strangers. Understanding—both in the sense of knowledge and in the sense of compassion—requires empathy.

FORGIVENESS

Life is too short not to be forgiving. An adult reaches out to people. She doesn't stand on ceremony. When she has the opportunity to make peace she seizes it. If someone important offends her, she doesn't sulk or give that person the cold shoulder in return. She tries to deal with the offence straightforwardly and to bridge the gulf between them.

I've seen a surprising number of people who have lost contact with a parent or sibling or, worse, a child who they think has been rude or unsupportive or ungrateful to them. It's true, of course, that there are injustices so egregious as to be unforgivable, but in most cases, the supposed transgressions that give rise to these rifts are remarkably trivial or stale. Still, because the wronged person is not mature enough to make the first move, the rift goes unhealed.

Some parents, for example, will tell their grown children not to come home if they do something that the parents disapprove of. Banishment is a pretty heavy sanction. It ought to be reserved for situations where continued living together would be truly destructive, but some parents use it if their children get their ears pierced, date a person they disapprove of, move out of the house without their consent or spend time with a relative with whom they're having a feud. These parents place a trivial principle ahead of an important relationship and end up losing out on both accounts. If they had really wanted to give their grown children the benefit of their wisdom, they would have stated their opinions straightforwardly and let the children decide for themselves, but since what they really want to do is prove that their children are disrespectful and ungrateful, they force their children to defy them by being arbitrary and coercive.

A good parent may be willing to acknowledge wrongdoing even when there is none in order to keep the lines of communication open with a distressed child. It is often hard to sit and listen to a child who is unjustly accusing you of harming her, when you believe you were doing your best to raise her. And there is a point at which some limits to this venting of anger have to be set. The reward for this patient listening, however, may be not just a better relationship with your child, but *a* relationship with your child.

An adult is willing to risk being seen a fool if it means she will be able to redress a wrong. She would rather risk being snubbed or rejected by the person she's trying to apologize to than miss an opportunity to build a bridge. She doesn't collect grievances in order to put someone in her debt, and she's willing to give more than she gets.

And all this magnanimity and generosity stems from a curious paradox: that, save perhaps for those dearest to her, an adult can live without any other *particular* person. Because she has survived (or seriously contemplated) the inevitable loss of people she loves, the psychologically mature person possesses the inner strength that goes with knowing she has the capacity to endure loss. She can contemplate the loss of her parents without feeling panic. This strength allows the mature person to be able to take the chance of falling in love, of laying her cards on the table and of risking rejection. The adult can admit that she needs certain people, because she knows that, ultimately, she does not.

SPIRITUAL AWAKENING

Many people undergo a spiritual awakening at the dawn of adulthood that continues and deepens throughout the rest of their lives. For some people this awakening may take place in the process of searching for a church or temple in which to give their children a religious education and identity, or themselves a sense of community. But for many others this spiritual awakening is internal, private, having very little to do with organized religion, of no immediate or obvious practical benefit, and unheralded by any outward sign of change.

I have placed spirituality at the end of this chapter for two reasons: The first is that, in a sense, spiritual awakening is more a consequence of becoming adult than it is a prerequisite. The second is that, compared to the other traits of adulthood we've considered, spirituality is simultaneously less necessary and more extraordinary.

Curiosity about spiritual matters doesn't begin in adulthood. Children, and especially adolescents, often have an avid interest in religion, philosophy, politics and science. The preoccupation with such topics provides an instance of the continuity between the pre-adult and adult phases of life. However, in association with the growing intellectual and moral autonomy of adulthood, interest in spiritual issues often takes on a more sophisticated and personal quality than it had before.

Heightened spirituality, as I mean it, is something that can be experienced even by non-believers. It may include, but isn't confined to, religious awakenings. It is certainly not limited to organized religious worship. It can take the form of an interest in a range of topics from astronomy to philosophy, and from ecology to yoga. Spirituality has to do with a desire to feel part of, and to understand, the transcendent: the universal, the grand, the enduring, the noble, the historic and the beautiful. The unifying theme here is the search for meaning and truth.

Why are these spiritual concerns developed or ascribed personal significance in adulthood? There are three reasons: (1) In adulthood we begin to have intimations of our own mortality. (2) We gain the freedom to go beyond our everyday concerns and needs. (3) We begin to assume responsibility for the welfare of the world outside our own small circle.

In early adulthood many people begin to lose close relatives—their grandparents and sometimes their parents—to sickness and old age. They realize, in a more immediate and personal way, how fleeting life and health can be. And as they become more intimately aware of the frailty and impermanence of the material world, they begin to shift their attention from a sole preoccupation with the physical (the body, possessions, the quotidien, the here and now) to a balance between the physical and the spiritual (the mind, the soul, the transcendent, the eternal). Adults turn to the spiritual not only because it gives them greater comfort and solace than the material, but, more importantly, because it offers them greater meaning and fulfilment.

Before most people can make their material concerns secondary, they must first go through a period during which they are primary. They have to feel free of insecurities about material deprivation. And it generally isn't until adulthood that most people begin to feel free of the fear of deprivation.

There are many people, of course, who achieve spiritual enlightenment *despite* being materially deprived, and there are many who achieve it *by* being materially deprived. But most people who are materially deprived have great difficulty in lifting their thoughts above their mundane concerns.

But spirituality doesn't just help us to rise above our everyday existence, it actually helps us to lead better lives. What we seek from spirituality above all is guidance. Whether or not we actually have children, at the threshold of adulthood we become the "parent generation." We seek to replace by an abstract relationship with parental ideals, values and wisdom the concrete relationship we had with our own real parents. To use a religious metaphor, the place in the psyche that was once occupied by our real parents is now filled by our spiritual parent—God. This occurs whether or not we believe in God. The point is we believe in something that exceeds ourselves—humanism, science, the civil religion of constitutional democracy, Nature, even Nothingness itself—and this something helps give meaning to our lives.

Spirituality reflects an innate yearning for something higher and greater than our mundane concerns—a yearning that links us with the historical past and the imagined future and connects our own microscopic selves with the vastness of the universe.

CHAPTER FIVE

WHAT DO YOU HAVE TO GIVE UP TO BECOME AN ADULT?

> When I was a child, I spake as a child, I under-
> stood as a child, I thought as a child: but when I
> became a man, I put away childish things.
>
> *I Corinthians 13 (11)*

If being a grownup is so wonderful, then why do so many people try to postpone it? A big reason is that becoming an adult
entails leaving adolescence and pre-adulthood behind. Not only
do these earlier periods have their own distinct charms—pleasures and privileges that have to be renounced before the transition to adulthood can actually take place—but they also have a
comforting familiarity that is anxiety-producing to discard.
Adulthood can seem intimidating to the uninitiated.

More importantly, becoming an adult requires the renunciation of pre-adult fantasies of ultimate and ideal happiness. These
fantasies derive both from our real and imagined early blissful
relationships with our parents and from our need to compensate
for the inevitable deprivations of childhood. But as these fantasies increasingly collide with reality, they produce the crisis
that gives birth to adulthood. Because the prospect and necessity
of having to give up these blissful dreams is painful, there is
nearly always an initial resistance to becoming adult.

Some people fear they will lose their creativity if they
become adult. If they're artists, they fear that maturity will rob

them of their passion for life and their willingness to take chances in their painting, composing, film-making or writing. This may be an understandable fear, but it is one that is mistaken. Though it is regrettably true that many middle-aged people do seem to lack passion, it is fortunately not true that all adults lack passion or that passion and adultness are necessarily in opposition to each other. After all, there are passionate adults and dull children just as there are passionate children and dull adults. It's usually the dull children, in fact, who become dull adults.

And passion alone is not enough to produce art anyway, otherwise every hot-head and manic would be a poet. The *content* of art may be passionate, foolish, wild, radical, reckless, antisocial or not. But the *process* of art, if it is art at all and not merely exhibitionism, has to be disciplined, thoughtful and self-possessed. The process of making art does require liberation from convention, but not of the sort we associate with adolescent rebellion. It requires the sort of liberation we associate with adult autonomy. It is inconceivable that any great artist would take social acceptability (or its converse, social unacceptability), rather than truth, as his guide. Yet only someone who had liberated himself from convention, who no longer needed to submit to or rebel against his parents or society—in short, someone who was an adult—would be capable of valuing truth over social acceptability or mere rebelliousness.

Creativity doesn't depend on acting like a child. What it depends on is the capacity to feel like a child—to recapture for as long as is necessary, but only for as long as is necessary, the forgotten sights, sounds, smells and feelings of an earlier period. It is the capacity to revivify, not to relive, childhood feelings of enchantment and romance, and the capacity to retrieve, not to inhabit, forgotten sensory impressions that is the key to both creating and appreciating art.

But the resistance to becoming an adult is not just due to the fear of assuming adult responsibilities or of losing pre-adult pleasures and creativity. It is also due to the fear of losing a coherent sense of self. The pre-adult is used to seeing himself as a pre-adult. It helps him explain his own behaviour and the way others behave towards him. Giving up this familiar vantage point on himself would be like losing his bearings or discovering that the magnetic poles have been reversed.

Faced with this potential disorientation, some pre-adults draw back from the brink of adulthood and return to an earlier, more secure, sense of self. They drop out, choose an "impractical" career path, hide in a co-dependent marriage or experiment with alternative life-styles.

Taking a breather before plunging into adulthood, however, can be a very good thing. George Bernard Shaw, for example, dropped out of a successful business career at age twenty and found himself through writing and intellectual exploration. The life-stage theorist, Erik Erikson, described Shaw's "prolongation of the interval between youth and adulthood" as "a psychosocial moratorium."[1] In Shaw's case, as in many others, this moratorium can be critical in helping the pre-adult to find himself. It's not a cop-out, in other words, but an opportunity for the person to re-examine the premises and values underlying his career and life-style choices before they become more fixed.

However, even if you declare a moratorium from your projected life path in order to find yourself, you do eventually have to settle on some path and resume the process of becoming adult. Because if you don't grow up, you'll feel like a perpetual adolescent and miss out on all the joys and challenges of adult life. Once you're teetering on the cusp of adulthood anyway, it's far easier to take the plunge than to continue dancing along the edge.

As you grow older, your familiar pre-adult persona starts to feel more and more constricting. Like an old pair of blue jeans that you love but can barely squeeze into, your old self-image has to be put away and a new self-image tried on. You can take your old persona out of the closet every now and then to try on; but you can wear it comfortably only when you want to be nostalgic or when you want to recapture the fun of being young. For everyday use, however, only the new adult persona will really fit.

A patient of mine compared the experience of shedding her childhood past in favour of her adult present to the process of molting. "I can see the new me beneath the old skin that's been rubbed away," she told me. "It feels tender, but very, very good."

To be more precise about this process, however, we really ought to say that something is being *renounced*, or given up, rather than put aside or rubbed away. The term renunciation gives proper emphasis to the fact that the "putting away" is active, voluntary and self-administered, that it's done with some feeling of loss and regret, and that the person doing the putting away has made peace with the process and recognizes its appropriateness.

THE CENTRAL RENUNCIATION OF ADULTHOOD

The central renunciation of adulthood is the letting go of our old relationship with our parents. It means giving up the old desires and beefs we feel towards our parents as well as our old dependencies and hostilities. It involves reinventing our relationship with them, and with the rest of the world, along new lines—lines that are more consistent with the new adult sense we have of ourselves.

How does the process work? Do we just decide one day to change our relationship with our folks? Not exactly. Deciding whether to give up such obvious forms of dependency as financial assistance, housing and parental advice may be relatively easy. These forms of dependency are at least clear-cut, are undertaken consciously and have simple remedies. But subtler forms of dependency, because they're disguised and unconscious, are harder to discover and harder still to decide whether to give up.

One of the subtlest and most persistent forms of dependency is the hoarding of old complaints. By keeping track of the ways our parents have failed us, we hope that we'll be able to invoice them for it sometime in the future. Then, if they can't make us happy when we present them with the bill, they will at least feel properly remorseful.

When we decide to renounce these claims against our parents, it means we now see ourselves as capable of satisfying our own needs. It means we've accepted the reality that our parents are no better at making us happy than we ourselves are. Before we can renounce our old claims on our parents, therefore, we have to be already happy. There has to be enough gratification in our current lives that we can afford *not* to collect on the old debts (real or imagined) owed to us by our parents. To extend the banking metaphor further: Before we can tear up the old IOUs from our parents and from the world, we need to have enough money in the bank—in the form of happiness and success—to make the sacrifice bearable.

Once we cut the umbilical cord—and this is the best thing about it—we can then control our own happiness. Happiness becomes something that we attain through our own efforts, rather than something we receive as a gift from our parents or from other people, and which can therefore be taken away.

Jody was a thirty-one-year-old high school teacher when she began therapy. She had been reasonably successful in her career, but not so successful in her relationships with men. She had no trouble attracting or falling in love with men, but having done so, she had considerable trouble trusting or talking to them.

She believed that the only thing men wanted from her was sex. And on the flimsiest of evidence, she felt free to accuse a man of being condescending towards her or of treating her as if she were stupid. Unfortunately, as Jody's accusations got more and more irrational and antagonistic, the man's responses got more and more ginger and placating—until, eventually, he really was being condescending towards her.

Jody blamed her father for her difficulty with men. She accused him of being interested only in how she looked and in how she acted with the boys she went out with.

"No wonder I don't trust men," she explained. "My father took no interest in my education at all. He treated me like a cute little fluff-head, and warned me not to get knocked up. He didn't even encourage me to go to college."

But Jody did go to college and she did very well there. She graduated with first class honours and, before training to be a teacher, earned a master's degree in English literature. At thirty-two she became the head of her English department; at thirty-three she co-authored a highly regarded report on the use of computers in the classroom that had been commissioned by the board of education.

The recognition Jody received at work made her feel more secure about her intelligence and her value to the community. As a result of this boost to her self-esteem, she became less mistrusting of men and more willing to believe that they respected her as a person and not merely as a sexual object.

She fell in love with a suitable man—who loved and respected her in return—and began a stable and loving relationship with him that eventually culminated in marriage. Feeling happy and appreciated allowed her to let go of her anger at her father and initiate a relationship with him that was much more balanced and mature.

To fulfil your potential, you have to be able to exploit your strengths. But before you can exploit your strengths, you first have to deal with your weaknesses—including those weakness that resulted from defects in your upbringing. The process of coming to terms with your limitations requires understanding. It requires understanding of yourself, and of your parents as well.

The following case illustrates how the process of understanding yourself can lead to a better understanding of your parents, and eventually to a more adult relationship with them.

Faith was a deeply religious forty-five-year-old woman, who lived with her two teenage daughters in a small suburban condominium. She had recently separated from her husband, an emotionally impoverished man fifteen years her senior, and because the condominium was the only thing she had received from him in the separation agreement, the former full-time homemaker had begun to work as a clerk in the office of a men's clothing store.

Despite her small income, Faith managed to save a little money. So, having devoted twenty-five years to furthering her husband's career and nearly twenty to raising her children, she decided that it was finally time to devote some effort to improving her own life. She enrolled in the divinity school of the local university and began a course of psychotherapy.

When Faith first began her therapy, she reported that she felt trapped inside herself. She was terribly inhibited in her seminars and froze whenever she was with more than one other person.

"I know there is something good and solid in me," she said. "I want to be able to express who I am without always stopping myself."

Faith had grown up in South Africa in a very deprived home. Her parents had emigrated from Poland before she was born. They spoke Polish at home and were very strict and very religious. Because Faith's mother had been physically and emotionally abused by her father, her mother had courageously separated from him when Faith was just over two years old. The father had moved to a different city, leaving Faith, her mother and her younger brother to fend for themselves. She never saw him again, and when she was seventeen, she heard that he had died.

They lived next door to her aunt and uncle and frequently had meals with them. At one of these meals, Faith's uncle hurled a plate at his wife during an argument, but ended up hitting Faith with it instead. Faith concluded that her uncle loved his wife too much to hit her, so he'd "accidentally" hit Faith instead. This perception of herself as someone unloved—a target for other people's frustrations—persisted throughout her life.

She felt stigmatized too. When the parish priest made his annual visit to bless the houses of the faithful (a custom at the time), he blessed Faith's aunt and uncle's house, despite their marital turmoil, but refused to bless her mother's house because she'd been divorced.

Luckily, Faith was able to call on some extraordinary inner resources to help her survive. She possessed an immense inner joy and enthusiasm, keen insight, intelligence and curiosity, an almost miraculous idealism, a highly developed appreciation of beauty—both natural and humanly created—a profound understanding of herself and genuine empathy for others. She had a lovely gentle manner and expressed herself with simplicity and grace. She could allow herself to be serious without needing to dilute it with irony, yet she could laugh at herself when she got too intense.

When Faith was in her early teens, her mother had the first of many paranoid psychotic episodes that resulted in her being given a diagnosis of schizophrenia. She was hospitalized repeatedly, but when she was at home it fell to Faith to look after her. Despite this partial role reversal, Faith continued to defer to her mother and tried her best to please her.

Both her mother and her aunt were very strict and critical concerning her manners, comportment, religious observance and propriety. They expressed oblique disapproval of her exuberance, creativity and precocious intellect.

"You may become something one day, Faith," her mother told her, "but will it be for good or for evil?"

Resentful of their put-downs and veiled envy, Faith decided to become "good" rather than "bright." She hid her inner light under a bushel, particularly when she was around her mentally ill mother, whom she easily surpassed in brilliance, and became the dutiful daughter instead.

Over the years, however, the fact that she had deliberately decided to conceal her brilliance and energy became repressed. Faith actually began to believe that she really was dull and limited. She became quiet, withdrawn and self-sacrificing. In order to help cope with her anger towards her mother, she tried to suppress anything "bad" in herself and worked hard to be seen as good. Yet, despite her isolation, she always had a few close friends. They saw her depth beneath the still waters of her adopted personality.

When she was twenty, the dutiful daughter transformed herself into the dutiful wife. She was full of hope and romantic idealism and, despite having no good examples to follow, tried her best to make her marriage work.

When she left her husband after nearly twenty-five years of unreciprocated effort, therefore, she was overwhelmed with guilt. True, he hadn't been capable of love, but that, so she reasoned, was not his fault. She was grateful to him for having removed her from the misery of her home and for taking her to America. And she felt responsible for him.

After a year of thinking about the matter, however, Faith realized that her guilt about leaving her husband stemmed from the fact that he reminded her of her hostile, pathetic mother. She concluded that, after nearly twenty-five years of nurturing and supporting him with very little in return, it was ethically defensible to finally move on.

As she understood herself better, Faith became more self-accepting. She was doing well at school, handling the emotional vicissitudes of her teenage daughters with empathy and skill, and feeling increasingly solid and at peace.

One day, while thinking about the plate-throwing incident, she had an insight: "There must be something about my quietness that provokes people," she said.

She recounted three incidents in which she felt she had been the target of other people's hostility: The first occurred at her cousin's birthday party when she was twelve. Her cousin seemed marvellously at ease with herself in a way that Faith could only envy. She was spontaneous and natural and, despite being the centre of attention, totally unselfconscious. Her cousin's social adeptness, however, only aggravated Faith's discomfort. She affected a haughty dignity and withdrew to a corner, like a princess waiting to be courted. But the courtship never came, of course. The children ignored Faith and gravitated to her confident cousin instead.

At the time of this episode, Faith blamed her cousin for humiliating her. She felt that she'd been deliberately shown up and ostracized. Looking back on it, however, Faith realized that her pain had been self-inflicted. It was her own defensive coldness and aloof demeanour that had alienated the other children, not her cousin's charm.

The second incident occurred when Faith was in high school. While she was sitting alone in the cafeteria one day, eating her lunch and reading a book, a boy threw an apple at her, which hit her on the nose. Though the attack was unprovoked by anything she'd done, Faith took it as evidence that there was something about her that incited hostility.

The third incident had taken place just a few days before her appointment. One of her divinity school classmates, a wealthy woman in her thirties, had made an excellent presentation in their "Feminism and the Church" tutorial. Faith felt so intimidated by the woman's polish and verve that she was totally unable to participate. She sat watching the proceedings in silence, while feeling more and more inadequate.

After the tutorial, the woman approached Faith and said, "Everyone has congratulated me on my presentation, but I want your opinion because I know you will tell me the truth."

Faith answered, "Your presentation was very polished and intelligent. Because you come from a privileged background, you come across as very confident and strong."

The woman walked away without making a reply.

"What happened?" Faith asked during her psychotherapy session. "I was being sincere. I thought her presentation was very good. Why was she angry at me?"

I told her that her comments to her classmate had implied the following: I've suffered and you haven't. My understanding comes from true suffering, whereas yours only comes from having had the opportunities of a privileged upbringing. I get to be eligible for sainthood; you only get to be a patron of the Church.

Faith began to laugh. "You're right," she said. "I was feeling envious of her."

Her silence in the tutorial, like her aloofness at her cousin's birthday party, was quite eloquent. Faith suddenly understood why the boy had thrown the apple at her in the high school cafeteria, and why she had acted like a wallflower at her cousin's party. She saw that her passivity and silence were meant as a reproach—first to her father for abandoning her, then to her mother for her cruelty and self-ishness, and finally to those in the world who were better off.

Before our next appointment Faith called her mother in South Africa. She told her mother that she now under-stood how difficult it had been for her to raise Faith and her brother all alone, without a husband and with her own problems. "I know you did the best you could," she said.

Her mother responded in an entirely new way too. She didn't justify herself, as she had in the past, or try to deny the many mistakes she had made. Instead, after a moment of silent thought, she simply said: "Faith, I love you."

Faith forgave her mother. Without minimizing her own suffering, she was able to stop reproaching her mother for it. Equally important, she didn't need to reproach her-self for her envy and silent hostility. She understood where it had come from—and she let it go.

For the first time in her adult life Faith was able to acknowledge the bad as well as the good in herself, and to allow herself to be strong and bright. She didn't need to hide her light under a bushel any more, or conceal her own strengths in order to make those weaker than herself feel stronger.

Despite her insecurities, Faith did well in school. As she gained confidence, she started to participate more in class and began to make friends with some of her class-mates. At the end of her first year, she won a scholarship that allowed her to complete her studies. And after gradua-tion she worked in a hospital as a chaplain.

RENUNCIATIONS IN RELATION TO THE SELF

What follows is a catalogue of attitudes that we have to give up in order to function optimally as adults. The more of these atti-tudes we've renounced during pre-adulthood, the easier it is to make the transition to adulthood. Let me emphasize, however, that it's not usually possible to renounce these habits, attitudes and desires merely by an act of will. The best way to change them, as illustrated by the case of Faith cited above, is by trying to understand and accept yourself, and by trying to understand and accept other people.

There is considerable overlap between the categories, and the list does not pretend to be comprehensive. It includes changes in attitude towards ourselves, our parents and the outside world. It involves giving up our unrealistic and infantile desires as well as our excessive passivity and dependence on others—especially our parents and spouse.

The obsolete pre-adult attitudes and behaviours listed in this chapter have primarily to do with the self. They include variations on the themes of grandiosity, self-indulgence and wishful thinking. The attitudes and behaviours listed in the next chapter have mostly to do with interpersonal relationships and our expectations of other people.

Renunciation of Grandiosity

Pre-adults often have a flimsy conceit—a grandiosity of *self-presentation*. As they approach adulthood, they feel a shaky sense of superiority that protects them from a dawning awareness of their own inadequacies. Like a party balloon that has been stretched so thin the slightest jab will pop it, their grandiosity is easily deflated. We all know people who act as though they're much smarter and more worldly-wise than the rest of us, but who get enraged or fall apart when they're challenged.

This is the most familiar form of grandiosity—and it's the easiest to give up once a certain quantity of real success has been achieved. Career satisfaction and a good relationship allow us to let the air out of our hyper-inflated narcissism with a minimum of pain. By generating genuine happiness and pride, they remove the need for compensatory grandiosity.

There is a second, and more insidious, form of grandiosity, however—the grandiosity of *self-expectations*. These are inflated notions of what success and achievement actually entail, inculcated by parents who are overly invested in their child's accomplishments. The inflated expectations are accepted on faith by the child, without examination as to their appropriateness, and then buried in the unconscious as an ideal to live up to. As a result, these children grow up with excessively grand and rigid ideas about what they will have to do to be worthwhile.

This grandiosity of self-expectations often accompanies the more familiar grandiosity of self-presentation. We all know people like this too. They can't settle for *trying* their best, they have to *be* the best—and they have to make sure everyone knows they're the best. They can't be content trying to become the best teachers, musicians or tennis players they can be, they have to become better than everybody else—and be recognized as such. Even their vacations have to be the best. They can't just go to Paris and enjoy it, they have to explore it so compulsively that they can claim to know it better than the Parisians themselves.

In order to be able to reflect on your actual accomplishments and find them worthwhile (so that they can be internalized as the core of a new adult sense of self), you must have realistic standards—criteria for success that are commensurate with your abilities. If they are too rigid or grandiose, you will constantly feel disappointed in yourself. Then, because you lack a core of self-worth around which to construct a more adult sense of yourself, you will have greater difficulty making the transition to adulthood.

This sets up a vicious circle: Because you feel like a failure, you raise the bar of success higher in the hope of regaining your self-esteem with one grand achievement, but when you can't vault over this new mark either (because it's too high for you), you feel like an even greater failure than before.

Renunciation of Entitlement

ENTITLEMENT BASED ON INDULGENCE VS. ENTITLEMENT BASED ON DEPRIVATION

Entitlement is a variation on the theme of unreasonable expectations. This time, however, it's our expectations of others, not ourselves, that are inflated.

People with a sense of entitlement feel that the world owes them something. They appear to be spoiled, but it isn't always the case that they're the product of too much unearned *privilege*. They can also be the product of too much unfair *deprivation*, which leaves them feeling entitled to lifelong compensation. Freud described these people as "exceptions"[2] because, having suffered enough already in their lives, they feel they deserve to have an exception made for them—they should be exempted from any further deprivation.

People seem to find it easier to renounce the entitlement resulting from indulgence than the entitlement resulting from deprivation. Life tends to dole out suffering and misery to everyone, randomly and on a regular basis. This "everyday" suffering undermines feelings of impunity and privilege on the one hand and reinforces feelings of vulnerability and deprivation on the other. In other words, painful experience offers a corrective balance for people who were spoiled, thus eroding their sense of entitlement, while it confirms the worst expectations of those who were deprived, thus leaving their entitlement intact or adding to it.

> Elizabeth was twenty-three years old and had just graduated from university when she came to see me "to get an objective opinion on what I'm doing wrong in my life." She had recently broken up with her boyfriend and was making enemies on the job. In both cases, her interpersonal conflicts stemmed from her conceit and her sense of entitlement. She expected to be courted and catered to by her boyfriend, and she expected special treatment at her job.
>
> Having been accepted into graduate school in creative writing to start that fall, Elizabeth had taken a temporary job as a receptionist in an accounting firm (except that no one but Elizabeth knew that it was only for the summer). After a few weeks of trying to ingratiate herself to the staff and clients, Elizabeth began to revert to her old personality. She was rude on the phone to clients who were anxious or demanding, high-handed with the other secretaries, whom she saw as beneath her, and devious with the office manager, who was her boss. Things were not going well at her job, and she sensed, correctly, that people there didn't like her.

She was also beginning to get an inkling that maybe she was the one with the problem, not everyone else. She had offended people with her arrogance and abrasiveness ever since she was a child, but in the past she'd never cared. Who cares about these people anyway, she would tell herself. They'll never have any impact on my life. I'm going to be a famous writer one day.

Now, however, she was less sure of herself. Her boyfriend had already left her, and she was on the verge of losing her job, which she needed to help pay for school.

When Elizabeth was seven, her parents had separated with great bitterness, and she was caught in the crossfire. She was alienated from her father for many years and was forced to live with her self-centred mother. The experience certainly hurt her, but she also learned to use her misfortune to play on the sympathy of others. People felt sorry for her, and she was given special privileges that started her on the road to a sense of entitlement: She was allowed phone calls home from camp, when other kids weren't; she was allowed to miss a lot of school; and she was given extra spending money by her grandparents.

Of course, Elizabeth was not entirely manipulative and mean-spirited. She could be charming and funny when she wanted to be, and she had a quick and facile mind. In high school she was placed in a "gifted" program, where she and her colleagues were told they were exceptional— budding geniuses who were destined for greatness. So even though Elizabeth didn't work very hard in school and didn't get exceptional grades, she never lost the conviction that she, herself, was exceptional. Between her sense of entitlement based on past suffering, and her sense of entitlement based on present intellectual superiority, she could be quite a princess.

During her first two years of therapy—concurrent with her first two years of graduate school—Elizabeth was rocked by several events that challenged her privileged view of herself; she lost her summer job in the accounting firm, her mother kicked her out of the house for being rude to her, she got low marks in several of her graduate courses, and her former boyfriend started dating a woman Elizabeth had always looked down upon. These narcissistic injuries had a predictable effect on her: They diminished her sense of entitlement based on her claim of superiority, and they heightened her sense of entitlement based on her claim of injury. As her conviction of intellectual superiority began to erode, she began to request special dispensation from her professors.

At the end of her first semester, for example, Elizabeth was having trouble keeping up with her schoolwork. She decided to ask me to write a letter to one of her professors, requesting an extension on an essay that was due.

"On what grounds? I asked her.

"I don't know," she said, beginning to falter. "Maybe you could just tell him I'm in therapy, or that I'm suffering from stress or something."

I explained to her that she would only ever develop any real self-esteem if she worked hard on her essay and completed it by the deadline. If she made excuses for herself based on bogus claims of mental illness, she wouldn't respect me or her professor. And, more importantly, she wouldn't respect herself.

She smiled while I was telling her this—not because she was embarrassed but because she already knew that what I was saying was true, and because she was glad that I was siding with the responsible side of her instead of with the irresponsible side.

This was a turning point for Elizabeth. She started to buckle down at school, and she began to confront her own history of exploiting people's sympathy to extract special privileges from them.

It's normally easier to renounce an indulgence during a period of feast than during a period of famine. That's why it's usually easier to reduce the use of alcohol when you're feeling happy than when you're feeling sad. When it comes to renouncing a sense of entitlement, however, the pattern is reversed—it's harder to give up entitlement when things are going well than when things are going badly.

For people whose sense of entitlement is based on a history of having been spoiled, good times are a confirmation of their right to special treatment—so they pursue further privileges. For people whose sense of entitlement is based on a history of having suffered, good times are a threat to the legitimacy of their claims to compensation—so they pursue further suffering as a way of restoring the legitimacy of those claims.

People who feel a sense of entitlement based on past suffering are inclined to excoriate themselves on the same painful experiences over and over again throughout their lives to prove that they still deserve special treatment. Because suffering has become a part of their identity—a red badge of courage—they can't resist tearing the scabs off their old psychic wounds. People who feel a sense of entitlement based on past indulgence are more fortunate. Because they don't draw their pride and identity from suffering, they don't need to pursue suffering as a way of feeling special. And because they generally have other sources of self-esteem to call on, they find it easier to drop their sense of entitlement than those who've been deprived or traumatized.

It *isn't* necessary to deny your past suffering in order to give up further claims to special treatment—your past suffering should be acknowledged and worked through. But it *is* necessary to renounce your sense of entitlement if you want to feel like an adult—and be treated like one.

Renunciation of Infinite Possibilities

To get something worthwhile, you have to be willing to give up something else. If you want to be excellent at one activity, you have to give up trying to be excellent at every activity. You can be an excellent surgeon and a very good amateur astronomer, for instance, but you almost certainly can't be an excellent surgeon and a professional astronomer. It isn't just a matter of talent; it's also a matter of time. Excellence takes focus and commitment.

Arlene, a young student in her last year of medical school, had to decide which specialty to pick for her postgraduate training. Her problem was that she liked a number of different specialties, all about equally well. She liked pediatrics and psychiatry, but also obstetrics and surgery.

Because she couldn't choose, she decided to become a family practitioner. However, after several years of family practice, she began to feel disillusioned. She wasn't doing interesting pediatrics or psychiatry, because the difficult cases had to be referred to specialists, and she wasn't doing any surgery other than suturing minor cuts. The only thing she was left with that she had any real fun doing was the prenatal care of pregnant women and the delivery of their babies. Yet even in this she had limitations. She was allowed to do only normal deliveries. The complicated ones she had to turn over to obstetricians.

To remedy her frustration, Arlene decided to do a second residency in obstetrics and gynecology. She figured ob/gyn would give her the chance to do some surgery, counsel a few moms and hold a few babies as well. When she returned to practice as the master of one branch of medicine, she felt much happier with her career.

The moral of this story is *not* that doctors should specialize. Some doctors love family practice and get to do more of the things they enjoy than Arlene did. The moral is this: In order to get really good at something, you have to be willing to sacrifice being an undifferentiated generalist. If you ask a boy what he wants to be when he grows up, he will tell you he wants to be a firefighter *and* a rock star *and* a teacher *and* a baseball player *and* a motor mechanic *and* maybe a ninja warrior. But, unless he's extraordinarily gifted, privileged and lucky, it's unlikely that when he grows up he'll be able to do all those different things well. He will have to make a commitment to two or three things at which he can excel. It's the rare person who can be master of more than one trade. But none can be master of all.

THE GRASS IS NOT ALWAYS GREENER
(ALTHOUGH IT OFTEN SEEMS THAT WAY)

Of course, there are more mundane examples of failure to commit than that of a doctor being unable to choose her medical specialty. Consider, for instance, the person who tries to reinvent herself over and over again by continually changing careers. The grass in her neighbour's back yard always appears greener to her, and she imagines that she can solve her problem simply by moving. But unfortunately, because she has to keep starting each new career from scratch, she ends up making very little progress in any of them. That she is the author of her own misfortune does not prevent her from getting dismayed, however, when some "plodder of lesser talent" works his way past her and ends up becoming her boss.

More common even than the people who can't commit to their careers, because the grass always looks greener somewhere else, are the men who can't commit to their girlfriends, because they're afraid that some more desirable woman may be waiting for them just around the corner.

What's wrong with these men? Why can't they make a commitment? There are many reasons, of course, but one that's usually overlooked or discounted is that they are excessively idealistic. They very much *want* to make a commitment, but they take commitment so seriously they just can't bring themselves to do it. They're afraid to make a mistake. Before they make the final decision, they want to be one hundred percent sure. But since they can never be one hundred percent sure—because no one can ever be one hundred percent sure—they can never make a decision.

Some men—especially those who've been dominated by their mothers—have trouble figuring out whether they're really in love. They're riddled with doubt. Having spent their lives trying to intuit other people's feelings, they've lost the ability to reliably intuit their own. They may be confident and aggressive during the chase, but they become anxious and bored during the relationship. They feel threatened by the intensity of the other person's love and burdened by the responsibility of having to return it.

There is one quality, however, that can save these men from themselves, and that quality is good sense. Not all men have it, of course, but many men do. And if a man does have good sense, then even if he's burdened with excessive idealism or doubt, he may eventually be able to come to his senses. He will realize that *not* committing to his girlfriend will mean losing her forever, and that losing *her* forever is worse than losing some fictional ideal. He will let go of the fantasy of infinite possibilities and hold onto the reality of one finite probability.

When Jared first came to see me, he spoke as if he were in a dream. He was coherent, articulate and even insightful, but there was no emotion. His speech was monotonous and drained of feeling, as if he were anaesthetized or half-asleep. And this surprised me because what he was telling me about was the break-up of a three-year-long relationship with Candace, the woman he loved and once thought of marrying.

Five days earlier Candace had told Jared that she needed time away from him to decide about their relationship. She told him—and not for the first time, either—that she wasn't sure about his commitment to her, or even whether he really loved her. She recounted some of the evidence: He refused to see her except on Saturday nights or holidays, was reluctant to socialize with her friends or family, seemed sexually bored and was indifferent to her reports about work or anything else that didn't involve him.

"We're twenty-eight years old," she said. "We've been dating for three years. We're supposed to love each other. And yet you haven't shown any interest in living together, getting married, or even in talking about living together or getting married. You've been taking me for granted, and now I'm not sure how I feel about you."

Jared protested, of course, but he knew that she was right about the facts and even about his lack of enthusiasm and commitment.

At first Jared blamed his work. He was trying to become a partner in a large corporate law firm and was expected to put in long hours. But he knew that this was only a rationalization and soon began to wonder whether his indifference to Candace might not be a reflection of his true feelings towards her.

"The funny thing is I always thought I'd marry her," he said. "I just never told her. I knew she loved me, but I kept her at arm's length because I wasn't ready to be tied down."

Jared believed in marriage in theory, but in practice he was dubious. His parents had undergone a messy divorce after his father discovered that his mother was having an affair, and it had divided the family. His older sister never spoke to his mother again, and Jared was pulled in both directions. Because he was only eleven at the time, he was forced to continue living with his mother and to become her unwilling confidante. He set aside his own needs and tended to hers, but he mistrusted his mother and resented her attempts to rationalize her infidelity by blaming his father.

Like many children who are obliged to parent needy parents, Jared became a good boy—and a bad boy too. He did well in school, helped around the house, practised his violin without having to be asked, attended Boy Scouts and church, and never gave his mother any trouble, but he became passive-aggressive towards her, withholding his love along with his anger, and he dreamed that one day he'd have a wife who would be beautiful and strong and who would love him completely. In the meantime, Jared suppressed his feelings and went through his life like a sleepwalker.

However, when Jared met Candace at the age of twenty-five, he underwent a momentary change. Because she was completely unlike his mother, he began to let down his guard. He responded to her warmth, thoughtfulness, generosity and fun with pleasure and enthusiasm, and he fell in love. But as time passed, and as their feelings deepened, Jared began to feel threatened. Having sacrificed his own feelings and needs as a child to look after his mother, he was afraid to be responsible for another woman's happiness. So even though Candace wasn't demanding anything unreasonable of him—and certainly wasn't expecting him to take responsibility for her happiness—Jared set limits on his contact with her, her family and her friends, and kept at bay his own feelings of tenderness and love.

In short, at twenty-eight years of age, Jared continued to behave like his mother's son. Without knowing it, he reacted to Candace as if she were his mother, instead of the woman he loved. He withdrew and turned off his feelings for her, and as a result of this self-numbing, he began to wonder whether she was really the woman of his dreams. To all the world he looked like a poised and successful young professional in love with a charming young woman, but in reality he was a detached and anaesthetized sleep-walker re-enacting a troubled relationship with his selfish mother.

Candace saw the emptiness and conflict beneath the façade, and when she finally summoned up the strength to confront him, Jared was forced to wake up. He saw what he was about to lose and what he'd already lost. He looked at his relationship and recognized that Candace and his mother were different people. He allowed his feelings to flood back into him and realized that he'd been taking out on Candace the resentment he felt towards his mother. He reviewed his life and realized that, if he wanted to make it his own, he would have to feel his own feelings and become his own person. He realized that he would have to come to grips with the childhood past and give it up. And he realized that he would have to stop looking for the ultimate woman and make a commitment to the woman he loved.

Jared honoured Candace's request to have some time apart from him. He stopped calling or seeing her, and he took the opportunity to learn about himself. He worked hard to figure out how he felt and what he wanted. And after six weeks of soul searching, he was ready to call her. He felt as if he'd grown up in those six weeks and that he knew what he wanted.

The change in Jared was apparent to Candace in his voice—it was animated and confident and alive.

"You sound different," she told him after several minutes of a mutual update.

"I feel different," he said. "I feel as if I've finally become a man. I feel as if I'm finally ready to live my own life, independently and on my own terms. And if you're still willing to have me, I'd like you to be part of it."

Candace took a minute to think it over before answering. "Jared," she said, "for now, let's take it slowly. After that, we'll see."

Women who can't commit—though perhaps rarer than men who can't commit—also have "grass is greener" fantasies. They are not immune from the temptations of holding out for a better offer or of trading up, but they are also no less immune from the temptation to sell themselves short. Whereas many men fear commitment because they're afraid of missing future opportunities, many women fear commitment because they're afraid of losing their independence and self-reliance. They either don't feel strong enough to retain their sense of identity while being part of a couple, or don't feel strong enough to keep a sense of their own power while being in love. What helps them overcome this fear is the confidence they get from their own achievements: The better they feel about themselves, the more secure they feel about their sense of identity and power, and the less vulnerable they feel about the process of falling in love.

Renunciation of Self-indulgence and Self-destruction

This is a bit of a grab-bag category under which I want to include all those minor indulgences that adolescents (and many would-be adults) seem to have trouble giving up. These are all the little pleasures of the culture of narcissism and materialism that are fine in moderation, but coarse in excess.

I have included in this category obvious vices such as drug and alcohol abuse and less obvious foibles such as smoking cigarettes, overeating junk foods, buying fancy foreign sports cars, getting friendly with the head waiter at expensive restaurants, sleeping until noon on weekends, procrastinating and being chronically late for work.

These are self-destructive, or at least self-sabotaging, behaviours. In most cases, they reach their zenith in adolescence and then decline during pre-adulthood. However, some people seem to have greater than average difficulty in giving them up.

There are four psychological conditions that may cause these self-damaging behaviours to hang on past adolescence:

The first is a desire to hold on to youthful feelings of indestructibility. The reasoning here is: If I can smoke cigarettes, eat junk food, rollerblade in traffic or defy my boss, it means that I'm still many years away from having to worry about the consequences of these actions—I'm still indestructible.

The second is a desire to "give up" on yourself in order to get revenge on your parents. This form of self-harm is a dramatized message to your parents telling them that they did a lousy job raising you. In spiteful imitation of your parents' alleged or actual negligence towards you, you behave with callous disregard towards yourself.

The third is a desire to turn passive failure into active failure. People who feel they were born with a limited amount of drive, perseverance or courage—and who want to earn failure themselves rather than having it thrust upon them by others—may launch a pre-emptive strike on themselves by engaging in self-damaging behaviour. This deliberate self-handicapping provides them with a ready-made excuse for their failures and lets them avoid the pain of unexpected defeat.

The fourth psychological condition that predisposes people to self-harm is a distorted desire to be "independent." Some people feel they can't take control over their lives in any other way than by wrecking them. Even though it is nihilistic and unimaginative, the temptation to wield this sort of self-destructive power over yourself can be nearly irresistible. For example, I know of a man who saw his marriage crumbling and—instead of trying to salvage it, which is what he really wanted—left his wife abruptly before she had the chance to leave him first.

RENUNCIATION OF ALCOHOL AND DRUGS

Drugs and especially alcohol are so widely used in everyday life that they have come to seem quite normal. But, at any level above moderate use, they have an insidious negative effect on the people who use them—and it's easy to slip unknowingly from moderate to excessive use. I'm not saying that everyone who drinks two glasses of wine at dinner every night will automatically become alcoholic, but try skipping those two harmless (or perhaps healthy) little glasses for a couple of days and see if you don't miss them. Alcohol is highly addictive. (Because wine enhances the enjoyment of food and is often rationalized on the grounds of connoisseurship, its regular use is particularly seductive, especially to those who would never dream of drinking "hard liquor" every day.)

People with family histories of alcoholism, with mood

disorders such as depression or manic-depression, and with past histories of addiction or chronic underachievement are particularly vulnerable to the effects of alcohol and need to be especially cautious about regular use—even moderate regular use.

Renunciation of Passivity

People are passive from temperament, from fear, from laziness and from habit. They are also passive from choice, especially when all courses of action seem futile or perilous, or when passivity is a welcome relief from intense activity. Passivity in one person is sometimes a fitting complement to activity in another. When you're sitting on an airplane or in the dentist's chair, when you're hungry, sick or exhausted, when you're trying to relax, and when you're trying to fall asleep, passivity is appropriate. But when you're trying to learn, accomplish or produce things, when you're trying to develop relationships, when you're trying to express yourself or to improve the world, and even when you're just trying to enjoy yourself, passivity is a problem.

Passivity is the twin of dependency. People who are passive usually rely on other people to do things for them. They tend to be observers of life rather than participants. Some pre-adults fall into the habit of being passive because they've been kept in a dependent state by their parents. Others don't feel powerful enough to take action. But since no one can feel powerful *until* he takes action, passivity is the first thing they have to overcome if they want to feel strong and independent.

Since no one is completely passive, of course, passivity is a relative concept. The main thing that distinguishes passive people is their preference for activities that have little impact on the outside world—activities that leave things pretty much as they were. Given a choice, passive people will substitute a lower impact activity for higher impact activity merely in order to avoid stress.

The model case of a passive activity that's substituted for an active activity—one that's harmless but ineffectual, and that's common in adulthood but feels distinctly adolescent—is masturbation. Masturbation? What's wrong with masturbation? The answer—from a psychological viewpoint at any rate—is that nothing is wrong with masturbation—provided it's not your preferred form of sexual activity.

Masturbation, in fact, has some definite advantages over intercourse: It doesn't require a partner (you can do it when you're separated from your lover, when your lover isn't interested in having sex, and when you don't have a lover); it generally takes less preparation and effort than intercourse and doesn't involve making a commitment to somebody else; there's less performance anxiety than with intercourse (if you have trouble achieving an orgasm, at least you don't have to fake it), no risk of catching a disease, and no acceptance of limitations (you can imagine doing anything with anyone). But these are also the disadvantages of masturbation. The same features that make masturbation convenient and easy make it *too* convenient and easy. Masturbation doesn't get you involved with anyone else, and it doesn't require much in the way of activity.

Masturbation is a metaphor for behaviour that is self-absorbed, harmless, passive and ineffectual. When someone is indulging in easy and ineffectual behaviour, we (the more crude among us, anyhow) accuse him of "just jerking off." And when someone is indulging in stimulating but ineffectual thinking, we accuse him of "mental masturbation." We expect to see a fair degree of this kind of behaviour in adolescence, but we don't expect to see as much of it in adulthood. Perhaps that's why people feel more embarrassed if they get caught masturbating than if they get caught having sex with another person: It's seen as immature. If we want to be effective adults, we have to devote less energy to the safe, passive, self-centred behaviours that lead to quick but shallow gratification and start to devote more of our energy to the adventurous, active behaviours that lead to delayed but genuine fulfilment.

Is there a place for masturbation in adulthood? Of course there is. As with all the other little indulgences of adolescence, when we reach adulthood, the golden mean applies: Moderation in all things.

Mario reported to me that his wife, Eleanor, came home early from a meeting one night and caught him watching a porno flick. The film's story-line (to the extent that it had one) involved two farm women coercing an "innocent" young farmhand into having sex with them.

Eleanor objected to his watching pornography for a variety of reasons, some ideological, some personal. Mario, however, was more concerned about what his preference in pornography said about his sexuality—the fact that he seemed to identify with the farmhand's passivity and disavowal of sexual desire as portrayed in the movie. It suggested to him that, even in fantasy, he couldn't accept responsibility for his own impulses, that he needed to displace his sexual desires onto someone else—the woman— making her the instigator of sex, and that he needed to make himself not the active initiator of sex, but the passive recipient of it.

Watching pornographic movies wasn't the only problem that Mario had with passivity and with clinging to pre-adult fantasies. His life seemed to be organized on the principle: "Why do in reality what you can more easily do in fantasy?"

Although he was bright, he had a checkered career both in school and in the workforce. He dropped out of college, and did an assortment of semi-skilled jobs before finally landing a position as an office-equipment salesman. Initially, he was enthusiastic, but as time went by he became increasingly resentful. Though he was good at sales when he put his mind to it, and had no other training, he found it demeaning to have to make cold calls on customers and tried instead to present himself as an expert in office integration. Naturally, he had very little credibility with his customers, his sales numbers began to fall, and when his industry underwent one of its periodic shake-outs, he lost his job.

But, of course, Mario's motto was: "Why do in reality what you can more easily do in fantasy?" So rather than looking for work right away, he decided to indulge in a long-shot fantasy of redemption and triumph instead. Hoping to make the big score that would turn around his

life (and feeding fantasies of laughing at his detractors—
mainly Eleanor), he spent seven months trying to develop a
computer game. When his game failed to win the interest
of any software company, however, he sank into a depression, and spent the next six months moping around the
house.

Like many pre-adults, Mario felt that if he didn't become a
star, he would become a nobody. He alternated between the
twin poles of perfectionism and cynicism. His greatest fear
was the fear of mediocrity. Because of his perfectionism, it
took him ages to get down to work; as a result of his procrastination, he never had enough time left to put forth his
best effort. He was a chronic underachiever.

He also tended to be very antagonistic to his wife. He
took every suggestion Eleanor made to him as a put-down.
He objected to her quite sensible expression of feminist
ideas as if he were being emasculated by them, a reaction
that only made her more strident. Naturally, their marriage
was in peril.

The turnaround in their relationship came when Mario
remembered how he'd felt as a boy when he was confronted by someone more assertive: He felt like a weakling and
a coward. He had been scrawny as a child and suffered
from asthma, which made it hard for him to compete in
physical activities. To make matters worse, his father had
been impressively robust, highly accomplished and difficult to please, and his mother had been excessively indulgent. Mario got quite adept at coming up with a variety of
cop-outs, including his illnesses, to avoid conflicts and to
avoid having to perform at the level his father demanded.

Faced with Eleanor's benign assertiveness, Mario
began to feel like a weakling all over again. He believed
that in order to be a man, he had to stand up to her. Once
he understood that she was his equal and that she was not
trying to emasculate him, he stopped feeling threatened by
her and became less antagonistic. Their marriage gradually
got back on track.

And so did his attitude towards work. Mario was able

to renounce his need to be a star (which had compensated for a lifelong feeling of inadequacy anyway) and to accept the kind of work he really was qualified to do well—sales. What's more, he was able to do it with enthusiasm and without procrastination or passivity.

Renunciation of Magical Thinking, Pseudo-naïveté, and Pseudo-cynicism

MAGICAL THINKING

There are people who believe for their whole lives that things turn out well or poorly because of fate, fortune, karma or magic, and not because of concerted action, perseverance, attention to detail or effective problem solving. They believe that some people (usually other people) have charmed lives, and some don't. There are no random events; everything happens for a reason. If someone has a problem in her life, it means that she's jinxed or has fallen out of favour with the gods. If she succeeds, it means only that she's lucky (which obviates the need to envy her). This is magical thinking.

Magical thinking is very common among young children. It helps them feel safe by allowing them to displace their belief in the mysterious and awesome power of their parents onto fate itself. Even among fairly rational adults, minor forms of magical thinking are quite common as superstitions and rituals. However, if major forms of magical thinking persist into adulthood, it indicates that primitive childhood fantasies of parental omnipotence continue to hold sway.

One young man, an aspiring actor, refused to go to auditions on days his psychic reader said were inauspicious. Whether this superstitiousness held him back very much in the long run, I can't say, because he could often try out for the same part on a different day. In the short run, however, it did cut him out of a few opportunities to showcase his considerable talents, and for a man just barely breaking even on what he earned by acting and waiting tables, this seemed an unfortunate sacrifice.

In most cases, naïve fantasies and superstitions are pretty harmless. In some cases, they're even helpful.

Dolores, an unfortunate woman with a long-standing depression that made her quite miserable, discovered a lump in her breast just after one of her periods. At first she refused to see her doctor. She was convinced it was "bad" and didn't want to face up to it. But after several weeks, she did go to her doctor, who sent her for a mammogram, which revealed a large, inoperable cancer. Dolores underwent chemotherapy to shrink the tumor and then started a course of radiation treatment—both of which she tolerated surprisingly well.

The really hard part was that she blamed herself for her cancer: "I've read somewhere," she mournfully told me, "that if you're depressed it can give you cancer—and I believe it."

When I asked Dolores why she believed it, she explained, "Things happen for a reason. I was on bad terms with my mother when she died, and I just knew I'd be punished for it someday. What goes around, comes around. I thought that the depression was my punishment, but now I know there was something more in store for me."

I tried to explain to Dolores that breast cancer is a common disease that many women get who are neither depressed nor estranged from their mothers. "You have enough to cope with," I told her, "without having to blame yourself for getting sick." But she never really stopped blaming herself. And although she had no other symptoms of depression, she clung to the belief, right up to the time of her death eighteen months later, that she "deserved" her illness.

I refrained from analyzing these superstitious ideas because, painful though they were, they seemed to give Dolores considerable comfort, and they didn't interfere with her willingness to seek treatment for her cancer. It was clear she needed to believe that "things happen for a reason." In the face of great suffering, this belief gave Dolores some reassurance that there was an omnipotent force in the universe that would ultimately comfort and protect her, and that her penance would allow her to be reunited with her mother after death.

PSEUDO-NAIVETÉ

Not all naïve thinking is sincere. On the contrary, there are people who consciously adopt a pose of naïveté in order to place themselves on the moral high ground. They disavow "worldly" impulses such as envy, greed, hostility, sexual desire and competitiveness in order to feel superior to the people around them. Their pseudo-naïveté allows them to feel self-righteous about their own behaviour and "shocked" about the behaviour of others. Not surprisingly, when they "discover" that other people have vices they've disavowed in themselves, they are secretly pleased. It gives them the chance to express all the latent hostility, indignation and outrage they claim never to feel.

The problem with pseudo-naïveté, of course, is that the person adopting it has to act like a babe in the woods. She can't just suppress her envy, competitiveness and anger; to be consistently convincing, she also has to suppress her ambition, sexuality, assertiveness and pride. In order to disavow the aggressive side of her nature, she is forced to discard the erotic side. And in order to disavow both, she is forced to renounce the prerogatives of adulthood.

When the façade of naïveté drops away, however, look out!

After twenty years of marriage, Gladys had returned to school to study social work. She revelled in the humanitarianism of her new career and began to look down on her husband, Dmitri, who earned his living as a corporate lawyer. She accused him of being interested only in making money and of being insensitive to the travails of the less fortunate. She depicted herself as unmaterialistic, sensitive and empathetic—as too fine for this world.

Midway through her training, Gladys fell in love with one of her therapy supervisors and began to have an affair with him. She concealed her affair from Dmitri on the grounds that she didn't want to cause him pain, and she rationalized it on the grounds that her new lover fulfilled the spiritual side of herself that Dmitri couldn't touch. But when Dmitri discovered the affair five years later and filed for divorce, Gladys dropped her naïve façade: She hired the most aggressive and materialistic lawyer she could find and went after everything she could get.

PSEUDO-CYNICISM

The flip side of pseudo-naïveté is pseudo-cynicism. Here the person affects a pose of world-weariness. The world, so she claims, is too much with her.

She has seen too much of the folly, pettiness, selfishness and meanness in the world to believe that anything good can be expected of anyone.

The pseudo-cynic has a great nose for hypocrisy and phoniness, her own included. If you ask her, "How are you?" she'll reply, "Do you *really* want to know, or are you just being polite?"

Under the guise of an unswerving "honesty," she can be ruthlessly blunt—not only with others, but with herself as well. But because she chooses to see only the negative side of things, her honest appraisal is ultimately quite dishonest. Film and theatre critics, book reviewers and journalists, because they're applauded for pointing out the negative side of things more than the positive, run a particular risk of falling prey to pseudo-cynicism. They are liable to get seduced by the clever put-down.

Pseudo-cynicism is the critic's trap—but not just the critic's trap.

Michael, a man in his late twenties, loved to make pronouncements on any person, place, idea, job or scene that intimidated him. Businessmen, for example, became "suits," people who weren't cool were "from the 'burbs," conservative elderly women were "bluehairs," accountants were "bean-counters" and so forth. Not only were his critiques lacking in cleverness and humour, they were also quite limiting to him. By dismissing virtually every sort of job and life style open to him, he painted himself into a corner. There was nothing Michael could do without feeling embarrassed or hypocritical. As a result, until he renounced his pseudo-cynicism, he was totally at a loss to figure out what kind of career he could safely pursue.

Pseudo-cynicism, unlike real cynicism, is not just the flip side of idealism, it's an excuse not to act. It is not the result of bitter experience, it is the result of fear. If pre-adults wish to overcome their fear and renounce their pseudo-cynicism, they need only act. Only action builds courage and restores faith in the self and in the world. Only action can transform a fearful, negative, pseudo-cynical pre-adult into a confident, positive adult.

Renunciation of the Need for Certainty

As Benjamin Franklin wrote to Jean Baptiste Le Roy, "In this world nothing can be said to be certain, except death and taxes." Life is full of uncertainty. Most moral issues are ambiguous. Most arguments have at least two sides. Most feelings about ourselves and towards other people are ambivalent. Children and adolescents may get to act as if life were perfectly clear, but adults do not. Adults must be able to accept life's uncertainties, yet still be able to act decisively.

Uncertainty doesn't exist only in the real world; it exists in the psyche as well. Between the desire for pleasure on one hand and the demands of conscience on the other, psychic conflict is inevitable. Pre-adults commonly respond to the challenge of having to resolve this conflict by diminishing or discarding the side of the conflict they'd least prefer to struggle with. They often recruit someone to confirm the wisdom of their choice by presenting that person with a skewed argument that forces him to favour one side of the conflict.

Veronica was angry and worried that her husband was abusing the pain killers he'd been given for his lower back pain, so she decided to confess her concerns to her sister. But when Veronica's sister advised her to force her husband to get help by giving him an ultimatum, Veronica turned around and accused her sister of a lack of compassion. Veronica wanted to get someone else—her sister, in this case—to express anger at her husband so that she could disavow her anger at him and focus exclusively on her love.

Ward wasn't sure whether to quit his job as a brands manager for a company that made processed meats. He'd worked at the company in various capacities for eight years, and although he was moving up the corporate ladder and making a good living, he felt unappreciated by his newly appointed boss. He applied for a transfer to a different division, but there were no openings anywhere else, so he was stuck where he was.

His family, some of his friends and the people in human resources all advised him to hang in and make the best of it until things changed for the better. But Ward wasn't sure he could wait. So he approached his girlfriend with his dilemma, telling her all the reasons that other people had given him for staying at the job—security, seniority, stability, status and so forth—but telling her this without much enthusiasm and with an air of resignation.

Hearing his explanation for staying at his job, his girlfriend, on cue, asked him if he were happy there. And when he replied, with evident pathos, "I enjoy it sometimes," she took him in her arms and told him that he just had to quit.

"Those other things aren't important," she chided him. "What's important is your happiness."

Ward was secretly pleased. Having got his girlfriend to insist that he take the course of action he wanted to take anyway, he said, "I guess you're right. I'll tell them tomorrow that I'm resigning."

Not-so-subtle manipulation of this sort takes place in therapy all the time. The person in therapy will try to get his therapist to take responsibility for an awkward decision by describing it in a tone that gives lie to the words.

He'll say about someone he's gone out on a date with, for instance, "I guess I should ask Mary out again. She's so *nice*—and so *appropriate*."

So that, picking up the meta-message, the empathic therapist will respond, "But you don't sound too enthusiastic about it. Are you sure you really want to?"

Which allows the person in therapy to reply—with a brightening mood because he's been given permission to do exactly what he wanted to do from the beginning but felt guilty about—"You know you're right. I'm not that attracted to her. Thank goodness I have someone insightful like you to protect me from my own selflessness!"

CHAPTER SIX

WHAT ELSE DO YOU HAVE TO GIVE UP TO BECOME AN ADULT?

It is unjust to claim the privileges of age and
retain the playthings of childhood.
Samuel Johnson

RENUNCIATIONS IN RELATION TO THE WORLD

In order to become adults, we have to be willing to give up our
pre-adult expectations of other people and of the world at large.
We have to be willing to accept responsibility for our own
actions, to stop blaming other people for things that go wrong
and to modify our demands in accordance with what is fair and
reasonable.

Renunciation of Externalization

Externalization is the opposite of taking responsibility for your
actions. It involves shifting responsibility—usually blame—
onto other people. A common example of externalization—one
that's almost always in fashion—is blaming your parents for
your own unhappiness. Renouncing externalization involves *not*
blaming others. It means taking responsibility for your own
actions and your own circumstances.

Renouncing externalization sounds easy, but it's harder to accomplish than you might think. The reason it's difficult is that most forms of externalization are unconscious. We're not aware we're externalizing; we really believe the other person is to blame.

For instance, when we blame our parents (or boss or partner) for our own unhappiness, we don't realize we're externalizing the responsibility. We believe we're placing the responsibility where it properly belongs. (And often, the responsibility does partly belong there.) The problem with blaming our parents, however, is that it cuts us out of the loop. If they're responsible for our unhappiness, then how are we going to be able to make ourselves happy? When we externalize, what we're saying is: We're not in charge; someone else is in charge—someone who's bigger, stronger, older and more responsible than we are.

Externalization keeps us dependent on other people, and it perpetuates a childish relationship to authority.

Harriet was a twenty-eight-year-old graduate student who came to see me because of ongoing conflicts with her mother. She felt that her mother had made lots of mistakes in the way she'd raised her—mistakes that continued to hold her back.

"My mother was too worried about everything when I was a kid," Harriet explained. "She fussed over things. If I had a problem at school, she'd rush right in to meet with the teacher. If I was unhappy at camp, she'd call the director. She was very insecure. As a result, now *I'm* insecure!"

Harriet's complaints continued along these lines for many months. She blamed her mother for making her insecure, indecisive and childish. She seemed to feel that she couldn't make her life better until her mother somehow changed. "That woman has stunted my growth," she lamented.

It occurred to me, one day, to ask Harriet how old her mother had been when she was born. (Harriet was the eldest child.) Her jaw dropped slightly, and she stopped herself in mid-lament. "Twenty," she replied, as if a light had suddenly come on in her head. "Eight years younger than I am right now."

After that things changed for Harriet. She developed a new empathy for her mother that allowed her to be more patient with her and more tolerant of her insecurities. Harriet renounced her tendency to externalize the blame for her own shortcomings, and she began to take responsibility for her own welfare. In short, she grew up.

Renunciation of Projection

Projection is an unconscious mechanism by which we attribute our negative feelings to other people. We project our negative feelings onto the other person and then react to her as if she had those very same feelings towards us. We do this as a way of disavowing those feelings in ourselves and as a way of expressing hostility towards the other person.

Here's how it works:

Bernice has doubts about her love for her boyfriend, Al. But Bernice can't accept the idea of having doubts about Al because (a) she feels dependent on him and doesn't want to have to break up with him, and (b) she has pledged her undying love for him and doesn't want to look like she didn't mean it.

In order to externalize these negative feelings, Bernice decides, unconsciously, to project her doubts about Al onto Al. As a result of this unconscious projection, Bernice now sees Al as the one having doubts. She can then say: "Al's having doubts about me—the bastard!" And because he's having doubts about her, she feels justified in having doubts about him in return.

The most likely targets for projection, naturally, are the people towards whom we're having negative feelings ourselves. Therefore, when we think that someone is having negative feelings towards us, it always pays to examine whether we've been projecting our own negative feelings onto him or her first. We do this by combing through our thoughts and feelings to see whether we can catch sight of those little tell-tale flashes of hostility that always accompany a projection.

PROJECTION LEADS TO PARANOIA

Most of the time we don't just feel negatively towards the important people in our lives; we feel positively towards them as well. We care too much to be merely neutral. In good, healthy relationships, the balance between love and hate is heavily weighted in favour of love. And the predominance of love over hate permits us to accept our inevitable negative feelings without undue guilt.

But if the balance between love and hate starts to tilt in the direction of hate—either because a particular person has made us angry or frightened, or because we're filled with more general feelings of anger or fear—then we will start to feel more and more guilty about our negative feelings and have to project them. And if we start doing this generally—if we start projecting our negative feelings onto everyone we relate to—then the whole world will start to look hostile to us, and we will have rid ourselves of hatred by putting paranoia in its place.

Paranoia is a frightening thing. It results from a malignant combination of projected anger and distorted perception. That's why people with severe chronic anger and people with impaired reality-testing are prone to developing it. If we want to reduce our paranoia, we have to understand why we're angry—which isn't always easy because the person we think we're angry at may not be the original source of our anger—and we have to correct the distortions in our perception of reality—which also isn't easy because the impairment may result from a mental disorder such as chronic depression. For these reasons, most people with paranoia—whether garden-variety suspiciousness or clinical psychosis—will benefit from professional help.

PROJECTION, PROTECTION AND POWER

Many psychological defence mechanisms start out as adaptive responses to childhood anxiety, but hang on into later life as maladaptive reflexes. The defensive use of projection often follows the same pattern. Besides making us feel virtuous (and sometimes paranoid), projecting our anger onto someone we love and need accomplishes two other things that are quite helpful to us when we're very young and vulnerable: First, it protects the person we love and hate from our destructive anger (since, as a result of our projection, it now appears as though it is he who is angry at us, instead of we who are angry at him). And second, by strengthening his image in our eyes, it allows that person to be a continued source of protection to us (because, having been transfused with our projected anger, he now appears less anemic). Our projection makes him seem "larger than life" and therefore more valuable to us as a governor and protector.

We use projection in this specialized way—to pump up someone we love in order to make him seem stronger than he really is—only when we feel perched on the edge of a psychic abyss and urgently need someone to grab onto. It is a desperate move, a last resort when the only alternative facing us is chaos.

A young child might use this form of projection, for example, to build up the image in his mind of an inadequate parent upon whom he still feels dependent. By giving the parent *his* strength (in the form of projected anger), the child hopes to stave off premature disillusionment. He hopes to extend his parent's shelf-life as a protector by lending some of his anger to the parent. And he may be successful...but not without a cost. For in order to strengthen *the parent* with his projection, he has to weaken *himself*. In order to make the parent seem powerful, he has to see him or her as a terrifying monster. And in order to believe that his parent really *is* stronger than he is, he has to deny two critical realities—the reality of his parent's deficiencies and the reality of his own strengths.

All things considered, donating your anger to someone who needs propping up is an expensive "gift."

RECLAIMING YOUR PROJECTED STRENGTH

Not surprisingly, unless the child can eventually reclaim the strength she's projected onto her deficient parent, she may have great difficulty in separating from her parent and feeling adult.

Louise, a thirty-six-year-old social worker, had this problem with her mother and decided to come for therapy to deal with it. She didn't know, of course, that she had propped up her mother with her projected anger; she thought that she still depended on her mother and that she couldn't separate from her.

When Louise was seven years old, her mother had the first of a series of rather serious depressions that, over the years, required many lengthy hospitalizations. Her mother would spend days in her room sleeping and crying and avoiding all contact with the family. When she finally did emerge from her room, she was apathetic, tearful, self-critical and suicidal. "You and your father would be better off without me," she once told Louise in a moment of despair.

Louise never forgot that threat. It frightened her, of course, because she loved her mother and depended on her, but it also made her angry, because it seemed so selfish. Her father, a shy and ineffectual man, was totally at sea without his wife around to direct him, and Louise worried about who would look after her if her mother killed herself.

In the early stages of her mother's depression—before it was diagnosed and before her mother was hospitalized— Louise had trouble understanding why her mother got angry at her when she was being at all demanding, and even when she was just being playful or exuberant. She didn't realize that her mother was so absorbed with her own pain and misery that she didn't have it in her to meet Louise's needs or to tolerate her normal childhood rambunctiousness. She felt hurt and rejected by her mother and started to become sullen and withdrawn in response.

But after her mother was hospitalized and found to have a clinical depression, Louise was able to gradually accept the fact that her mother had been ill, not just self-absorbed and cranky, and she began to deal with her mother in a different way. For example, rather than trying to be lively and talkative, she tried to be quiet and helpful. And rather than permitting herself to be angry at her mother for "abandoning" her, she tried to be obedient and deferential towards her.

But it didn't work. Louise still felt frightened. What would happen if her mother killed herself one day, as she had threatened? Who would take care of her father? More important, who would take care of her? And with her mother so fragile, how was Louise supposed to deal with the anger she still felt towards her?

The problem was so desperate that only one solution presented itself to Louise's unconscious mind: She had to project her own strength onto her mother. As a result of this unconscious decision, Louise started to see her relationship with her mother in a different light. She no longer saw her mother as pitiable and weak, but as hostile and intimidating. And she no longer saw herself as robust and angry, but as needy and fearful.

By the time Louise came to see me for therapy, she no longer needed a hostile and critical mother to lean on. She needed an accepting and friendly mother to separate from. More important, she needed the chance to feel strong and grown up herself. But old patterns don't change just because they're no longer useful, and Louise still felt dependent on her mother and frightened of her mother's moods. She had long since repressed the fact that her mother's apparent strength came from her and still consciously believed that her strength came from her mother.

The first crack in this ancient repression took place eighteen months into the therapy. I had just returned from a two-week vacation, and Louise seemed guarded and defensive with me. She explained that, while I was away, she'd been worried I was angry at her for some sarcastic remarks she'd made about me just before my vacation. And, in truth, I had been a little miffed at her during that last appointment. When I thought about my irritation, however, I realized that my leaving Louise to go on vacation reminded her of her mother leaving her to go into the hospital.

When I pointed out this similarity to Louise, it rang a bell with her. She remembered feeling angry at me during that last appointment and realized that her perception of my anger, though partly accurate, was largely a projection. We figured out that she had projected her anger onto me because she was afraid I was abandoning her to go on vacation. She needed to pump me up with her projected anger to reassure herself that I would be strong enough to cope with her when I returned from my vacation.

Of course, this was precisely the same tactic—projection—that she had used at age ten to deal with her fear of losing her mother. And once she saw that connection, she understood why she hadn't been able to separate from her mother, and why her mother seemed so angry at her. More important, she discovered that deep down she was not fearful and intimidated, as she'd always believed, but strong and brave, as she'd thought of herself before her mother got sick.

In time, Louise began to put her long and stormy relationship with her mother into an adult perspective. She forgave her mother for her illness and began to separate from her. She reclaimed the strength she had donated to her mother during her childhood and, for the first time in her life, began to feel adult.

DEALING WITH PROJECTION

Despite its shortcomings, people deploy projection to handle their anger in all sorts of situations where the direct expression of anger would seem to be too risky. For example, children whose parents are very rejecting may decide unconsciously to project their anger onto them instead of expressing it directly. They avoid provoking their parents by doing this, but they end up believing that their parents hate them instead. Similarly, patients who feel too dependent on their doctors to risk expressing their complaints about them directly may project their anger onto their doctors and end up feeling persecuted by them. Wherever negative feelings, like anger, are too threatening to enter consciousness—wherever they're too threatening to be "owned"—they may be projected.

Angry people always seem to imagine that others are angry at them—and sometimes they're right. Because, if the other people don't recognize they're having anger projected onto them, they may really be feeling angry. It isn't easy to identify when you've become the unwitting object of someone else's projected anger, and it's even harder to deal with once you're aware of it. The natural reaction is to actually feel the anger (as if it did originate inside you), and then to direct it back at the person who projected the anger onto you in the first place. If this happens in therapy, however—if the therapist boomerangs the person's anger right back at him, as I did for a time when I was treating Louise—then the therapist will inadvertently validate the paranoia of the person he or she is treating and risk producing a therapeutic stalemate.

If projection is an unconscious defence against internal feelings, then how can you recognize and deal with it? (The Unconscious, after all, is unconscious.) Let's say you're worried that your co-worker, who just got promoted to a position you applied for too, is angry at you for failing to support his position in yesterday's meeting. How can you decipher whether he seems angry at you because you failed to support him or because you're projecting onto him your resentment at not being promoted? Here are some suggestions:

STEP ONE: First, assume that you're *not* projecting. Mature people use projection as a defence against anger relatively rarely. If you're getting the feeling that someone has negative feelings towards you, you're probably right—he does. But remember, nobody likes to be painted as a negative person. The person you're worried about may sense your projected hostility and resent it. He may be feeling negatively towards you because you're projecting negative feelings onto him. Check out your perceptions with someone impartial. If he or she doesn't think the person in question is angry at you, go on to the next step.

STEP TWO: Are you obsessing about the person you believe is being negative towards you? Projection is always accompanied by—and always caused by—an excessive preoccupation with the object of your concern. If you're obsessed by this person and what he's thinking about you, or if you're fascinated with him and can't get him out of your mind, then it's a good bet that what you're sensing from him are the negative feelings that you're projecting onto him.

STEP THREE: Mild hostility towards someone is less likely to result in projection than intense hostility is. So if you feel intense hostility towards someone you suspect of having negative feelings towards you, look for evidence of projection in yourself. Projection always leaves a residue of anger in the mind of the person making the projection. If your anger is excessive (whether or not you feel it's justified), consider projection as the probable cause.

STEP FOUR: Look for evidence of intense love. Though it may seem paradoxical, hate is often projected to preserve feelings of love. Ask yourself why you care so much what this person thinks of you? (Do you have a crush on your co-worker, for example?) If the answer is that you want to have a special relationship with him, then projection may be playing a role in your perceptions of him.

STEP FIVE: If you've diagnosed yourself as projecting negative feelings onto someone, then it's time to do a little self-analysis or to get some help. What are your true feelings towards that person? Why is he so important to you? Have you experienced similar feelings towards other people now or in the past? And do those people remind you of him? What do they all have in common? Do they remind you of one of your parents or siblings? Are you re-enacting with the present person a relationship from the past? What frustrations are left over from that earlier relationship that you may be trying to deal with now? If the person in question doesn't remind you of anyone from your past, could you be displacing negative feelings from someone else in your current life onto him? Why is it so difficult to feel angry towards this other person?

Is he too vulnerable, or are you afraid he'll lash out at you or reject you if he knows you're having negative feelings towards him?

STEP SIX: Once you recognize that your feelings towards the person in question are inappropriate—or at least exaggerated—try changing your attitude towards him. Recognize the ways in which he's different from your projections. Give him the benefit of the doubt. Treat him as if you believe he'll give you a fair shake. If your perceptions of his negativity subside, then you've successfully worked out your projection (and you've learned a lot about yourself). If your perceptions about him don't change, then seek professional help. You may not be projecting, but even so you'll probably benefit from further analysis of the situation.

Renunciation of the Expectation of Unconditional Acceptance

There is a brief wonderful moment in early infancy when, if we're lucky, our parents enjoy us unconditionally. The moment passes all too soon, but the memory of it lingers like the vision of a sunny country cottage that we've only seen in a magazine, but always dream of coming home to. We could call this brief shining moment the Edenic period, because it's an innocent and idyllic interval of time when everything is given to us without our even having to ask for it. It is the only time in our lives when we're admired and adored simply because we exist: "I am, therefore I get."

Very soon, however, we're forced to leave the sacred garden to wander in the real world and earn our way there. The Edenic period is supplanted by the achievement period. By the end of the first year of life, we're forced to wait for our meals, sleep through the night and communicate our needs other than by crying.

Being expected to "behave" is a painful fall from grace, and many of us never quite accept it. We want to be special because of who we are—because of how promising, or cute, or talented we are—and not because of how we act. The fact that we have to actually fulfil our potential, that we're no longer given credit merely for having it, can be a bitter pill to swallow. It makes many thirty-year-olds feel quite desperate. They have trouble giving up the role of fair-haired girl or boy. They feel cheated that they can't still be someone's talented protégé, a gifted up-and-comer.

Some putative adults have trouble giving up the expectation of unconditional acceptance too. They expect to be enjoyed and appreciated unconditionally, not only by their parents, but by the rest of the world as well. Parents should love their children unconditionally, but it's unfair to ask them to accept their children's actions unconditionally—especially when their children aren't children any more. Children, after all, don't accept unconditionally everything their parents do. Nor should they. But likewise parents should not be expected to accept unconditionally everything their grown children do. If we were to start setting up one standard of conduct for parents and another for their grown children, then we would be admitting that children can never become adults like their parents.

It's true that parents are authorities to their children in a way their children can rarely be to them, but that imposes no requirement on parents to accept everything their children do. And the same, of course, applies even more strongly to the rest of the world. The world is under no obligation to appreciate and enjoy us just because we exist.

Ed was a criminal lawyer like his father. He'd gone into his father's firm at twenty-eight, after working for the Crown Attorney's office for two years, and quickly established himself as a whiz kid. He won tricky cases, cultivated the media and brought lots of money into the firm. He drove a Porsche, wore expensive suits and drank only the finest wines. By the time he was thirty-five, however, Ed was no longer the fair-haired boy. There was a whole new crop of rising stars, each just as smart he was, and many just as stylish.

For a brief period Ed didn't know what to do. He liked being thought of as a whiz kid. But he wasn't a kid any more, and the whiz-kid image no longer seemed to fit him. He felt jealous of the new kids on the block—of the attention they were getting from the older lawyers and judges— and found himself getting depressed.

Ed began to use cocaine, which he obtained from a former client, and before long was using it every day. His personality underwent a dramatic change. He started getting into the office late, and in poor shape to work. His health began to deteriorate: He sniffled all the time, had chronic back pain and complained to his family doctor that he was having frequent bouts of the flu. His mood flip-flopped between hyper and giddy on the one hand, and sad and irritable on the other. He needed sleeping pills or wine to fall asleep, and coffee or more coke to stay awake. Naturally, the quality of his work and his relations with the staff began to go downhill. He fobbed off his research onto junior associates without providing supervision, then blamed them when the results fell short of his expectations. Because he often entered the courtroom unprepared, he ended up losing straightforward cases that should have been a piece of cake and difficult cases that he would have won in the past.

Finally, one of his clients told Ed's father, who was the firm's senior partner, that Ed was using cocaine. Ed's father called him into his office and read him the riot act: "I want you in a drug rehab program within thirty-six hours or you're fired! Don't come back to the office until you're clean and ready to work. If you use drugs or alcohol again, I'll inform the law society and see that you're disbarred."

Ed was outraged. He couldn't believe that his father would threaten him with dismissal. He drove to his parents' home that afternoon and began weeping to his mother: "He's my father. He's supposed to support me. I'm going through a difficult time. I'm in constant pain with my back. I have allergies…"

His mother cut him off. She told him that she agreed completely with his father, and that they were being tough on him for his own good. She offered to help him find a drug rehab program and to attend family sessions with him if they were required.

Ed spent the next twenty-four hours raging at his parents, but when they refused to back down, he made arrangements to enter an in-patient program near his home. He returned to work six weeks later, no longer the fair-haired boy but grateful to his parents and ready to act his age.

There are limits to what even a parent will tolerate. Acceptance, appreciation, enjoyment, approval, pride and support are conditional. If we think otherwise, we're destined to be unhappy. The world is surprisingly tolerant of a wide variety of behaviours, but it can never be as indulgent and unconditionally loving as our parents were when we first entered their lives.

Renunciation of Old Claims for Compensation

Life is not always fair. We are all the victims of numerous injustices—some petty, some serious. Some injustices can be remedied through social action, and some by individual assertion, but many injustices can't be remedied at all. It's unfair that some people are born into less nurturing families, are given fewer opportunities or have poorer health. It may even be unfair that some people are born with less raw intelligence, talent or drive.

One universal "injustice" is that our parents don't always place our interests ahead of their own. Even the best parents sometimes place their own interests first. (Even if they did always place our interests first, that too would be an injustice because it would make us monsters of entitlement who were incapable of deferring gratification.)

We all leave childhood with deficiencies and strengths attributable to our upbringing. Coping with the strengths is fairly easy, but what are we to do with the deficiencies? The worst strategy is to dramatize your deficiencies in order to be able to seek compensation for them from your parents or from the society at large. Not only is compensation rarely forthcoming, but any compensation that is exacted is invariably paltry compared to the benefits of a life well-lived. Nevertheless, despite the low rate of return, there are plenty of people who will exaggerate their psychic deficiencies in order to extract pity, guilt or an apology from their parents. They will lead perversely miserable lives merely in order to make others miserable or to be let off the hook for their own failures.

Horror movies are almost entirely populated by such characters—monsters who take revenge on the rest of the world because they've once been the victim of some cruel accident of science or nature, or madmen who terrorize the countryside because they've been humiliated or shunned. Their appearances and their crimes may strike us as bizarre, but their motives are entirely familiar.

It's comforting, of course, to have your suffering validated by the person responsible for it, or even by someone else. And in cases where the damages were egregious and where the compensation being sought is realistic, this strategy can be an important part of the therapeutic process. Children who were the victims of physical or sexual abuse, for example, may feel liberated by an acknowledgement of their ordeal. But a lifetime spent nursing old wounds generally produces very little in the way of compensation.

Once the need to have your childhood grievance acknowledged has been met, the best strategy is to set aside your claims for compensation and try to make the best of the rest of your life. Since no one can ever be adequately compensated for their childhood pain, serious problems arise when people refuse to let their old wounds heal and make a career of grievance collecting. Making every random misfortune into an actionable grievance adds to the reservoir of pain. Like the child who murders her parents and then requests clemency on the grounds that she's been made an orphan, grievance collectors cut themselves off from their families and then expect to be catered to on the grounds that they've been made an outcast.

Ironically, people who waste a lifetime seeking reparations from their parents for past injuries often have parents who did the very same thing with *their* parents. Because grievance collecting is the child's way of trying to maintain a close relationship with an aggrieved parent, it tends to get handed down from generation to generation. Grievance collecting is the tie that binds.

Grievance collectors are unwilling to become autonomous of their aggrieved parents, whom they both hate and love. They're afraid to renounce the safety and luxury of a psychological disability pension, funded (metaphorically) by their parents. Grievance collectors, by definition, refuse to think of themselves as adult.

Renunciation of Hypochondria

Imagine you're back in school. Read the short passage below, and answer the multiple-choice question that follows it.

It's a grey Thursday morning in February, and you have a history test scheduled for ten o'clock that day. Last night, however, you talked on the phone to your friends until eleven, and by eleven-thirty felt too tired to continue studying. You decided, therefore, to get up early and cram. With good intentions, you set your alarm for five a.m., but when it rang this morning, you kept on hitting the snooze button. It's now seven-thirty and you're in a panic.

In all probability, you would:

(a) Go to your history class and do the best you can on the test, resolving to study more thoroughly for the next one.
    OR
(b) Miss the beginning of school and cram like crazy until ten, skipping breakfast, taking out your frustration on the rest of your family, and complaining about how busy you are.
    OR
(c) Discover that you have a sore throat and mild fever and ask your parents to make a doctor's appointment for you at ten that morning. (It's probably the beginning of the same cold that made you feel preternaturally sleepy after hanging up with your friends at eleven the night before.)
    OR
(d) Try (c) first, followed by (b) when (c) fails to persuade your parents, followed finally by (a).

If you didn't grow up to be a hypochondriac, you probably would have chosen (d) as your answer. But if you did grow up to be a hypochondriac—in which case your parents would have believed your illness story—you almost certainly would have chosen (c).

FEIGNING ILLNESS

All of us, at one time or another, have tried to avoid doing some unpleasant task by feigning or exploiting minor illness. Since illness is one of the few "legitimate" excuses most people will permit themselves, a certain amount of minor malingering is probably normal. And as long as the fraud is *conscious*, it's still fairly easy to give up. Once the fraud becomes *unconscious*, however, it is much harder to give up and may even produce "real" illness.

What makes fake illness go underground—become unconscious—and then re-emerge as "real" illness? The answer, of course, is shame. The fact that the symptoms are being consciously manufactured for some dishonest purpose produces shame. In order to cope with this shame, the psyche represses the origin of the symptoms, which, because their cause is now unconscious, seem "real." Shame is likely to arise when we're really trying to bamboozle someone, or when we're trying to get out of a serious responsibility. As long as the feigning of illness is done with a wink—as long as the person we're trying to convince we're ill knows we're faking it and is willing to go along with the ruse—then shame is not a big problem. Since that's generally the case when children try to "fool" their parents into letting them stay home from school, the shame in that situation is minimal, and the fact that the illness is a fraud is likely to remain conscious.

Once we leave childhood, however, the stakes involved in feigning illness get higher. We're either trying to wiggle out of obligations that are more serious, or the people we're trying to bamboozle (usually ourselves, sometimes our employers) are less indulgent. In either case, when we set out to manufacture symptoms in pre-adulthood, we always end up feeling ashamed. If that shame gets unbearable, we have to repress the fact that we're faking or exaggerating our illness and convince ourselves that we're *not* faking it—that, in fact, we really are sick. And if the selling job we're doing on ourselves is convincing, then we really do feel sick.

In other words, if we use sickness as a cop-out frequently enough, and in enough important situations, we may eventually succeed in making ourselves sick. And adults have better things to do.

SHOOTING YOURSELF IN THE FOOT

Illness can be used as a symbol. This is especially true of neurotic illness. Some people use neurosis as an emblem of their pre-adult status. They claim, for example, that they can't ask their bosses for a raise because they're too intimidated by authority, or they can't meet their deadlines because they're too inhibited by perfectionism, or they can't attend to their own personal grooming because they're too depressed about breaking up with their lover. By displaying their symptoms, they're saying in effect, "Give me a break. I'm emotionally impaired. I can't be expected to fulfil my responsibilities."

The use of neurosis as a cop-out is quite common. It's one reason why neurosis doesn't always clear up even after it's been analyzed. One patient, for example, told me that he couldn't look for a job until *after* he got his head straightened out in therapy (which, as a result, took him much longer to do). And another patient told me that she couldn't date seriously until she'd completed treatment because she always chose inappropriate men (which meant that, in the interim, she shouldn't be expected to exercise any kind of reasonable judgment whatsoever). In a criminal justice setting, this defensive strategy is referred to as copping an insanity plea.

There are people, of course, who are truly ill, but they usually try to minimize or conceal their debility. People who are using their illness as an excuse, by contrast, tend to maximize and trumpet it.

Because hypochondria always involves eliciting a response from some parental authority figure, it perpetuates the early parent-child relationship. Though the hypochondriac may start out trying to fool his parents, teachers and bosses into letting him off the hook, he ends up fooling himself instead. By refusing to accept age-appropriate responsibilities, he throws a roadblock in the path of his own development.

HYPOCHONDRIA AND DENIAL OF THE NEED FOR TLC

There are more subtle cases of hypochondria where, for example, a real illness is prolonged in order to gratify embarrassing dependency needs. Here too the motivation is unconscious. The symptoms can't be renounced until their psychological origins have been made conscious.

Low-grade viral illnesses are notorious for producing chronic fatigue syndrome in people who've previously been very active. Despite years of living independently, many of these people return to their parents' home in order to convalesce. Although the acute illness may be a bonafide infection (with hard medical evidence such as elevated liver enzymes and white blood cell counts, or rising and falling viral antibodies), the chronic illness is often harder to verify and may be prompted by an ambivalent, though unconscious, desire to be nurtured. College students who've just left home for the first time are especially prone to this kind of tenacious, ill-defined syndrome.

Why are these psychosomatically ill people unable to get their dependent and passive wishes gratified more directly? The reason is that they feel ashamed of these wishes. If they don't suppress or conceal any behaviour that smacks of neediness, they feel inadequate. These needs, which are actually quite normal, don't disappear, of course. On the contrary: Because they're being dammed up, they get even stronger. And when the person's shame can no longer keep these unmet needs in check, they burst forth in a torrent, overwhelming the psyche and forcing it to find some extraordinary means of gratifying them.

An episode of acute illness may be just the tiny additional force that's needed to burst through the barriers. Even under normal circumstances, the need for nurturing is increased by illness. However, in these extraordinary circumstances where the weight of unmet needs has been built up to the point of bursting (as it has in these fiercely help-rejecting people), the first "legitimate" opportunity to get these needs met breaches the psychic dam and releases a cataract of dependency. When it comes to providing opportunities for gratification, there is no more legitimate candidate than a bout of illness. As a result, what may have begun as an acute, self-limited illness can start to drag on and on and eventually becomes chronic.

It is easy to understand why first-year college students might be susceptible to psychosomatic illnesses. They're trying to cut the umbilical cord in the face of academic and social pressures that encourage them to think of themselves as adults. The more straightforward methods of obtaining TLC—like admitting they're homesick or lonely or overwhelmed—can be threatening to their self-esteem. Given their narrowed range of options, some college students find it more acceptable to have their normal dependency needs met by falling ill (or, just as effectively, by falling in love).

The circumstances that give rise to psychosomatic illnesses later in life are more pathological than the conditions that give rise to them during college. Adults who can't accept normal nurturing are often quite lonely and emotionally isolated. Their problem is not a surfeit of affection as it is for college freshmen separating from their parents; their problem is a dearth of affection. These adults are often so needy they develop perversely hostile relationships with the very people who *could* give them love.

Both groups of debilitated patients—the away-from-home students and the lonely adults—need to learn to accept and express their dependent wishes in healthier and less self-destructive ways. And they need support and encouragement to return to their studies or jobs before their illnesses become self-perpetuating and their disabilities irreversible.

Renunciation of Pretending

There are some clichés that, despite being trite, succinctly capture a profound idea. One is: "Life is not a dress rehearsal." Obviously, this aphorism means that you don't get a chance to live your life over again once you've finished this one. But is it sensible to compare life to a theatrical performance?

In some ways it is. We perform on the stage of our own imaginations in our fantasies and in our dreams, and we perform before the people in our lives in our everyday actions. True, for most of us, the play is appearing off-off-off-Broadway, but we are, nevertheless, the heroes or heroines of our own private dramas. At the same time, we can't be overly conscious of acting, or our performances will be forced and wooden. We can't be especially conscious of the audience either, or we will start trying too hard to please it instead of ourselves.

Yet, if we fully inhabit our role, then acting—in both senses of the word—is a joyous experience. And it remains joyous even when the play itself is a tragedy. The word "play" is significant here because the elements of experimentation, self-expression and freedom that it implies are the hallmarks of a life well-lived. We never want to stop playing.

The distinction between acting and pretending is a subtle one. To be an actor, you must choose the correct role at the correct time. The correct role is the one that best fulfils your true self, the one that permits you to "act natural." To be a pretender, you must choose the wrong role at the wrong time. The wrong role is one that you think the audience expects, but that doesn't feel natural because it isn't you.

Adam was a poet. He came to see me because he was feeling terribly depressed in the aftermath of a tempestuous love affair with a separated woman. The woman he had been dating was a sexual dynamo. She loved to be tied up and stimulated for hours. She dressed provocatively and flirted shamelessly with everyone. Adam was enthralled. He couldn't imagine ever finding another woman who would turn him on the way she did. Unfortunately, she abused cocaine and alcohol and had great difficulty remaining faithful. Echoing her motto, Adam tried to tell himself that jealousy was only a petty emotion.

Adam's paramour taunted him. She accused him of cowardice, temperance and frugality. "You don't know how to let go," she advised him. So, against his better judgment, Adam started using cocaine and drinking too much and began frequenting trendy clubs and restaurants whose prices were not geared to the poetry set. Even so, after several on-again-off-again months, his sexual playmate went back to her estranged husband.

Not surprisingly, Adam's poetry turned to the topic of obsessive love.

As we talked, it seemed apparent that, during his love affair, Adam had been pretending. He'd been playing the role of the romantic poet, but this role was not an expression of his true self. He imagined that if he played the role of a poet living on the cutting edge of life, his art would be improved. But the reverse happened: His poetry became theatrical, garish and derivative. It lacked the ring of truth that art conveys. He had chosen the wrong role for himself in order to impress his girlfriend. He had ceased to be an actor in his own life and had become instead a pretender in hers.

THEATRICALITY

We could argue that, by definition, it's impossible for a person *not* to express her true self. After all, where else could a person's motivation be coming from if not from her true self? Wasn't Adam fulfilling his sexual fantasies and his idea of what it is to be a poet by participating in his romance? Does the mere fact that it ended badly necessarily negate the fact that, at least for the moment, his tempestuous relationship expressed who Adam thought he was?

Adam is not alone in preferring theatre to reality. There are other people—many in fact—who make their lives into a kind of melodrama for the delectation of their parents and everyone else. Their behaviour is histrionic, self-dramatizing and overblown. Every trivial event gets blown up into a crisis of epic proportions.

They express themselves in three-inch headlines. If they meet someone they're attracted to, they aren't just attracted, they're "head over heels in love." If they flub an exam, they didn't flub an exam, they "blew it big-time." Because *everything* is exaggerated, nothing has its true value, and everything ends up trivialized.

Are these histrionic characters acting out their true selves? Sometimes. But most of the time they aren't. They are using their hyper-emotionality to *prevent* the emergence of their true selves. They fear the real feelings beneath the fake ones, so they hype the fake ones as a diversion. You can tell these feelings are fake because, despite the surface appearance of great conviction, they are surprisingly shallow and fickle—they appear seemingly out of nowhere, change abruptly and evaporate when any light but limelight is focused on them. The hyperbolic feelings are used primarily to engage other people, to create the illusion of passion and to keep the troublesome real feelings repressed.

Their theatricality is ultimately a defence against growing up. Because becoming a grownup would entail facing up to the very feelings and responsibilities they're trying to ward off by their hysteria, they prefer instead to present themselves (to themselves as well as to the audience) as excitable children. They do have genuine feelings, but the feelings and issues they hype are not necessarily the ones they care most about. Those issues—having mostly to do with mature relationships and sexuality—they find much too threatening to express or even to acknowledge.

If exaggerated feelings seem real when you're experiencing them, then how can you figure out if you're pretending? The answer is you *know*. You may not know in the heat of the moment. But if you think about them afterwards, you will, like Adam, have the sensation of faking it, of playing to an imaginary audience. (In Adam's case, the imaginary audience was his future readers.) In acting a role that expresses your true self, the principal component of the imaginary audience is you. If you are only pretending to play a role, the imaginary audience is composed primarily or exclusively of other people.

Eventually, you will learn to detect pretence not just after the fact, but while you're doing it. You'll become an actor instead of a pretender.

Willa lived her life as if she were on stage. An attractive woman in her early thirties, her chief complaint was that she had never been able to have a successful relationship with a suitable man. Willa used her sexuality to seduce men, then ignored them once they had become interested in her. The men soon got into the act. They played games with Willa in return, until soon the relationship had self-destructed. This pattern was repeated over and over again to the point where Willa's friends and family worried whether she'd ever be able to find happiness.

When therapy began, I thought that Willa had some kind of unconscious hostility towards men, and indeed she was highly competitive with everyone. She had to come out on top of every encounter. Yet I felt there was something more. Willa seemed to enjoy recounting her misadventures with the men she met. She was even able to look at herself with a kind of bemused detachment, as if to say: "There I go again. I guess I'll never learn." It was clear that Willa didn't really want to change—at least not then. She was getting something out of her failed relationships—a chance to star in her own long-running soap opera.

Willa had been the prima donna in her family. Her mother, who was very dramatic herself, indulged Willa's theatricality. She was maternal only when Willa was hurt or sick. When Willa became a teenager, she took delight in trying to provoke her parents by dating wild boys, staying out past her curfew and generally defying their rules.

Willa left home early, but continued her melodramatic life. Her fantasy, which had once been conscious but was eventually repressed, was that her parents would say to themselves: "What went wrong with Willa? She's so pretty and bright and personable. Why can't she find happiness? Where did we go wrong?"

She wanted her parents to worry about her. She made her life into a drama in which they were the troubled audience. Though she was pretending to be living her own zany, heartbreaking life, she was, in reality, performing for what she imagined were interested onlookers.

The great irony of a life dedicated to pleasing (or provoking) the members of an audience is that *they* have a life, and you don't. After the performance ends, they go home to their own lives and quickly forget about you. Willa's parents may have been concerned about her miserable life, but she was the one actually leading it. And after they stopped worrying about her life, they went back to enjoying theirs.

Willa, on the other hand, had no real life to return to. She was like the actress in the movie, *Sunset Boulevard,* who stayed in character long after her career had ended. Willa imagined that her parents were more worried about her than she was herself, but this was only a way of denying her own deep fears. Beneath the pathetic illusion that she was the star of a melodrama she wrote, produced and directed was the stark realization that she was, in truth, all alone. She was the star of her parents' life in her own imagination only.

PRETENDING MAY BE A REHEARSAL FOR ACTING

One reason it's so hard to distinguish between pretending and acting is that pretending can be used as a developmental stage en route to acting. In the early phases of discovering and learning our true roles, we sometimes have to pretend. The part is too new to feel completely natural. We're still very much aware of the audience; we can't seem to remember all our lines; our actions are awkward and stiff; we feel slightly fraudulent when we put on our costume and make-up; and the props still feel unfamiliar. (By the way, having the correct costume and props doesn't hurt. Wearing a white coat and dangling a stethoscope from your neck doesn't necessarily make you a doctor, but it sure does help you to feel like one.)

In time, however, our role becomes so familiar that we can lose ourselves in it. Because the outside audience is different every performance, *we alone* become the true judge of our accomplishments. We are able to forget the audience and become our true selves. We stop pretending and start acting.

Being a parent, for example, may feel awkward when you first take on the role (though there are people who've been rehearsing for it all their lives), but before you know it, you can't remember what it was like to sleep through the night.

Pretending is an early phase in the process of learning a new part.

Lou's chief complaint was anxiety, which resulted from the fact that he played two roles that were in conflict. Outside his home, Lou was a hard-boiled, austere businessman. Inside his family he was a warm and emotional husband and father. However, when he was emotional he felt weak, unmasculine and dependent; when he was cold, tough and rational, he felt isolated and lonely.

As a boy, Lou had been skinny and weak. Though he was naturally sensitive and affectionate, he became disdainful of those feelings in himself because his parents regarded them as unmanly. Lou began to emulate his father, a tough, unemotional man, and hide his "feminine" side even from himself. It was only much later, after he'd got married and had children, that he permitted his softer side to re-emerge. Yet he didn't know how to handle it. His feelings made him feel vulnerable and ashamed.

By the time he came into therapy in his mid-forties, Lou had almost forgotten the fact that he had adopted the role of tough guy in childhood. So familiar had this role become over the years that he actually believed the hard-boiled Lou was his true self and the soft-boiled Lou an impostor. Only his anxiety tipped off the fact that he was pretending to be tough.

Once Lou understood the history of his tough-guy persona—that it was a role he had learned in childhood to fend off feelings of inadequacy—he was able to renounce the pretend parts of it. He became a more integrated and balanced person. He was still able to be resolute and assertive when the situation demanded it, but when the situation didn't demand it, he could now be warm and gentle without feeling weak or unmanly.

Lou started to enjoy the people he worked with. He took an interest in their lives and got to know them as people. When he had to correct them, he did so honestly and straightforwardly, but with tact and consideration of their feelings. He became more affectionate and patient with his wife too. He showed his affection not just by initiating sex, but also by refraining from initiating sex when she wasn't in the mood.

Lou didn't adopt this kinder and gentler façade wholesale—that would merely have been a new pretence. But he was able to renounce the old hard-boiled role, which had never been totally comfortable anyway. By understanding himself better, Lou was able discover his true self and become comfortable expressing it in his daily life.

Renunciation of the Tendency to Take the Path of Least Resistance

There are people who are phobic of any situation where they might be called upon to perform to some objective standard. They fear failing. They fear having to submit to the will of others. They fear being challenged or humiliated or defeated. They do everything they can to avoid or postpone coming up to bat. They always find the path of least resistance. They may not end up feeling fulfilled, but they do manage to avoid the bugaboos they fear.

People who take the path of least resistance focus on the activities they enjoy and at which they excel, and avoid the activities they dislike and at which they look awkward. They always work well within their comfort zones. And they always manage to get someone to let them off the hook of having to fulfil unpleasant responsibilities. They are very good at making "arrangements." In return for performing the duties they and their parents consider important, they will try to negotiate an exemption from the duties they consider unimportant. In every school there's a brainy kid who gets a doctor's note exempting him from gym class, or a budding musician or athlete who's allowed to give his academic subjects short shrift.

A penchant for finding the path of least resistance can lead in one of three directions: to devaluation of the goal, to fudging or to larceny. These strategies build on a child's facility for shirking responsibilities. To feel like an adult, therefore, he will have to renounce them.

DEVALUATION OF THE GOAL

People who take the path of least resistance often employ a psychological rationale that is similar to the feeling of sour grapes—devaluing what they lack the ability, courage or perseverance to achieve.

Let's look at an example of devaluation of the goal that will be familiar to anyone who's ever taken piano lessons. Most children (and adults) don't really like to practise the piano. They would like to be able to *play* the piano, they just don't want to have to perform the tedious work necessary to do so. That's why most children quit.

Here's the rationalization: I'm never going to be a concert pianist, so why bother trying to master the instrument? I can learn to appreciate music by listening to records.

This excuse does, of course, contain a sizable grain of truth—just enough to convince some parents to let their kids drop their piano lessons. Often, though, the child really would enjoy playing the piano (granted not at Carnegie Hall), but is devaluing it—convincing herself that those sweet grapes are really sour—as an excuse not to practise.

Many adults who put in a mediocre effort at their jobs use the same sort of reasoning. They rationalize that their job isn't really what they want, that it's not stimulating or fulfilling, or that it's menial and beneath them. They always manage to convince themselves that it isn't really worth their while to try something difficult or unpleasant. However, since all worthwhile goals and activities *do* require effort to achieve, they soon find themselves at the end of a dead-end street. The only option left them is to devalue everybody else's goals as well.

FUDGING

Fudging is a type of cosmetic surgery. It is used to make something *look* better than it really is. It's the metaphorical rounding off of numbers that shouldn't be rounded off. Examples include doctoring account books to hide revenues and beef up expenses (this is called creative accounting), massaging experimental data to produce more impressive results (this is called scientific fraud), and discarding bolts unaccountably left over after assembling the barbecue (this is called masculine pride).

Fudging is a time-honoured method for taking the path of least resistance. It often seems innocuous, and sometimes it is. But most of the time, it's nothing less than cheating and deceit. The purpose of fudging is to get a good-looking result without having to put in the required effort. The fudger hopes to avoid embarrassment by performing a sleight of hand.

Fudging is a habit that begins early in life. It usually continues until one of two things happens: (1) the fudger gets caught and humiliated, or (2) he overcomes his feeling that work is done primarily for show and becomes self-motivated.

Gary was a clever but lazy kid who could always be counted on to find some way of avoiding work while looking diligent. He'd clean up his room, for example, by throwing everything into the closet, but he'd make his bed with perfect hospital corners. He'd do his homework assignments on a different topic than the one assigned, but they'd be too clever to warrant penalizing. In order to impress people with his intellect, he'd read a wide range of subjects, but he'd only skim the essence of each subject and refuse to learn the "unimportant" (i.e., difficult) details. As a result, he was a bit of a dilettante.

Because Gary didn't want his parents, teachers, bosses or girlfriends to become disillusioned with him when he fell short of their expectations, he began to embroider the truth. If he got an A-minus on an exam, he reported it as an A—and said it was the highest mark the teacher gave out, even when that wasn't true. If he once lived in Little Rock, Arkansas, he would have claimed to know President Clinton. If he earned exactly $100,000 per year, he'd tell you his income was "in the six figures."

Caught in a squeeze between the pressure to perform and the fear of working, Gary invariably procrastinated. He began his first assignment late and then spent too much time on it so he could avoid having to go on to the next one. When he applied for a new job or for a spot in graduate school, he beautified his résumé—adding an unearned degree and attaching a forged reference letter.

Some of the most tragic cases of fudging are those of potentially brilliant medical researchers who doctor the results of their experiments in order to make a breakthrough discovery. At first they're hailed as messiahs, but very soon, when their findings are found to be bogus, they're vilified as pariahs.

The typical fudger is the apple of his mother's eye and intensely competitive with his father. His father is generally a stolid, hard-working, honest, well-liked and respected man, who may be successful, but lacks pizzazz. Furthermore, because his father is either considerably older than the fathers of other boys or because he lacks the energy and desire to do things with his son, the boy has difficulty identifying with his father's positive qualities. Those middle-aged virtues seem impossibly remote to the boy. Because he can neither compete nor identify with his father, yet is afraid to be judged on his own merits, the fledgling fudger resorts to flash.

As a result, the potential fudger can't develop autonomy. He is too keenly aware that his parents, teachers and others have high expectations of him and is in constant fear that he won't measure up. He may pursue a career that his parents think is prestigious—like science, math, business, medicine, law or engineering—but that he lacks a real feel for. Nevertheless, he'll seek out the most rigorous or prestigious institution in which to train—compounding the pressure on himself and increasing his feelings of inadequacy. He won't be able to admit his self-doubt to anyone (including himself), however, because he's afraid he'll be disgraced. Not only is he unable to seek therapy or change careers, he can't even ask for help with his work. He feels like an impostor.

Having set this trap for himself, fudging seems like the only way out. Between daunting effort and shameful mediocrity, fudging is the path of least resistance.

Over time, however, he starts to find the pressure and the guilt of fudging unbearable. He wants out. He unconsciously begins to court disaster. He gets reckless. He even fudges in foolish ways that are easily discovered. And sooner or later, he gets caught.

Of course, to someone so desperate to impress other people, the initial trauma of public exposure is devastating. But once he is out of the spotlight, the defrocked fudger often feels a profound sense of relief. Having been stripped of his burdensome pride, he can finally be free. Having been battered a little by life and feeling less like a child, he can begin to identify with his father's virtues. Feeling a new sense of adult autonomy, he can start his life over again as someone he's never been before—himself.

LARCENY

Larceny is another of the paths of least resistance that, at one time or another, tempts all of us. Like devaluation of the goal and fudging, larceny begins early in life. Many children will try lying, stealing or cheating at least once, but very few will attempt to make a career of it. And even those children, when confronted with their delinquency by a responsible adult, will usually bring their crime spree to a halt.

Some children, however, learn that crime pays and that punishment can be avoided. They discover that it's relatively easy to conceal their crimes, to bamboozle honest people and—on the rare occasion that they are caught—to avoid or minimize punishment by lying shamelessly. These neophyte con artists misconstrue mercy as weakness and trust as stupidity. They get used to finding the expedient path to gratification. When working for the things they want seems too difficult, when the opportunity for larceny presents itself, or when they can salve their conscience by sharing the blame with a group of co-conspirators, these children won't shy away from breaking the law. Unlike true psychopaths, they know the difference between right and wrong and feel guilty for their misdemeanours. But somehow or other, they find a way to rationalize their dishonest acts. In other words, they learn to cheat with impunity. That's how juvenile crooks grow up to become adult crooks.

Annals of Larceny

At the end of the eighties, during the height of the insider-trading scandals on Wall Street, people found it hard to understand why someone who was making millions of dollars a year would cheat to make a few million more. I don't purport to know for sure what their motives were, but I do know that their larcenous habits didn't begin when they got a call from Ivan Boesky.

All career criminals get started as children. A typical history of petty larceny, told to me by a man who was seeking therapy because of career problems, illustrates this axiom.

Calvin began his criminal career, as most children do, shoplifting candy and trinkets from the local variety store. By interspersing his thefts with legitimate purchases paid for with change pilfered from his father's wallet, he got pretty proficient at evading suspicion. However, he did get caught stealing a chocolate bar at the age of ten and was severely reprimanded by the store's owner.

In the annals of crime, this kind of event is regarded as a critical turning point. The child felon has a life-determining decision to make—he can give up shoplifting and go straight, or he can get better at it.

Here's what Calvin did: He went home that evening and tore a hole through his pants pocket, so that his pocket communicated with the lining of his pants and formed a hidden reservoir in the leg. Next day he returned to the same store, shoved a chocolate bar into the torn pocket and then wiggled the hot candy into the secret compartment in his pant leg. This time, when the store owner accused the lad of stealing another chocolate bar, he was prepared with a defence. First, with a look of wounded innocence, he denied any suggestion of wrongdoing, and then, to prove his innocence, the youthful perpetrator turned his pockets inside out and began to cry. Despite his well-founded suspicions, the store owner had no recourse but to let the suspect go. Calvin left feeling flush with excitement and eager to hatch his next scam.

In the long run, Calvin's preference for larceny over legwork didn't pay him very well, which was the reason he decided to seek therapy. He did poorly in college and dropped out before completing his degree. He performed below expectations at a series of jobs, culminating in two years of unemployment. And he exploited his hard-working wife, until she finally threatened to leave him out of frustration at his lack of initiative.

Larceny leads to larceny not only because it's easier than hard work, but also because the perpetrator of the larceny lacks confidence in his ability to succeed by any other means.

Leo, who came to see me after having been fired from his job for forging sales contracts, told me that his history of cheating went back to childhood too. When he was thirteen years old, he'd applied to a high school of art and design in New York; the school required him to submit a portfolio of his artwork as part of the application process. Although he was a pretty good artist, Leo wasn't sure he had the goods to get in. His portfolio was a little thin, and the quality was uneven. So, to solve his problem, he decided to trace drawings from books and magazines and submit them as his own.

Leo's first foray into forgery was never discovered. He was admitted to art school, presumably ahead of other children who had refused to cheat, and he learned two lessons that stayed with him throughout his life: The first was that it's easy to pull the wool over people's eyes if you show them something tangible—like a traced drawing or a forged contract—to back up your lie. The second was that it's difficult to develop any confidence in yourself when you've been able to achieve your goals only by cheating.

Both these men began to cheat when they were children and continued to do so well into middle age. Yet each of them—unconsciously—found ways to punish himself for his crimes. Calvin did so by floundering in his career, and Leo did so by getting caught committing a forgery.

Some people commit crimes in order to be caught. By getting themselves punished for a conventional crime, they hope to atone for imagined "crimes" that as children they considered even more grievous—wanting to torture their neighbour's younger brother, for example, or wanting to sleep with their Sunday school teacher.

But just because many crimes have an unconscious as well as a conscious motive, it doesn't follow that we need to understand the motive for the larceny before we can renounce it. And the motives underlying larceny are neither obscure nor unique to the criminal. They are universal. All of us would love to get away with things or get something for nothing.

The principal difference between those who succumb to temptation and those who resist it resides not in motivation but in impulse control. Larcenous people don't cheat more than the rest of us because they have less insight, they cheat more because they have less restraint. The final barrier to dishonest behaviour isn't conscience, it's continence.

The fact that most of us *do* renounce larceny—despite the

ubiquity of the temptation to do otherwise—is the best illustration of the principle that we intend to be judged, not by our intentions, but by our actions.

Renunciation of Self-deception

Larceny isn't the only form of dishonesty that you have to give up in order to feel adult—it's only the most concrete. You also have to be prepared to give up being dishonest with yourself. After all, it isn't possible to act honestly towards others while lying to yourself. Self-deception makes it too easy to rationalize your bad behaviour.

Perfect self-honesty is extraordinarily difficult to achieve. Very few of us have the courage to examine our actions in the cold hard light of our ideals. Most of us flinch. We look away or make excuses. Yet, without honesty, it's impossible for us to overcome the psychic obstacles that stand in the way of our growing up. For that reason, the renunciation of dishonesty is *the* pivotal act in the process of becoming adult. This lesson was brought home to me by a twenty-six-year-old college teacher named Phoebe, who came to see me because she was having trouble sorting out her life.

Phoebe was bright, well-educated, stylish, friendly and generous, yet totally unable to advance in her career or to find a suitable partner. And, for many months, the reason for her turmoil remained a mystery. One day she'd teach a brilliant class, and the next day she'd call in sick. For half a year she'd date a terrific man, then in one night she'd dump him for a stranger she met at a bar. All of it was discussed with great drama and "insight," but none of it ever changed.

Then one day Phoebe missed her second consecutive appointment without notice, and I called her at her home to find out what was wrong. The phone rang about nine times before she picked it up, and when she did I couldn't understand her. Her speech was slurred and rambling and silly, and when I asked her directly, she admitted that she'd been drinking with a man she barely knew.

At her next appointment, Phoebe admitted that she

was an alcoholic and that she had lied to me when I'd asked her about it in the past. It took her a little longer to accept the fact that she needed to enter a treatment program, but when she finally did so, her work and relationships improved dramatically. She became much less dramatic and "insightful" in her weekly psychotherapy, but much more honest and mature in her daily life.

THE TRADE-OFF

The reason we renounce pre-adult vices when we become adults is not because we like pleasure less as we get older, but because the old indulgences have become less pleasurable. It's a trade-off. We give up the old pleasures of our formative years to make room for the new pleasures of our mature years. It takes faith to trade the angel you know for the angel you don't know. But if you do so willingly—if you make this trade-off with bravery and conviction—the transition to adulthood goes much more smoothly and the process becomes much more satisfying.

Although we normally view renunciation as an act of negation, it is, in fact, an act of affirmation. It is a positive and progressive choice: a decision to grow and mature and become better people. We don't become adult by passively sitting back and letting it happen to us; we become adult by actively stepping forward and making it happen. We become adult through our words and through our deeds. And renouncing immature habits is one of those deeds.

CHAPTER SEVEN

BECOMING ADULT BY WORD AND DEED

> You don't learn to hold your own by standing on guard, but by attacking and getting well hammered yourself.
>
> *George Bernard Shaw*

Becoming an adult is not something that is thrust upon you; becoming an adult is something that you earn. But it is not a goal in itself; it is the reward you get for achieving the goal. The goal itself is happiness. And happiness can be achieved only by living up to your own standards; fulfilling or struggling to fulfil your own ambitions; enjoying, preserving and creating beauty in the world; loving and being loved by other people; and doing something worthwhile and doing it well. So although feeling adult is something that you have to earn by your words and deeds, it is a pleasure to work at and a joy to achieve.

ACHIEVEMENT
The Importance of Achievement

If there is one factor more than any other that makes a person feel like a grownup, it is achievement—particularly when the achievement involves the fulfilment of a cherished dream. This is quite fortunate, because achievement is also something over which we have a degree of control; to a large extent it's a function of our own efforts. If, instead of achievement, feeling adult depended on factors outside our control—such as the amount of encouragement we received from our parents, the depth of our potential, or the grandeur of our dreams—we'd be more at the mercy of fate, and feeling adult would be a hit-or-miss affair. It's good to have these other things, of course, and they can make it easier to have real achievements, but by themselves they don't make you adult.

In Chapter One of this book I compared the act of becoming a grownup to the experience of learning to ride a bicycle. The comparison is particularly apt because learning to ride a bicycle, like learning to become a grownup, is an age-appropriate achievement. Any number of other complex and uniquely human accomplishments besides learning to ride a bike—from learning to walk or throw a ball, to studying geography or mathematics, to mastering the violin or the game of golf—could have served just as well as analogies to the achievement of becoming an adult.

They all have in common the following elements:

The person seeking to achieve the goal—whether learning to ride a bicycle or becoming an adult—must be physically and psychologically ready to do so.

She needs a guide, mentor, teacher or hero to model herself after. And if suitable role models can't be found in person, they can be sought in books, films or other media.

The task being learned, though challenging and complex and composed of many parts, can eventually be integrated into a smooth and unselfconscious unity, the attainment of which is accompanied by unique feelings of pleasure, accomplishment and growth. This sensation of "getting it" applies as much to the process of becoming an adult as to the more discrete tasks of learning a sport or a musical instrument.

Once the task has been achieved, the person achieving it starts to feel an increased sense of freedom and autonomy. New worlds of opportunity open up to her.

Success leads to a permanent change in the person's self-image. She now thinks of herself in a new way—as a cyclist, musician or adult.

There is a sudden gain in effortlessness, after the rudiments of the task have been learned. Yet there will always be room for further practise and improvement. And because of this, the novice may eventually be able to surpass the master.

Nearly everyone can acquire enough facility in riding a bicycle, playing the piano or becoming an adult to be able to employ that skill and enjoy it. But not everyone can become a star at it. Talent, opportunities, luck, the capacity for perseverance and levels of attainment are unevenly and unfairly distributed across humanity. We can probably all learn to pick out "Chopsticks" on the piano, but we can't all become Herbie Hancock. We can all draw pictures of flowers with our crayons in school, but we won't all grow up to be Georgia O'Keeffe. Most people can learn to throw a baseball, but only a few can pitch in the same league as Sandy Koufax. And we can all learn enough math to figure out how to make change, but no matter what we do, we aren't ever going to be Stephen Hawking.

However, if we work hard at playing the piano, painting, throwing a baseball or learning mathematics, we can achieve a great deal. And we can see what would be required to truly excel at each of these activities or, by extension, any other activity. Achievement, therefore, turns out to be a lesson both in humility and in the appreciation of excellence.

The achievement of adult stature—like the achievement of excellence in other fields—is easier for some people than for others. Just as some people have a talent for music or sports or mathematics, some people have a talent for being adult. Most people, of course, have a talent that is middling. Here, however, the analogy between most other types of achievement and the achievement of adulthood starts to break down: Because, while only those with extraordinary talent can become an excellent musician, athlete or mathematician, even those with middling talent can become an excellent adult.

FAILURE

The only thing that makes you feel more like an adult than achievement is achievement alloyed with failure. The two are stronger together than either is alone. Making your company successful again after a stint in bankruptcy is more affirming than making it succeed in the first place. Returning to play in the major leagues is that much sweeter after you've been demoted to the minors. And the triumph of discovering the cure for an illness, solving a mathematical problem or learning to paint is even greater when you've been told that you won't be able to do it.

When failure is added to success, it strengthens the will, builds character and increases appreciation for the achievements of others. Failure gives you empathy, humility and a feeling of maturity. Surviving failure makes the pain of disappointment gentler and the pleasure of success sweeter. Your healed scars are the reminders of battles won and lost—of a life lived bravely and to the full.

Evaluating Achievement

Why is achievement the key to feeling adult? Because feeling adult involves changing how we see ourselves, and how we see ourselves is determined, more than anything else, by how we act. It would be a reasonable approximation of the truth to say that self-image is the sum of our actions. If you wish to see yourself as a good person, then you have to perform good acts. If you wish to see yourself as a grownup, then you have to act grown up.

But what if you perform adult deeds and have childish motives? Will you still see yourself as an adult, or will you see yourself as a child instead? If you perform good deeds with selfish motives, for example, will you think of yourself as a good person or as a bad person? If you rescue a child from a burning building, will it matter to you why you did it? Will you feel less like a good person if your reason for doing so was more to look like a hero than to save a life?

The answer to all these questions hinges on the issue of consistency. If each individual positive act is a rare and isolated event, then the reason you're doing it will probably make a difference to the way you see yourself. But if these acts are a frequent occurrence and are part of an overall pattern of positive action, then your motives for performing them will diminish in importance. What will count is the nature of the acts themselves. Naturally, if you have good thoughts, you'll be more likely to perform good deeds than if you have bad thoughts. But having the thoughts—good or bad—won't, in itself, take you very far. You need action. The road to a bad self-image is paved with good intentions that were never translated into good actions. Remember, *self-image is the sum of our actions.*

When you're trying to decide what kind of person you are, you won't look at each individual act as if it were taking place in isolation; you will look at all of your actions *in toto* and in context. No one is always good or always adult. Each of us is a mixture. If we had to be perfect in order to feel good about ourselves, then none of us would ever feel good. If we had to act grown up all the time in order to feel adult, then none of us would ever feel adult. In order to feel adult, it will be enough that most of our actions are adult.

The idea that good (or adult) deeds are diminished if our motives are bad (or childish) is based on the naïve assumption that our motives can ever be unmixed. It assumes that there are actually deeds that have purely good motives. This may be possible in theory. (There have been saints, after all.) But, in practice, it's never the case. In reality our motives are *always* mixed. Even the motives for our most noble actions contain some element of self-interest. It would be disingenuous to deny it. We don't need to be particularly ashamed of this fact, however, because the truth is, the more willing we are to acknowledge the ambivalent nature of our motivation, especially the negative component of it, the more altruistic and uninhibited our actions will become, and the less power the negative side will have over them. For example, we may start out working for a charity because we want to meet eligible people to date or in order to network for our business, but end up working for the charity because we see how it benefits the people it was created to help.

Does the same principle apply to acting adult? Will you automatically feel grown up if you behave like a grownup? Again the answer is yes—eventually. You will reach a critical point—after your actions have been consistently grown up for some time—when the clash between your previously held pre-adult self-image and your growing adult one will become too strong to deny. You will then decide that the emerging adult self-image more precisely describes your actions than the pre-adult one that's been holding sway, and you'll start seeing yourself as a grownup. In other words, acting adult does eventually result in feeling adult.

There is a mental component to the establishment of self-image. But it's not the act of having good thoughts; it's the process of comparing your actions to your ideals to see how your actions measure up. If they measure up, then you feel good about yourself and you have a good self-image. If they don't measure up, you don't feel good about yourself, and you have a bad self-image. If you believe in working hard at your job, for example, but take it easy whenever your boss is out of the office, you're less likely to feel good about yourself than if you work hard all the time.

The same principle is applied in determining whether you view yourself as an adult, except that, whereas other self-images can fade and need constant reconfirmation, once you see yourself as a grownup, the image is pretty much set. Perhaps that's why trying to feel like an adult is a more complicated change in self-image than trying to feel like a hard worker or a competent tennis player.

STANDARDS

If self-image is the sum of our actions, then why do some seemingly good people still manage to feel bad? I'd like to be able to say that it's because they're applying overly strict criteria of goodness to themselves, that they're "hard markers" who always give themselves bad report cards. Unfortunately, however, it's usually the other way around; they're falling short of standards that are too low to give them a valid feeling of achievement. And they're falling short of even these low standards because they're not prepared to make the sacrifices necessary to reach them. People who live up to the letter but not the spirit of their obligations at home, at work or at school won't feel good about themselves. They don't feel badly because they're doing bad things, they feel badly because they're not doing enough good things. I have yet to meet anyone whose standards were so high that they prevented him from achieving happiness.

Many people deal with the shame of failing to meet their own reasonable standards by unconsciously copping to a lesser plea.

They plead guilty to a trivial misdemeanour in order to conceal or repress the fact that they've committed a more serious one. If a kid steals change from his father's dresser to buy candy from the candy store, for example, he may feel less guilty confessing that he ate junk food between meals than that he took money that didn't belong to him.

By transferring the guilt from the serious transgression to the trivial one, plea bargainers hope to convince themselves and others that their guilt really isn't warranted. If they succeed in making this transfer of guilt, then their guilt will no longer appear to fit their crime. Because their real crime is now repressed, it creates the illusion that their standards are too high and that they're being too hard on themselves.

Unfortunately (or fortunately), the illusion rarely lasts. Their plea bargaining eventually breaks down. Even if they manage to fool everyone else into thinking they're too hard on themselves, they can't ultimately fool their own consciences. Their displaced guilt comes back to haunt them, and, despite their efforts, they end up feeling just as badly as before.

Ironically, when the repressed "crimes" they feel so guilty about are finally brought to light in therapy, they often turn out to be no more serious than the ones they've already owned up to. They're usually misdemeanours or conflicts from childhood that were repressed before they had a chance to be resolved— guilty fantasies or mild displays of aggression, perhaps revolving around Oedipal or sibling rivalries, that are reawakened when the contemporary situation starts to resemble the childhood one.

Vince told me that he was sure everything he tried would end in failure. "I always screw up!" he said dejectedly. He was feeling quite downcast that day in therapy because he'd had a fight with his wife, Rena, the night before and was feeling guilty about it. Rena had asked Vince to go to the store to get a carton of milk, but he had refused, claiming that since he'd already stayed home that night baby-sitting while she'd gone to a movie, it was her turn to run an errand. Nevertheless, Vince knew his quibbling had been petty, and he felt ashamed of it.

Considering the trivial nature of Vince's bad behaviour, his claim that he was a screw-up seemed a trifle harsh. Was this a case of someone whose standards of marital conduct were too high? Should I tell him not to be so hard on himself? I didn't think so. Vince's dejection seemed a tad too ostentatious and disproportionate to be due to the kerfuffle with his wife.

I asked Vince if anything else had happened recently that he felt ashamed of. After some thought, he admitted that he'd handed in a work assignment one month late. Was this the true cause of his apparently exaggerated self-criticism? I still didn't think so, but it certainly seemed to be a better candidate for explaining his shame than did the tiff with Rena. I felt sure, however, that Vince was repressing something even more embarrassing than the late assignment—something that, in his mind, justified his shame and made him confess his inadequacy.

He couldn't get to the source of this repressed guilt during those initial sessions, but several months later he had a breakthrough that brought these feelings to the surface. During a discussion we were having about why he'd been arriving late to several consecutive psychotherapy sessions, he suddenly became conscious of the fact that he'd been repressing intense feelings of rivalry towards me—feelings that made him want to resist coming to his appointments, but that also made him feel guilty and ashamed when he finally got there. Getting to his appointments late allowed Vince to express his rivalry with me and to cope with his guilt about his rivalry with me at the same time. He could express his resistance towards me by keeping me waiting, and he could avoid talking to me about his rivalry by cutting down on the amount of time left in the session to do so.

Of course, as Vince quickly realized, these feelings and actions—resistance and avoidance—didn't begin in his relationship with me. They were precisely the same rivalrous feelings and actions that he'd had towards his father when he was growing up—feelings that had made him both intensely guilty and fearful of losing his father's love.

These feelings were stirred up whenever he had to deal with an authority figure whom he both liked and feared.

None of us quite lives up to our own standards. We all expect to fall short of them to some degree; that's what spurs us on to try harder and do better. But provided we've made a credible effort to reach those standards, we generally won't punish ourselves unduly for falling short.

When people do punish themselves unduly for falling short, however, it may not be because their standards are too strict, as it sometimes seems; it may be because they're having to constantly fight the temptation to ignore those standards. They want to rebel against the standards and rules they've established for themselves because they still feel as though they're being imposed from outside. They need to be more repressive because they're constantly putting down incipient uprisings within their own psyches.

Why do they still feel as though their standards are being imposed from the outside? One reason is that they may have internalized their parents' rules of conduct without, at some point, having adapted them to fit their own personalities. They have not yet established moral autonomy. As a result, when they start doing things their parents might have disapproved of, they feel as though they're rebelling against their own rules of conduct. And the more they want to do their own thing, instead of their parents' thing, the harder they have to be on themselves, until, eventually, their behaviour can start to become quite compulsive.

Ali couldn't accept an invitation to a friend's summer cottage without first making up some excuse about why she'd have to leave before the end of the weekend. At first she would claim that she had to get back to work, but she stopped using that excuse when she decided that it made her look too self-important. Of course, by staying the entire time once she got to the cottage, she'd expose the fact that she had been making excuses anyway.

Yet, despite this, Ali kept on performing the charade of having to leave early until her friends actually began to make fun of her for it. She then became embarrassed enough to want to figure out why she needed to put herself through a ritual that even she knew was empty. It didn't take her long to do so. She remembered that her mother had drummed it into her head, as a teenager, never to overstay her welcome. Because she was a little overweight at the time and not feeling very good about herself, and because she was pretty insecure about imposing herself on her girlfriends, she accepted her mother's advice without much question. But because she was also very gregarious and sensitive and responsible at the time, she was hurt by her mother's advice and wanted to resist it.

As a result of these conflicting feelings, Ali continued to be at war with herself even after she left home. On one hand she was afraid to overstay her welcome; on the other hand she was afraid to leave too soon and miss out on some of the fun. By declaring her intention of leaving early, Ali hoped to reassure her hosts—and herself—that there was no danger of her overstaying her welcome. Then, if her hosts coaxed her to stay she could do so without feeling guilty, and if they didn't she could leave before they were sick of her.

In order to feel an allegiance to any set of standards—even our own—we have to see them as legitimate. We have to understand the rationale behind them and agree with it. If we don't believe in the standards we're striving to achieve, then we'll resist trying to meet them, or we'll make it sheer drudgery trying to do so.

For most of us, the standards and rules we've been living by are a mixture of parental judgments; aphorisms from school and religious teachers; homilies gleaned from television, magazines and movies; and pronouncements made extemporaneously by our peers. The rationale behind them will be either fairly obvious or completely unexamined. But before we enter adulthood, it's important to take a fresh look at these received notions—modifying or discarding those that don't stand up to scrutiny and adopting as our own those that prove more durable and valid. Because, once having performed such a reassessment, we'll find it much easier to harmonize our actions with our beliefs and, as a result, much easier to feel good about ourselves for having lived up to our own standards.

The brief example that follows, though relatively trivial, has the virtue of being quite concrete.

Andrea had been dating a man for several months. He was very attractive, but not especially hard-working, and worst of all he had a terrible temper. Very early in their relationship, Andrea had given him the key to her apartment. Before long he was regarding her apartment as his own. Although he didn't pay rent or contribute in any other way to its upkeep, he felt free to come and go as he pleased.

Andrea's boyfriend was also very jealous. He grilled her if she were late returning to the apartment, called her at odd hours to make sure she was at home and sulked if she innocently talked to other men. After several weeks of this treatment, Andrea decided that she had to break up with her boyfriend. But she was afraid to confront him and didn't want to do it in person.

The problem was that she had an unexamined rule that governed this predicament and seemed to take precedence over any other rule. It was: YOU NEVER HAVE IMPORTANT CONVERSATIONS OVER THE PHONE. YOU ALWAYS HAVE THEM IN PERSON.

"Does this rule apply even when you feel emotionally threatened?" I asked her.

"You mean, if I'm feeling intimidated, I *don't* have to speak to him in person?" she asked me in reply.

She had to admit that, upon reflection, this ironclad rule of engagement didn't seem to make much sense in the current situation. She felt much relieved.

Andrea phoned her boyfriend and asked him for her key back. He was quite angry that she hadn't broken up with him in person, but when Andrea explained that she'd been frightened of his reaction, he calmed right down and actually understood why she might have felt that way.

In fact, her decision not to meet with him face to face actually underscored the gravity of her assertion, and he resolved not to be so inappropriately jealous in future relationships. The break-up went without incident, and whenever their paths happened to cross, he continued to be friendly towards her.

Once we've decided what standards make sense to us, we have to work hard to try to meet them. We can't achieve happiness by lowering the bar whenever we run into difficulty; we can achieve it only by trying to live up to tough, objective standards. Failure in the pursuit of high standards is less likely to lead to unhappiness than success in the attainment of low ones.

Impediments to Achievement

It's not enough just to undertake worthwhile deeds. If you want to feel like an adult, you have to actually accomplish those deeds as well. Actions have to be thoughtful and nuanced. Their likely consequences have to be considered along with their desired ones.

> Erin wanted to make her boyfriend feel cared for and comfortable—a perfectly laudable goal—but she did so by killing him with kindness. If he was contentedly watching television, she would walk in and say, "Why don't you put your feet up?" And later, if they were sitting side by side on the couch, she would twirl his hair. At first Erin's boyfriend found these little endearments endearing, but after awhile he found them irritating. When he pointed this out to her in a loving fashion, she took offence and told him to accept her the way she was.

Erin may have intended by her actions to express her affection for her boyfriend, but by not accepting that his actual reaction to them was different from her intentions, she actually ended up annoying him. The intended effect of an action and its actual effect are not always identical. What counts in the long run is the actual effect. Part of performing good actions is evaluating whether they're having the desired effect.

Some people who perform nominally good actions are actually interested in getting *bad* results. They have another agenda altogether. What they're really interested in is proving that life isn't fair. In order to make this demonstration, they undertake actions that seem always to be above reproach but that lead inevitably to some sort of disaster—resulting in their own misfortune.

It's the old problem of confusing intentions with actions: Their intentions are ostensibly positive, but their actions are invariably negative—for them. The way you're able to tell that their misfortune is premeditated is that they strike out every time they get up to bat. If their bad luck were really due to bad luck, they would have gotten on base by chance alone at least once. Even the unluckiest baseball players get on base once in a while. If they aren't pitched four balls or hit by a pitch, they'll at least reach base on a throwing error. As Fred's story shows, only people who really *want* to strike out bat zero.

> Fred was a young lawyer who kept losing cases. He worked hard on the research, but when he argued his case in court, he invariably got the judge angry at him. He would challenge the judge's rulings and raise questions about his or her ethics or knowledge. Before long, the judge was negatively disposed towards Fred and disinclined to rule in his client's favour. Fred couldn't understand it. It seemed so unfair. He was trying to do good, but he was actually doing bad.
>
> Of course, unconsciously, Fred was arguing a different case before a different tribunal. He was trying to prove to his parents that life isn't fair—and he was winning that case, while losing all the others. Fred's real beef was with his father, whom he felt never adequately appreciated him. By arguing with the judge and getting the judge to punish him, Fred was able to re-enact the conflict with his father over and over again in the courtroom.
>
> On occasion, Fred actually won a case. When he did, it sent him into a depression. Winning in court made it much harder for him to argue the case that life isn't fair. It meant that he could no longer blame everything on his father and that he had to accept responsibility for himself. It meant, in short, that he had to grow up.

People like Fred who "can't win for losing" do something else that explains why they fail so often: They keep a mental ledger of how they've been treated. On the credit side are the things they do for other people; on the debit side are the things other people do for them. By doing things for others, while preventing others from doing things for them, they make sure their account is always in the red. As a result, they constantly have other people in their debt.

If you do something generous for this sort of person, your generosity has to be negated by devaluation or neutralized by the commission of an act of greater generosity in return: If you buy them a book, they've already read it. If you treat them to an ice cream, they treat you to dinner. By running a chronic deficit, these book keepers are able to confirm their innermost conviction that life has shortchanged them.

People who keep such fastidious records tend to collect a lot of IOUs. Naturally, they feel angry that a lot of the time these IOUs aren't being repaid. Yet they wouldn't have it any other way. A "legitimate" reason for righteous indignation is like money in the bank to them.

One woman told me that she knew the birthdays of all her friends, though none of them seemed to know hers. Obviously, she was running a huge deficit in the gift-giving department. Though she lamented the unfairness of it all, she really preferred it that way. Despite the fact that her gestures were rarely reciprocated, she never missed a chance to send one of her delinquent friends a birthday or get-well card.

GRIEVANCE COLLECTORS

Grievance collectors collect injustices the way the national treasury collects debt. They love to feel aggrieved. Though they like to protest loudly about how they've been shafted, nothing delights them more than to feel they've got the short end of the stick. They keep an inventory of grievances as a pretext for expressing hostility, especially towards their parents. They feel cheated by their parents (often because they were displaced by a younger sibling), and they are unwilling to forgive their parents until their parents make restitution. How do they get revenge on them in the meantime? In the most perverse way possible: by

cutting off their noses to spite their faces. They behave virtu-
ously only when it will result in their own martyrdom, or when
it will make someone else look bad.

Here's an illustration of their self-destructive virtue.

Jack, a chronically depressed but very bright young man,
told me one day that he was upset. His boss had criticized
him for being late with a report that she needed in order to
complete her own submission on time. Jack felt that it was
unfair of her to criticize him because she had taken too
long to give him feedback on his first draft.

After the meeting in which she'd reprimanded him,
Jack sent his boss a note pointing out that she'd failed to
return some necessary revisions to him on time and hinting
that he didn't intend to put up with this kind of treatment.

It was a fact that Jack's boss could be tough to work
for. She was so busy herself that she had very little time for
reviewing the work of her assistants, and she left them
pretty much to their own devices. Nevertheless, she gave
them lots of opportunity and responsibility, and lots of
credit for the work they did.

She answered Jack's long, somewhat impudent letter
with a terse eight-word note: "Should I assign the report to
someone else?"

Her reply may have been a trifle brusque, but it was
not exactly devastating. Jack had made his point. He
should have let the matter drop and asked her to let him
finish the report. Instead, he dug himself in deeper. He
wrote her an even longer memo beginning with the sentence, "Can we stick to the topic?" and ending with the
sentence, "Perhaps we can do better in the future."

Now, in a perfectly egalitarian world, it shouldn't
have mattered that Jack was a senior medical student and
that his boss was the chief of medicine at a major teaching
hospital; nor should it have mattered that the report in
question was an article she was planning to submit to a
prestigious medical journal, and that it would have placed
his name alongside hers in the scientific literature. What
should have mattered was that he was "right" and that she

was "wrong." Right? Wrong! What matters is that his behaviour was incredibly self-destructive.

When I told Jack that the last sentence of his note had been patronizing and that his whole approach had been poorly conceived, he seemed genuinely surprised. "But I thought I was taking the high road!" he protested. "I let her know how I honestly felt, instead of swallowing my anger."

"No doubt," I answered, "but you didn't use your head. You might end up winning the battle and losing the war. You might have been narrowly within your rights, but you didn't consider what the outcome of your actions was likely to be. Perhaps your real goal was to prove that, no matter how much you try to do the right thing, you always end up getting hurt."

Jack didn't agree with my interpretation at that point. But eventually he reconsidered what I'd said to him—after he found out that his boss hadn't accepted him into the medical residency program that she supervised. At that point, he agreed that he had an axe to grind with the world, and that he seemed to want to hone its edge on his own hide.

It is very difficult for grievance collectors, like Jack, to allow themselves to be happy. Because, if they ever admitted to themselves that they *were* happy, they would have to renounce their long-standing claims to compensation. Their mental ledger would run a surplus, and they'd have to tear up the IOUs from their parents for the "unfair" treatment they'd received as children. Like most other neurotic habits, litigating a suit for damages against your parents is hard to give up, especially when you've been prosecuting it since childhood. Because these self-destructive patterns confirm the child's view of the world and because they help her to consolidate a sense of her own identity, they tend to become self-perpetuating and deeply ingrained.

When grievance collectors come to see that the advantages of happiness far exceed the payoff of reparations, they will sometimes drop their case against their parents and permit themselves to be happy and successful instead. Happiness, after all, is the best revenge.

Developing the Capacity to Achieve

There are people who believe they should be judged according to who they *are* rather than what they've *done*. They believe that approval should never be contingent on performance. They cling to the notion that potential is more meaningful than achievement.

If you think about it, that's how we all must have felt for a brief shining moment during infancy. Our parents approved of us unstintingly, regardless of our actual behaviour. They had a twinkle in their eyes for us. We were the repository of their dreams.

At some point, however, we were expected to perform. We had to *earn* our privileges. We had to accept certain household rules of conduct. We had to do our homework. We had to acquire the skills to play games and obey the rules. We had to compete against our peers in school, in sports and in lots of other ways. And we had to accept the harsh fact that even our parents weren't automatically enthralled by everything we did. We had to give up the illusion that there is such a thing as unearned merit.

Children who are especially cute, charming, winsome, precocious, amusing, adorable, bright and articulate often find it possible to maintain the illusion of unearned merit for a much longer time than is normally the case—sometimes well into pre-adulthood. Because they're able to get by on the strength of their personalities and potential, they're rarely asked to perform. But this "free ride" comes at a cost: They're generally forced to carry the burden of their parents' self-aggrandizing expectations—expectations they have little hope of fulfilling. The extra burden causes many of them to avoid the tough but important challenges they need to build real self-esteem. They start to shed whole categories of activities that are competitive or risky—categories such as mathematics, sports, foreign languages and music, where they lack talent or where talent isn't enough, and where they're not guaranteed success. Since they can't build self-esteem through their actions, they are forced to inflate the importance of just *being* special. They adopt a feeling of innate superiority and attribute their failures to a lack of support by parents, mentors and the world at large.

If they're bright (or more importantly, if, because they're articulate, they *seem* bright) their day of reckoning may be postponed. But, sooner or later, their sense of superiority and exemption from the need to achieve collides head on with reality. People of "inferior" talents and beauty begin to surpass them in both accomplishments and happiness. These fair-haired boys and girls start to stagnate. They lose their golden touch.

If they have certain inner resources or a record of having risen to meet some challenges when the day of reckoning comes, or if their grandiosity is deflated gingerly so that they don't feel totally defeated, these once-precocious pre-adults can generally sit down and start to work. Parents, teachers and coaches can play a positive role here by insisting that all young people, regardless of wealth, talent or beauty, perform to objective standards, that they participate in activities that don't come easily to them and that they persevere at tasks that are within their capabilities. These charming youngsters shouldn't be allowed to skip school or to drop difficult subjects without having first given them the old college try. They should be told that it's not important to *be* the best; it's important to *try* your best. Happiness and self-esteem aren't achieved through winning praise; they're achieved through striving to fulfil your potential.

Unfortunately, too many of these former "stars" continue to cop out. They become embittered and envious. Deep down they think of themselves as lazy and inadequate, when they're really only fearful of discovering that they might have limitations. In psychotherapy they wish to be appreciated by their therapists regardless of how they conduct themselves. They resent being told that their problem is a lack of effort and not a deep-seated neurosis inflicted on them by their parents. (Of course, their parents have contributed to their problem by loving them not wisely but too well.)

The truth is that they, like everyone else, must earn their self-esteem. Having ability and dreams is not enough. You have to have accomplishments as well. It's a tough lesson that is learned most easily early in life. Fortunately, it can still be learned even at the threshold to adulthood.

Iris refused to participate in sports. She was a tall, willowy and graceful woman, but too vain to allow herself to participate in anything that might make her look goofy in the eyes of other people. One day, however, one of Iris's friends invited Iris to take a dance class with her, and Iris reluctantly accepted.

At first Iris felt awkward and frightened, but the instructor, perhaps sensing her discomfort, gave her lots of encouragement and praise, and before long she was enjoying the music and keeping up with the other students. She returned to the dance class with her friend several more times and each time felt less and less inhibited. Eventually, she started attending classes regularly on her own and working out on the days in between. Noting her hard work, the instructor gave her lots of extra attention to help her improve. When she performed a movement that seemed to express the music especially well, he'd ask her to demonstrate it. Through his enthusiasm and support, Iris gradually lost her self-consciousness and started to enjoy the pleasure and beauty of dancing.

Later on, Iris also tried cycling, swimming, skating and softball. She never became an outstanding athlete, but she became a lot less vain and a lot more willing to risk appearing silly or inept while learning a new sport. She learned to take chances, to tackle new challenges and to work at improving her skills regardless of her ability. Learning to dance made Iris feel happier and more secure, and it taught her that real self-esteem is something you earn.

PERSEVERANCE

Everybody is told that success is 1 percent inspiration and 99 percent perspiration. We don't believe it, though, because we're only too aware that it's more like 1 percent inspiration, 49 percent perspiration and 50 percent luck. However, since our own effort is the only part of the formula we can actually control, it isn't a bad idea to act *as if* success were 99 percent perspiration.

Some children, like the precocious kids mentioned above, grow up believing that perspiration is only a tiny part of success. They work only at tasks at which they have talent.

Rick was such a person. He had charmed his way through home and school. Because he was a superior athlete, he practised his hockey and baseball, but not his French or math. By the time he came to see me, at twenty-six, he was feeling depressed. He was unable to get his delivery business off the ground. He had already spent about six months doing a business plan and couldn't seem to move forward.

When Rick asked his father to invest in his business, his father refused—claiming that he didn't have the money. Rick felt unsupported and decided that his father's lack of support was the real reason for his paralysis in life.

Rick lacked any experience with having to persevere at a difficult task. He believed that success came, not as the result of effort, but as the result of being motivated, clever or "living right." He believed, in other words, that success came by magic. So he tried a little magic: He began to do Tai Chi regularly, eat macrobiotic food, meditate daily and work out at the gym. But the magic, unfortunately, didn't work. He felt better temporarily, but because he hadn't made any headway with his business, he soon relapsed into depression. The disciplines of exercise, diet and meditation—because they represent tiny triumphs over passivity—can help a little bit, but they can't, by themselves, lead to success. The only route to success is through perseverance at the central task.

Rick hoped that I would agree with him that his father was the main reason for his lack of confidence. He hoped that I would tell him he was neurotic, and that if he submitted to therapy, he could, after many years, eventually be successful. He hoped that he could put off having to actually act until some moment far in the future, when acting would be effortless and painless, and when he'd automatically know what to do and be supremely self-confident.

It was a fond hope, but unfortunately, I had to disappoint him. Instead of "doing therapy," I gave him some advice. I told him that if he persevered with his business, he might succeed despite being neurotic, and that if he succeeded, he'd find that a lot of his paralyzing self-doubt would become irrelevant. I told him that trying to be an entrepreneur—taking a business idea and making it into a reality—was extremely difficult for *anyone* to do. I suggested that a work-day structure—getting up early and putting in a full day, just as if he were working at a job—might help him overcome his temptation to procrastinate. I told him that even if he failed at this project, he would still learn a great deal that would eventually help him to succeed at something else. And I told him to start, not tomorrow, but today.

Rick listened to what I had to say with appropriate scepticism. Nevertheless, he did create a loose structure for himself and begin to plug away at his business day by day. Did he succeed? No. He couldn't get his margins up high enough to make his business profitable. The premise underlying his business turned out not to be sound. Perhaps a more experienced business person would have recognized this before getting started and chosen a different idea. However, Rick had to learn from experience, and the lessons he learned could be learned only in the doing.

Nevertheless, despite having tried and failed, he felt better about himself than he ever had before. More important, he disabused himself of the idea, which had always paralyzed him, that success comes by some kind of magic, rather than by plain old hard work.

Which Achievements Help Us to Feel Adult?

Not all achievements contribute equally to the development of an adult self-image. To be image-building, the achievements have to be age-appropriate and worthy of an adult. They have to foster independence, autonomy and competence and lay the groundwork for the assumption of responsibility for others. The three achievements that contribute most to the development of an adult self-image are: (1) career competence, (2) economic self-sufficiency and (3) living independently.

CAREER COMPETENCE

Achieving competence in a career will eventually make anyone feel adult. Competence at school will not. Although school achievement is certainly worthwhile and builds a feeling of accomplishment that can be carried forward into the work arena, it does not, by itself, make people feel grown up. That's why people who've finished school, but don't yet know what they want to do for a living, feel and often act childish, defensive and inadequate. Even graduate students, who may be in their late twenties by the time they finish their doctoral degrees, typically don't start feeling adult until they've begun working competently in their chosen fields. One reason is obvious: By itself, scholastic achievement doesn't produce economic self-sufficiency.

The developmental benefits of career competence, however, are not reducible to those of economic self-sufficiency. Career competence produces changes in self-image that go beyond those associated with earning a living. Career competence is conducive to the development of an adult self-image, in a way school can't be, because it involves a privileged, adult transaction with the real world: You contribute your work to the world, and the world rewards you for your work. In school, you are waiting to make your contribution. In work, you are making it. In school, you are mostly taking. In work, you are mostly giving.

But it isn't enough to work. Your work has to be competent. Work that's incompetent is generally the result of inability, inexperience or lack of self-respect. Whichever is the cause, incompetence is incompatible with an adult self-image. Work that's competent is the result of ability, experience and a sense of responsibility and pride. As such, it is highly reinforcing of an adult sense of self.

Doing Work You Love (Or at Least Like)

Of course, it's much easier to achieve career competence in something you love (or at least like) than in something you don't. And falling in love with your work is not unlike falling in love with another person—you can feel immediate chemistry for your work or you can learn to love your work gradually. Of the two, immediate chemistry is the more unequivocal, but even love-at-first-sight is not without its complications. You might decide to become a stockbroker, for example, because you liked making money and selling things when you were working at your summer jobs, but discover, after actually being a broker for a year or two, that you find it unfulfilling.

On the other hand, if you choose a sensible career in which you have an aptitude and at least some interest, you might very well learn to love it, but always wonder whether you should have held out for your one true love. Should you follow your heart or your head?

This question isn't easy to answer, of course, because in our careers, as in our relationships, things are rarely that simple. Sooner or later any career, whether it began as instant love or took time to develop, will go through a period of doubt, disenchantment and boredom. We might love our work, but not at every moment. Sometimes we become bored with it and cast longing glances over at the people who seem to be having more fun. However, if our choice of career was at least wise to begin with, we will probably regain our enthusiasm for it or find some new way to make it more fulfilling.

Doug was a star athlete in high school. He played football, baseball and basketball and excelled at all three while maintaining a high academic average. During his senior year, he was scouted by several colleges in each sport; when he graduated, he accepted a full scholarship to play baseball and study business at a first-rate university.

Once he got to college, however, Doug made a stunning discovery: He didn't have the talent to become a professional athlete. He made a credible contribution to the varsity baseball team, but was never a standout, and wasn't drafted by a big-league team after his final season.

Doug didn't despair for long. He used his business training to get a marketing job with a company that made athletic shoes. His work allowed him to combine his love and knowledge of sports with the demands of reality and the necessity of making a living. And because his job gave him a great deal of pleasure and satisfaction, he was able to perform it with enthusiasm and success.

Managing Other People

One aspect of career competence—the opportunity to manage other people—is especially helpful in fostering a feeling of maturity. Being a good manager exercises the capacity of putting aside your own narrow interests in order to foster the aspirations of others. In this respect, managing resembles child-rearing.

Most people don't really get a chance to manage until they're in their early thirties. On the other hand, many people avoid managerial positions because they're afraid of the responsibility. They don't like having to handle the feelings of the people who report to them, and they don't like having to set goals, plot strategy or give the final answers to important questions. They prefer the safety of answering to someone else who will make those decisions for them. Fortunately, in most organizations the positions of leadership are graduated: the level of responsibility and the number of people being supervised increase with each promotion. By the time you become a senior vice-president, you're ready for the responsibility.

Of course, some people aren't interested in managing because they prefer focusing on their primary skills or working on their own. But it's good to keep in mind that learning to become a competent manager is a skill in itself. And that being a competent manager can add diversity and enjoyment to a career that has reached a plateau.

Economic Self-sufficiency

To most of us, the value of achieving economic self-sufficiency seems pretty uncontroversial. But consider how tempting it must be to try to finagle your way out of supporting yourself if you have the chance of letting someone else do it for you. In this regard, having wealthy parents can be a mixed blessing. For many children of the rich, the desire to take their parents' money will come into conflict with the desire to become their own person—to become an adult. Perpetual adolescence is the occupational hazard of the hereditary rich.

Wealthy children who succumb to the disease of living off their parents often compensate for this humiliation by adopting an air of importance or by affecting an insouciant superiority to the grubby business of making money. They get involved in the arts or philanthropy, start biospheres or manage their investments. By looking busy and important, they hope to get credit for career competence without actually having achieved financial independence on their own.

On the other hand, some scions of wealthy families are quite driven to make their own fortunes. They show a strong desire to become independent, perhaps an over-reaction to the temptation to live off the fat of the land. But whatever the motivation, the act of becoming independent increases the likelihood that the wealthy child will eventually feel adult.

If money is a complicated issue for the children of wealthy parents, it isn't so complicated for the rest of us. Not only does money provide us with a degree of material comfort and security and make us independent of other people and the state, but it keeps us from becoming excessively dependent on other potentially more infantilizing forms of reward—such as recognition, acclaim, praise, fame, position and prestige—that often involve pleasing other people, doing their bidding or currying their favour.

Praise and love are the currencies of interpersonal relationships; money is the currency of social recognition. Praise makes you more dependent; money makes you more independent. You know this intuitively. If you give your daughter an allowance for doing the dishes or cutting the grass, for example, she will feel more grown up and independent. But if you pat her on the head and praise her, she will feel like a good little girl who still has to come to you whenever she wants to buy herself a treat. Making your own living frees you from undue allegiance to any other person in particular and from the need to remain subservient and juvenile in general. Money—though not good as an end in itself—is at least a more impersonal and neutral reward than praise.

LIVING INDEPENDENTLY

Although it might seem to North American readers that living independently of your relatives is an obvious prerequisite for feeling adult, it's actually not. Consider some examples of people who might be unable or who don't choose to live independently: There are young couples who are forced to live with their parents or in-laws for a period of time after they first get married so they can save money to get their own place. There are adults who are forced to return home to look after their parents or whose parents have to look after them because of some illness or disability. And some grown children don't leave home, even when they're well into their thirties, because they're not married and see no reason to waste money on having their own place, or because they can't get a job. Is it impossible for any of these people to feel adult?

One way of thinking about this question is to examine the motives of those who don't live independently of their relatives. Let's start with the premise that if their reason for remaining at (or returning to) the parental home is beyond their control—say on account of illness, or housing shortages or high prices—then their living arrangement shouldn't interfere with their feeling adult. Sounds reasonable enough, but there's a hitch: People who don't leave home *always* claim that there are external reasons for doing so. It's very hard to admit to yourself that you're hanging around the nest because you're afraid to test your wings.

In North America, living with your parents—regardless of your reasons or age—signifies pre-adult status. When people who are still living at home at twenty-five tell me their life still hasn't got off the ground, I'd like to be able to tell them they'll be able to feel adult without actually having to move out—but I can't. I'd like to believe (and so would they) that feeling adult is just a matter of attitude and not also of external reality—but it isn't.

Theoretically, if a person *feels* autonomous, then whether or not he's living independently shouldn't matter. But it does matter—*to those who feel it matters.* In other words, if it matters to you that you're still living at home with your parents, then you are precisely the person for whom living at home means not being an adult. If it really doesn't matter to you, then you might be able to feel adult despite living with your parents and having others view you as juvenile. Even then it's a long shot.

Some people try to get around the issue of living with their parents by paying them rent. They believe this arrangement will make them more independent than living rent-free would. Unfortunately, the distinction is trivial, because, unless the person is paying his parents a full rent, he's accepting a subsidy that vitiates his independence. And if he is paying his parents a full rent, then there's no reason for him still to be living with his parents other than the fact that he's having trouble separating from them. Except as an interim arrangement, paying rent to parents gives only the illusion of independence.

OTHER ACHIEVEMENTS

There are other achievements that can contribute to making you feel grown up or that can push you into adulthood if you're wavering on the edge. Depending on your character and your capacity to respond, they may or may not serve as rites of passage into adulthood. Each challenge—whether coping with illness, surviving a loss or resisting aggression—requires courage in the face of danger, loss or suffering.

One reason that these challenging experiences can't be mandatory prerequisites for feeling adult is that not everyone has occasion to confront them. They happen mostly by chance. People rarely go out of their way to look for hardships, so not everyone will get the opportunity to grow by them. Furthermore, in order to really benefit from one of these chance experiences, you have to meet its challenge and transform brute adversity into something personally meaningful. In other words, if the challenge is something you're going to make into a valid achievement, you have to actively engage it and allow it to change you. If you only passively endure the misfortune, no matter how awful, it will remain mere bad luck and have no educational or developmental value whatever.

A second reason that these hardships and trials can't be made requirements for feeling adult is that they don't occur only in the pre-adult period. Yet even when they occur early in childhood, they can still engender strengths that will make the later transition to adulthood that much easier. Triumphing over adversity, facing danger or defending something of value all produce a quiet pride in people, based on moral strength, that makes them feel adult. This quiet pride shouldn't be confused with the reckless bravado of adolescence (though it may start out that way). It is instead the reasoned willingness of an adult to take action because of overwhelming necessity or because it's the right thing to do. It often therefore involves a grownup sense of justice.

There are some challenges that we don't seek but can't avoid. They are hell to endure and rarely have a silver lining. Yet they have to be endured, and in many cases enduring them makes us stronger and more independent.

Coping with a serious illness, injury or handicap, for example, is always terrifying. It forces us to confront our own physical limitations and mortality and in many cases to cope with lengthy and painful treatment. But if we're fortunate enough to survive the bodily damage without too much mental or physical pain and with our spirits intact, we can sometimes appreciate our lives more fully than before, put minor problems into their proper perspective and strengthen our desire to live.

Surviving the loss of a parent, spouse or sibling is very painful too, but it's also very sobering. It brings home the fact that we've moved up a notch—that we're no longer in the on-deck circle, but at bat—and that we have to make the most of every day. It reminds us of the fragility and preciousness of life and of the importance of kindness and love. Surviving the loss of a child, however, offers no such consolation. It is a pure and unmitigated ache that never goes away. In most cases, it offers no lessons and no redemption. Though it can be endured, it can't be overcome.

Overcoming the emotional pain of a collapsed love affair or marriage, however, can be overcome and usually is. It can be overwhelming to have to make a new life, find a new home, meet new people, perhaps even start a new job, but it strengthens our sense of responsibility and reminds us that we can take care of ourselves.

There are other challenges that we seek because we believe they will help us to grow, and some that we know might befall us if we undertake other challenging but risky activities. We might, for example, try to climb Mount McKinley and end up having to fight for our lives because of an unexpected snow storm. We deliberately sought the first challenge but knew we might have to deal with the second as well.

Enduring physical hardship, especially a struggle with the forces of nature—like learning to survive in the bush or coping with prolonged periods of hunger, physical exertion and exhaustion—allows us to test our mettle and prove that we can overcome adversity.

Standing up to a threat or resisting a bully or oppressor is almost always frightening. When it involves protecting those who are too weak to defend themselves, it solidifies our sense of responsibility for others and our self-esteem, and strengthens our sense of moral strength and autonomy. Going to war may be hell—there is little good that can be said for it. But fighting for your country and your ideals is sometimes necessary, and those who go to war are inevitably transformed by it. The soldier goes to war a boy and returns a man. It is rarely the way he would have sought to grow up, but it forces him to do so nonetheless.

Performing an arduous public service is a different kind of challenge. Working for the Peace Corps, the public health service or in the inner city may delay advancement in civilian life, but it exposes us to people and circumstances that are different from those we're familiar with. It certainly fosters self-reliance, responsibility for others and appreciation of our own good fortune, but is also reinforces the connection between people of different backgrounds and the importance of social responsibility.

Giving birth to or adopting a child and raising it differs from the other potential rites of passage because, although it takes courage and strength, it isn't normally considered a hardship or misfortune. It requires tenderness and fortitude more than assertiveness and bravery. Yet, because it requires both selflessness and responsibility, it is undoubtedly one of the most powerful forces for nurturing a sense of maturity. Since this is a responsibility that has often fallen more on women (and even girls) than on men, it may explain why women seem to find it easier than men to feel grown up. It follows that as men begin to take a greater role in childrearing, they too will experience its maturational benefits.

LOVE AND MARRIAGE

Marriage is one life experience that contributes to the feeling of being grown up almost as much as achievement (and failure) does—especially if the marriage is a good one.

In fact, the complete interpersonal progression—from serious relationship, to marriage, to childrearing—is a powerful maturational stream. Each successive step reinforces the one before. Of the three, however, marriage is perhaps the most pivotal.

There are two factors that give marriage its transformative wallop: love and duty.

Love

Keith, an engineer in his late thirties, came to see me because of anxiety caused by his work. He had recently been appointed chief engineer of a large auto parts manufacturer that supplied components to the "Big Three" auto makers. In his new position he was responsible for maintaining the quality and efficiency of the various manufacturing processes that produced these parts and for assuring that everyone below him was doing his or her job properly.

Because he had been promoted from within the ranks, his new power was resented by some of the people who had previously been his equal, and he was having considerable trouble knowing how to deal with them. Keith hoped to win them over by being friendly and modest, and by adopting a management style that was open and collaborative rather than dictatorial and "top-down." His biggest problem, however, was in figuring out how to deal with the plant's general manager, an authoritarian man like his father, whose steely demeanour and sudden outbursts of anger intimidated everyone in the place. The general manager was a very able man, but he came from the old school of management and funnelled all his criticisms through Keith. His tirades were so awful that they made Keith feel like a naughty ten-year-old, sitting in the principal's office waiting to be suspended.

Over the years, Keith had been very devoted to his job. He'd dated many women, but he'd never had any long-term relationships and had never fallen in love. Many of the women he went out with were tempestuous, moody and vain. They appeared to be very sexy, but when they began to make love they were not very sexual. Their feelings tended to run hot and cold, and they were frequently angry or disappointed. For his part, Keith seemed unable to reconcile passion with tenderness. Once he had sex with a woman, he started to find fault with her, and, before long, found an excuse to stop seeing her.

About a year into his treatment, however, Keith met a woman on a business trip and fell in love with her. She wasn't as sexy and vain as the women he was used to, but she was just as attractive and more sexual. She was also much easier to get along with: she wasn't moody or angry, her feelings were dependable and constant, she was straightforward and honest, and she didn't play games. Keith felt more sexually alive with his new girlfriend than he'd ever felt before. And this time, instead of dampening his affection, sex made his feelings stronger. The more time they spent together, the more intimate and comfortable they became. He noticed his girlfriend's shortcomings, of course, but they didn't bother him. They elicited a bittersweet feeling of protectiveness towards her that made him feel even more tender.

And Keith's girlfriend reciprocated his feelings. She loved and accepted him in an entirely new and convincing way that made him feel more poised and mature. For the first time in his life, he felt that he could be himself and that he didn't need to impress or baby his girlfriend.

In the midst of this love affair, Keith began to undergo a subtle change at work. He became more confident in dealing with his subordinates and less intimidated in dealing with the plant manager. Although he was unaware of it, he started to seem more grown up to his co-workers, and they responded by treating him with more co-operation and respect.

Over the next few months, Keith's anxiety level fell to the point where he was finally able to enjoy his new position. And shortly after that, he terminated his therapy and married his new girlfriend.

What does this anecdote tell us about the transformative properties of serious love? It tells us a number of things: It tells us that exuberant sex improves your sense of well-being, and that an improved sense of well-being increases your acceptance of other people. It tells us that giving love to someone you value makes you feel more valued, and that feeling valued allows you to accept responsibility and to make commitments. It tells us that finding a suitable partner (as opposed to an unsuitable one) makes the relationship go more smoothly and allows it to get better and better. It tells us that loving someone who loves you for yourself—for the real you—helps *you* to feel more comfortable with yourself and therefore with other people. And finally, it tells us that when you're poised on the doorstep of adulthood, being loved in this way—with appreciation and understanding—helps you to feel adult.

SELF-LOVE IS NOT ENOUGH

Many people seem to be under the illusion that the truly secure person requires absolutely no affirmation from any other person. They get down on themselves for feeling hurt by someone else's indifference or neglect, or excited by someone else's praise. They may even believe that, if they undergo psychotherapy, they will be able to overcome human nature and be an island sufficient unto themselves.

While it is true that your self-worth can be *too* dependent on the opinion of others, it is not true that it can be totally independent of the opinions of others. We all need external affirmation. During the first part of our lives, this affirmation comes from our parents and other family members; later it comes from teachers, friends, acquaintances, coaches, mentors and peers. We internalize this affirmation in our psyche, which makes it possible for us to maintain a good sense of self even when the external sources of affirmation have temporarily dried up. We are able to carry with us the memory of being loved (by our parents and others) and of being lovable, even when we're alone or among strangers. In other words, the conviction that we're worthy of love doesn't evaporate just because we're away from the people who love us. It's transported in our psyches.

But life can be harsh, and in most cases no one loves us as much as our parents do. So as we stray farther from home, our feeling of being lovable can take quite a beating. That's the reason why being loved by another adult—who really knows us and accepts us—is so affirmative and so important. It reinforces our own beleaguered sense of worthiness.

The love of a spouse isn't the only kind of adult love that's affirming. The writer Philip Roth, in his autobiography *The Facts,* notes that, among other things, it was the acceptance of his friends that allowed him, at age thirty-four, to accept himself and to find his true voice in the novel *Portnoy's Complaint.*

But being loved and accepted by our mate (as Roth also notes) has an even greater impact on our sense of self than being accepted by our friends does. Because our new dependence on affirmation from our mate supersedes our old dependence on affirmation from our parents—a dependency that is often restrictive and conventional, and that may no longer fit us—it helps us to loosen the bonds of our childish view of ourselves and to strengthen the bonds of our adult view of ourselves. Our affectionate tie to our parents (assuming it was there to begin with) and our fondness for our childlike selves are never lost. They merely assume secondary importance. The tie to our mate and our fondness for our adult selves liberate us from a childish dependency on our parents.

Duty

Marriage is a contractual as well as an affectionate relationship. It is contractual not just in the narrow sense of a legal contract (although the legal status of a formal marriage does have psychological significance), but also in the sense that it engenders a sense of duty and commitment.

The wedding ceremony, the exchange of vows, the imprimatur of state and church, the recognition accorded by parents, friends and the community, the joyousness of the occasion, and the rights and privileges accorded it, all serve to reinforce the special importance of marriage. However, it is the understanding between the two partners that is paramount.

Marriage, unlike lesser relationships, requires a degree of duty and selflessness that we associate only with adult status. In marriage, regardless of the vicissitudes of our feelings or fortunes, we are strongly encouraged to make the union greater than the sum of our separate lives. To do this successfully we need more than love, or even self-sacrifice; we need maturity.

You can't make another person become an adult. That's why it's less risky to choose a partner who has *already* made the transition to adulthood or is on the threshold of making it than one who hasn't. If you marry someone who already has the qualities of an adult, then marriage itself will consolidate her feeling of adultness. If you marry someone who does not yet have those adult qualities—even if it's just because she's young—then you're making more of a gamble. Even so, taking the obligations of marriage seriously can help a person to accelerate the process of achieving an adult sense of self.

Marriages between people of very different ages can sometimes be quite fulfilling—but they can also have their problems. In many cases, when a pre-adult hooks up with an adult, the pre-adult is trying to avoid growing up, and the adult is trying to avoid having to deal with someone who's an equal. The pre-adult is looking for a surrogate parent, and the adult is looking for admiration, power or a feeling of youthfulness.

For example, a man who marries a much younger woman (often in a second marriage) may be trying to recapture the lost passion of his youth. A women who marries a much older man may be trying to find a father figure to look after her. This is a highly volatile arrangement, of course, because the young woman will eventually grow up in spite of herself and then want to be treated as an equal.

In the reverse arrangement, where an older woman marries a younger man, many of the same dynamics initially apply: The younger man wants to find someone who will mother him, and the older woman wants to find someone who will fulfil her need to be needed. The difference between the two arrangements lies in their different outcomes; in marriages between older women and younger men, the men sometimes refuse to grow up. They remain great passive-aggressive children forever, relying on their wives for direction and for care.

All marriages are something of a *quid pro quo*—both parties get something from the deal, and both parties give something to it. In marriages where the woman is forced to mother the man, the woman has generally made a bad deal. She may have felt that she had only her caretaking to offer a man, for example, but regardless, by underestimating her true value at the beginning of the relationship, she ends up with someone who has very little to offer her.

ACTING ADULT

The foregoing discussion on the maturational benefits of marriage illustrates another point about the process of becoming a grownup: If you're on the verge of becoming an adult anyway, it is possible to consciously "make yourself" into one by envisioning how an adult ought to behave, by acting like an adult and then by discovering that you've actually become one.

In other words, you can *act* like an adult so diligently—by seriously fulfilling the responsibilities and prerogatives of marriage, for example—that you will end up genuinely *feeling* adult. Of course, you have to be ready to make the transition to adulthood, otherwise you'll end up being a pseudo-adult instead of a real one. This is the unfortunate fate of a few very precocious children, who *act* adult before they're ready to *be* adult, and end up being neither. They may have had to care for a sick or alcoholic mother, for example, and learn to suppress their own childhood feelings and needs. They look like mature adults on the outside but continue to feel like needy children on the inside—a split that can persist throughout their lives.

People can apprentice for the job of grownup, just as they can apprentice for any other job. A lot of learning in every sphere takes place that way. A new medical graduate, for instance, may begin his internship acting *as if* he were a doctor, without really feeling like one, but end his internship feeling like a doctor and really being one. Of course, this can happen only if he has really developed the competence to be a doctor. If he hasn't developed that competence, then just acting like a doctor won't make him feel like one at all. It will make him feel like an impostor instead.

Good Role Models

Apprentices need masters, and pre-adults need mentors. If you want to learn a new skill, it helps to watch a master perform it first. This applies even when the skill you're trying to master is the skill of becoming an adult. The process of becoming an adult is not radically different from the process of becoming a doctor or an electrician. Both sorts of apprenticeship involve the acquisition of skills and attitudes. You have to put considerable time and effort into completing school, gaining occupational competence, becoming self-reliant and assuming responsibility for others. But the final "inhabiting" of the role—the conviction that you really are a doctor, electrician or grownup—takes place, after a period of "playing" the role, when there is a sudden change in self-image.

Some young people become disillusioned if their mentors have any imperfections. They are never satisfied and end up discarding potential role models wholesale. It's worth remembering that no mentor can be a role model for everything. A satisfactory mentor doesn't have to be a role model for all of life, but only for the part of life that you're trying to master. In other words, each mentor has her strengths and weaknesses. You have to choose the behaviours and attitudes that are worth emulating and ignore the behaviours and attitudes that aren't.

The best mentor is someone you respect and who respects you. She has to appreciate what's special about you and want to foster your talent. She has to encourage you when you lose faith in yourself. She should have high standards but should never undermine your faith in your capacity to meet them. And she should be patient with your shortcomings and mistakes.

James Watson, the Nobel prize-winning molecular biologist who, along with Francis Crick, discovered the chemical structure of DNA, had this to say about what it takes to succeed as a scientist:

> You've got to try and be with people who are brighter than yourself... You've got to be prepared sometimes to do some things that people say you're not qualified to do.... Since you know you're going to get into trouble, you ought to have someone to save you after you're in deep shit. So you better always have someone who believes in you.[1]

If you feel inadequate after you spend time with your mentor; if you think *she* thinks you're inadequate; if you get down on yourself and she doesn't buck up your spirits; if you feel you're a low priority to her, that she doesn't like you, or that she's exploiting you solely for her own ends; if her attitude towards you implies that she believes you can *never* be as good as she is—then you need a new mentor. The problem lies not with you, but with her. She may be a great doer, but she's a lousy teacher. If your mentor doesn't convey an interest and belief in you, then you will eventually lose interest and belief in yourself and, ultimately, in your work.

We find occupational mentors at work, of course, but where do we find mentors in the skills of adulthood? Ideally, we'd find them in our own homes—in our own mothers, fathers and older siblings. But not all parents and older siblings are necessarily good role models, and given the conflicted nature of our relationships with them, it isn't always possible to appreciate them even if they are.

Bad Role Models

Most pre-adults do rely on their parents and older siblings as mentors to some degree, but they usually try to find other adults to mentor them as well. Their choices can sometimes be quite idiosyncratic. If they've had a relationship with their parents that left them disillusioned, for example, they may find role models who are more "ideal" than their parents were, but less grounded in reality. There are false messiahs of all kinds who appeal to young people searching for someone to believe in. There are cult leaders and gurus, leaders of radical political cells and just plain drop-outs.

The most dangerous "ideal" mentor, however, is the one who mixes theory with romance—the teacher/lover who seduces his students with simplicity and a kiss. Eroto-philosophical pressure of this kind can take someone who was thoughtful, independent and level-headed and turn him into someone who is simple-minded, platitudinous and boring.

Pre-adults are often very concerned with authenticity. Adult role models who seem inauthentic—who don't exemplify the "correct" ideals or who don't seem "real"—may provoke resistance to the very notion of growing up. Many young people felt this way during the 1960s. They viewed their governments and their college administrations as inauthentic and actively rebelled against the values of the adult world.

Most pre-adults, however, don't have to venture so far from home, or to such exalted heights, to find grownups who are selfish or hypocritical. They may have parents who are remote and hostile, or who demand obedience because they're unable to encourage emulation. They may have teachers who play favourites and are uninterested in their students, or coaches who emphasize winning over good sportsmanship. And they may have religious leaders who preach humility while leading lives of opulence and grandeur, or political leaders who claim to be populists but who really pander to the fears and prejudices of ignorant people.

Whatever its cause, though, disillusionment with role models can produce resistance to entering adulthood, and thus to a lengthening of pre-adulthood. The psychologist Erik H. Erikson labelled this prolonged pre-adult phase a period of "moratorium."

The greatest harm, however, comes from role models who are *mistakenly* believed to be authentic and do not, therefore, produce disillusionment, but who are terribly destructive nonetheless. These are the mentors who are experienced, competent, esteemed and sometimes even famous, but who are ungiving, critical and unsupportive. They are especially harmful because the destructive effect of their lack of affirmation is so insidious. While purporting to give their protégés the best possible training, these selfish or limited mentors are actually giving them a feeling of inadequacy and robbing them of a belief in themselves.

Here's an example of a young person whose belief in herself was nearly destroyed by callous mentors.

Alice was an architect in her early thirties. She was a senior associate with ten years experience in an internationally famous architecture firm. She came to see me because she felt burnt out. She said she wasn't enjoying designing buildings any more and felt "shafted" by her bosses who had kept her out of the limelight. Yet she was afraid to leave her firm because they did more interesting projects than anyone else, were the most prestigious firm in town and paid her reasonably well. Most important, she *felt* that she wasn't a very talented designer on her own and would lose whatever credibility she had in the profession if she were to leave this prestigious firm at which she still unhappily toiled.

One day, on a visit home, Alice mentioned to her mother that she was thinking of buying a piece of property on a lake. She planned to build a house that would show-case her ability and that she could then sell at a profit.

"You don't have enough money for that!" her mother blurted out before Alice had even finished. "What if you can't sell it? You'll lose everything you have!"

When Alice told me about this interchange, she said, "I don't know what to do. I can just afford to do it, but what if my mother is right? I could blow everything—my savings and my reputation. Maybe I don't have the talent to do anything worthwhile anyhow."

Alice was depressed. Her idea for the house had seemed promising, and deep down inside she believed she could pull it off. And yet she admitted that she had approached telling her mother about her plans with consid-erable trepidation. She knew what her mother's response was likely to be and was half hoping that it would discour-age her—as indeed it did—so that she could give up before having to take any risks.

"Isn't this the same sort of interaction you have with your bosses?" I asked her.

She admitted that it was. Throughout her career at the architecture firm, her bosses had been hot and cold in their enthusiasm for her work (despite giving her a whole lot of it to do). They would rave about something trivial, while expressing reservations about something important, or praise someone who had only helped her, while criticizing her. Sometimes, after she'd been ignored or damned with faint praise, Alice would find out that her bosses had pre-sented her ideas to the clients as if they were their own.

Over the years, Alice had gradually begun to lose a sense of the value of her own work, any pleasure in doing it and any faith in her own gut feelings about how to solve design problems. This lack of support and encouragement had gradually eroded her enjoyment of architecture, to the point that she now felt burnt out and unable to make a move.

But she now also understood that her faith in herself had begun to be damaged by her parents while she was still a child. When she was growing up, her mother constantly second-guessed her, as she'd done when Alice told her about the proposal to build a house. Like many children, Alice got used to checking with "adults" before making any kind of move, and she learned to suppress her own gut feelings. Because her decisions didn't come from her own intuition, Alice had more regret when things didn't work out and less satisfaction when they *did*.

Contrary to what you might expect, it's actually easier to accept a bad outcome when you've made a decision based on your own judgment than when you've relied on the judgment of others. You may be able to shift some of the blame this way, but when compared to the damage it does to your own sense of adultness, this little cop-out is a faint consolation.

In fact, sometimes that's precisely the motive people have for following bad advice—they want an excuse to be angry at the person who gave them that advice. The strategy is as follows: You take bad advice from someone, usually a parent, even though you know it's bad advice. Then, when the outcome turns out to be bad, you punish the advice-giver with your conspicuous misery.

This was the strategy that Alice unconsciously employed when she sought her mother's advice about building the house. She wanted to punish her mother by having a miserable life based on her mother's negative advice.

Alice soon recognized that by choosing mentors who were as undermining to her professional development as her mother was to her social development, she was repeating at work the same masochistic relationship that she'd had at home. Her firm did offer her certainty and cachet, but unfortunately, these modest benefits had to be purchased at the expense of her own autonomy and self-esteem.

Having understood all this, Alice *did* go ahead and build her lakeside home. But she didn't sell it. She moved into it with the contractor whom she'd hired to build it. They married soon after the completion of the house and formed their own partnership to design and build homes.

CHAPTER EIGHT

BECOMING ADULT IN HEART AND MIND

> To be a man is to feel that one's own stone con-
> tributes to building the edifice of the world.
> *Antoine de Saint Exupéry*

How do the experiences of childhood and pre-adulthood—the achievements, ideas, challenges, relationships and losses that we have before we're thirty or forty—prepare us to become adult? What lessons do they teach us that prepare us to function in an adult fashion and that make us feel adult?

The experiences of childhood and especially of pre-adulthood teach us three key lessons:

The first lesson is that we are not the centre of the universe. This lesson is a blow to our narcissism, and we never quite learn it fully, but to the extent that we do, it equips us to deal with frustration and helps us to avoid bitterness and despair. It teaches us that other people have needs, that we have to share love and the other good things of life, that love and the other good things of life don't always come unconditionally but have to be earned, that life isn't always fair and we don't always get what we want, and that giving is often as gratifying as getting. It provides us with a moral compass and with respect for the feelings of other people. Discovering that we're not the centre of the universe is a lesson that begins in infancy and continues throughout our lives, but it is a lesson that is learned almost entirely in the classroom of love. And the better we learn this lesson, the greater our capacity for love will be.

The second lesson is that we are equal to our parents and, therefore, by extension, to all other adults. This lesson is a blow to our sense of security and our desire for authority, but it frees us to pursue our own aims and desires, convinces us that we can look after ourselves and imbues us with a sense of our own authority and power. It gives us the confidence, backbone and sense of self-worth that we need to function comfortably in the world, and it reassures us that we can survive without our parents. It is a lesson that we learn primarily in the context of the parent-child relationship but that we can apply well beyond the domestic arena in the world at large. The better we learn this lesson, the stronger and more fulfilled we'll be.

The third lesson is that we are part of civilization. This lesson is a blow to our sense of uniqueness, but it helps to embed us in the flow of history and in the world as a whole. It teaches us that, although we may be able to become independent of our parents, we can never become independent of civilization. It reminds us that we are part of something larger than ourselves, makes us into social beings and empowers us to assume our social rights and responsibilities. It is a lesson that we learn at home, in school, in religious institutions, in politics and in the world at large. And once we've learned it—once we've become civilized—we are truly adult.

LEARNING THAT WE ARE NOT THE CENTRE OF THE UNIVERSE

Almost everything we know about love we know from painful experience. The first time we feel love is when we're being nurtured by our mothers or primary caretakers. But the first time we learn about love is when we want nurturing and are unable to get it. And the first time we really understand love is when we discover that it's a two-way street—that having love doesn't depend just on what we want and need, but on what the other person wants and needs as well.

If we're fortunate, we learn this lesson slowly and by

degrees in the context of a loving and generous family. If we're unfortunate, we learn this lesson prematurely and traumatically in the context of a destructive and unstable family. If we don't learn this lesson at all—if we have too much love or too little and leave childhood still believing that love is entirely within or entirely outside our control—then every other thing we try to accomplish, from school to work to sports to friendship, will be subordinated to the goal of trying to win the admiration and the love we crave.

We learn, for example, that sharing, consideration, kindness, gentleness, patience and co-operation will generally gain our parents' approval, but that greed, selfishness, impatience, violence and rebelliousness generally won't. We learn that our parents consider some behaviours to be good and others to be bad, and that they'll reward us for the good and punish us for the bad.

But the big breakthrough comes when we discover that we can't have our mothers or fathers all to ourselves, and that, when it comes to getting their love, we're not always at the front of the line. This is the first time in our lives that we discover we're not the centre of the universe, and it's the first time the sweetness of love is tainted by the bitterness of rivalry, jealousy and hate. From the moment we realize we have to share our mother with our father, our father with our mother, and our parents with our siblings, all passionate relationships become triangular, and all deep feelings of love become mixed with some modicum of jealousy and fear.

What is it that we fear? We fear that if we behave badly we'll lose our parents' approval, and we fear that if we encroach on their romantic relationship we'll be badly—even physically—punished by the parent whom we perceive to be our rival. It isn't necessary for this parent to actually *be* jealous of us in order to appear threatening, it's only necessary for us to be jealous of her and to assume that she feels the same. Nevertheless, whether real or imagined, it is the desire for approval and the threat of a jealous parent that compels us to develop a conscience.

Conscience

In order to make peace with our rival parent—to reduce the likelihood that he will want to punish us—we try to identify with his rules and values by creating a proxy for him in our psyches. This new mental structure—the superego—speaks to us with the parent's voice and authority and guides and punishes us as he once did. After we've acquired a superego, we no longer fear the disapproval of our parents only; we fear the disapproval of our superegos too. We don't need our parents to tell us not to hit our sister or brother; our superego will tell us for them—and make us feel guilty if we disobey. We'll feel guilty, in fact, even if we only *think* about hitting someone. Because, although we may be able to conceal our thoughts and actions from our parents, we can never conceal them from our superegos. Once we have a superego, we have the beginnings of conscience and of moral autonomy.

During childhood, our superego is harsher than it will be later on. In the beginning, it is composed mainly of rather frightening memories of our parents with our own anger projected onto them, and of their disapproval of us when we break their rules or fail to live up to their expectations. But during pre-adulthood, as we get stronger, braver and wiser and, therefore, less jealous and resentful, our superego starts to moderate. It begins to include memories of interactions with our parents and other authorities that are less frightening and less invested with our own hostility. By the time we're ready to make the transition to adulthood, our superego has not only become more moderate, but has expanded to include both other authorities besides our parents and the abstract principles of moral conduct, including the rule of law.

Love

The love-hate relationship that we have with each of our parents is, of course, the basis of the Oedipus complex. And it is the initial resolution of the Oedipus complex at the age of five that teaches us that we can't have romantic feelings towards our parents (this is the origin of the incest taboo), that we have to share good things (like our parents' attention) and sometimes even give those good things up, that we have to respect parental authority, that we have to consider the rights and privileges of other people, and that we have to follow social rules or risk punishment.

The initial resolution of the Oedipus complex changes our relationship with our parents. We renounce our passionate feelings towards them and begin to develop a romantic interest in people outside the family. It's after the age of four or five, and especially after puberty, that we start to have crushes on teachers, rock stars, athletes, actors and other children. As a result of our Oedipal guilt and fear, we suppress our competitive feelings towards the parent whom we perceived to be our rival (the parent of the same sex), and we begin to identify with and model ourselves after him or her instead.

What happens if we don't successfully resolve our initial Oedipus complex? What happens if, as in the case described below, our rival parent is eliminated from the equation by death or divorce, or our parents show us that they love us far more than they love each other?

Astrid was a bright and attractive twenty-one-year-old college student. Her father was a successful surgeon who valued academic achievement above everything else, and her mother was a teacher who, after Astrid was born, stayed home to be a full-time homemaker. They had married when they were both very young, started fighting almost immediately and finally separated when Astrid was twelve.

Astrid had always been the apple of her father's eye. He was especially fond of her precocious charm, quick intelligence and excellent performance at school. He lavished on her the affection that he couldn't lavish on his wife, and when he and his wife separated, Astrid and her brother went to live with him.

Astrid's father began dating fairly soon after the separation but didn't remarry until Astrid was seventeen. During the time they'd been on their own, Astrid and her father had developed a very special relationship. So when her father remarried, she became intensely jealous of his new wife and competed with her for his attention. When her father and stepmother had a baby boy, she felt even more jealous, but she took consolation from the fact that at least the baby wasn't a cute little girl who might steal her father's affection.

At nineteen, Astrid went away to university and made the Dean's List every year. But Astrid had a problem: She seemed to be attracted only to men who were married or already had girlfriends. When unattached men called her for a date, she brushed them off, claiming they weren't very interesting or mature. But the relationships with attached men never lasted for more than a few dates either, because, in Astrid's opinion, none of these men measured up to her father anyway. When she came home for summer vacations, she immediately fell back into the role of surrogate wife. She rose early in the morning to make breakfast for her father, ran errands for him and met him at the door when he came home from work at night.

Astrid didn't understand why she had a problem with men. But one day, while she and her mother were out shopping, her mother expressed concern about what she viewed as Astrid's unhealthy attachment to her father, pointing out that this seemed to her to be the likely root of Astrid's difficulty in forming relationships with unattached men. She encouraged Astrid to get into psychotherapy and invited her to move in with her until she was able to afford her own apartment.

After a period of time in psychotherapy, Astrid accepted the legitimacy of her stepmother's role in her father's life, she got closer to her mother, and she eventually fell in love with a suitable, unattached man.

REJECTION

The next big blow to our romantic narcissism comes when we're rejected by our first real love. This is one of the most painful experiences of pre-adulthood, and it always makes us question our attractiveness, sexual adequacy, social value and sometimes even our intelligence and character. Most people take at least a year to recover from this rejection, and depending on their own resources, their degree of isolation and support, their maturity and their past experiences, they may be more or less vulnerable to rejection and wary of relationships for many years afterwards.

The trick is to recover from this first rejection with a

renewed sense of self-worth, with optimism and courage, and without a feeling of bitterness or paranoia. This requires a solid base of self-esteem established in childhood and adolescence, and it requires some positive friendships and dating experiences in pre-adulthood. Those who fail to learn the lessons of the Oedipus complex during childhood, or who feel rejected by their parents in favour of a sibling and can't get over it, may be unable to regain their equilibrium after their first painful rejection and may end up repeating similar experiences of rejection over and over again throughout their lives.

Bernie was a mechanical engineer who had been prescribed a variety of different antidepressant medications by the time he came to see me at the age of thirty-two. He was indisputably depressed, but none of the medications had worked because his depression stemmed from a sense of inadequacy and alienation, not from a disordered neurochemistry.

Bernie was the eldest of four children. His father was a chiropractor and his mother was a homemaker who wanted her children to be "real" professionals like *her* father, a prominent orthopedic surgeon, not "fake" professionals like her husband. Unfortunately, Bernie was not the academic star of the family. That honour went to the next sibling in line, his sister Gabriella, who, although eighteen months younger than Bernie, quickly took his place as the standard-bearer for the family's dreams of professional prestige.

Bernie languished in Gabriella's shadow and grew progressively more bitter, sullen and resentful. While she garnered a scholarship to an Ivy League college, he "only" gained admittance to the local university. While she attended a famous medical school and eventually joined its faculty, he "only" completed an undergraduate degree in engineering and got a job at a tiny consulting firm. Of course, by all objective evidence, Bernie was anything but a failure. But in his own mind, his place in the family pantheon had been usurped by Gabriella, and he was a disappointment to his ambitious and overbearing mother.

The situation was exacerbated when his girlfriend of two years broke up with him while he was out of town consulting on the construction of a stadium. Although she refused to specify the reason for her decision to end the relationship, beyond saying that she felt abandoned by him, Bernie suspected she had met someone else while he was away (a suspicion that was subsequently confirmed), and he was understandably hurt, angered and depressed by her cold treatment of him.

Unfortunately, his anger and depression never went away, and he began to see rejection in every relationship he had. He felt slighted by his management at work and thought constantly about quitting. He futilely pursued women who had no understanding or appreciation of him—hoping consciously to win their approval, but trying unconsciously to demonstrate their perfidy. And he expressed open hostility towards his mother for her disapproval and overbearingness, and towards his father for permitting her to manifest those traits.

Bernie tested nearly all the people of importance in his life to see if they approved of him. If they occasionally wavered in their hosannas—as they inevitably did—he took the opportunity to sulk ostentatiously in front of them and to feel vindicated in his mistrust. It became a self-fulfilling prophecy: He expected to be undervalued and rejected, and by virtue of his sensitivity and sulking, he was. This was why he felt depressed.

Luckily, Bernie had a lot going for him. He was insightful and motivated to make his life better. Once he understood that his bitterness was the cause, as well as the consequence, of his being rejected, and once he understood that the reason for his vulnerability was his jealousy of his sister, he was able to treat his feelings of depression himself and to regain his sense of confidence, optimism and self-worth. He interrupted the vicious cycle of rejection and paranoia he'd been re-enacting since childhood, and he started to enjoy his relationships and to feel more stable and mature.

People who fail to learn the lesson that they are not the centre of the universe often end up seeing the world as a cold and frustrating place. They spend their lives either trying to gain approval or trying to demonstrate that the opinion of others is of little importance. They are narcissistic and incapable of loving other people, but easily deflated and hungry for love themselves. Because life is continually disappointing them, they can never abandon their quest for ultimate happiness and perfect love. And because they can't accept reality, they can never be happy for very long or feel confident of their value or maturity.

People who succeed in learning this lesson, however, are able to find, to feel and to sustain real love, and they're able to achieve real happiness. They're able to cope with life's inevitable disappointments and rejections without becoming bitter or cynical, and they're able to develop a sturdy sense of self-esteem and a valid sense of being adult.

LEARNING THAT WE ARE EQUAL TO OUR PARENTS

Despite the fact that we all want to be treated as equals by our parents, we find the idea profoundly threatening. We're afraid to give up the security and protection of being able to look up to them, and we're afraid to run the risk of provoking them by challenging their authority and their superior position. But before we can feel equal to other people and therefore be adult, we first have to overcome these fears and begin to feel equal to our parents.

In order to overcome the fear of losing our parents' protection and support, we have to acquire enough independence and self-reliance that we can survive without them. And in order to overcome the fear of their authority and power, we have to acquire enough authority and power of our own that we can stop feeling intimidated by them. The rate at which these two developmental milestones are achieved depends to some extent on the type of parents we have. If our parents are fun to be with, open-minded, non-authoritarian, non-judgmental, generous and easy-going, then it will be easier to overcome our fear of their authority and power, but not as easy to overcome our dependence. If they are strict, rigid, intimidating, authoritarian, punitive, dogmatic and stingy, then it will be easier to overcome our dependence on them, but not as easy to overcome our fear.

Achieving equality with our parents doesn't mean that we can start treating them cavalierly and disrespectfully; equality means that we can start treating *ourselves* seriously and respectfully. Nor does it mean that we should treat our parents just like everybody else—we should continue to treat them specially, with love and honour. What it means is that we should stop expecting them to meet our childish needs and that we should start trying to meet their reasonable and appropriate adult needs, as we would for anybody else we love.

Independence

We need to be able to maintain bonds of support, loyalty, respect, duty and love with our parents, but not at the expense of our own autonomy. In this respect, wonderful parents can sometimes be a mixed blessing. Just by virtue of their generosity and the pleasure we get from their company, they make it harder for us to break away and to become independent.

> Bradley lived at home with his doting mother and father until he moved in with his girlfriend, Lydia, during his last year of law school. He was unable to make up his mind about marrying Lydia because he was still very much attached to his parents, and because she was less proper and dignified than his mother, whom he adored.
>
> Nevertheless, before they'd been living together for more than a month, Bradley began treating Lydia as if she were his mother anyway. Despite the fact that she had a demanding job too, he let her cook all the meals, do the cleanup and laundry, plan their social engagements and vacations, buy gifts for his parents on their birthdays and anniversary, manage the household finances, deal with the apartment superintendent and hire all the repair people. He devoted his time to reading his law books, watching television, visiting his parents and complaining about Lydia's relatives. At first Lydia wondered whether Bradley would

ever get around to proposing to her. But after many months
of worrying about whether she measured up to his mother,
Lydia began to wonder whether Bradley measured up to
her.

Fate intervened, however, when Bradley was hired by
an out-of-town law firm, and they moved farther away
from his parents. The geographic separation helped him to
feel more independent of his mother and more appreciative
of Lydia. It also motivated him to start pulling his weight
around the house and to become more self-reliant. These
changes reassured Lydia that Bradley was someone she
could spend her life with. So when he finally proposed, she
was happy to accept.

Here are some of the techniques that pre-adults use to put psychic distance between themselves and their parents in order to
be able to survive on their own whether or not their parents are
still around to help them.

GEOGRAPHIC SEPARATION

Though it's not strictly necessary or always effective, as Bradley
and Lydia discovered, geographic separation is a valid method
for achieving independence. In order to separate from his parents, the pre-adult child moves out of their house, into a different neighbourhood, out of town, across the country or even to
the other side of the planet. In his new home he's free to develop
his own personality and relationships. The process may begin
when he goes away to college, but it doesn't get going in earnest
until he no longer returns home to live during the summers.

In geographic separation, loneliness is the scalpel that severs
the umbilical cord. It is a sharp and brutal instrument, but it
usually works. The danger, though, is that the pre-adult child
will feel so lonely and adrift that he will become depressed or
form attachments to destructive people. He will be unable to
make any further steps towards autonomy and fulfilment until
the loneliness problem has been solved.

There are two things the pre-adult has to do in order to solve
the loneliness problem, and both are required before he can feel
loved and appreciated in his new home. The first is to become

self-reliant and able to enjoy his own company. And the second is to establish good, sustaining friendships and supportive relationships with parental surrogates—mentors and bosses—who can help him heal the wound of separation.

ADOPTING A DIFFERENT PHILOSOPHY OR DIFFERENT VALUES

Like geographic separation, adopting different values or a different philosophy, religion or life-style is a tried and true tactic for establishing independence. In many cases, this tactic amounts to nothing more than rebellion. But when it's not prompted primarily by hostility, adopting a different point of view can be a sincere attempt by the pre-adult to find a world view that fits better with her outlook and personality than the one taught to her by her parents.

> Phyllis, for example, was raised in a non-religious home. But when she moved to a new city after college, she decided to join a church. She felt the need for more order and tradition in her life, and she wanted to establish a sense of belonging to her new community. Her parents, though surprised by her decision, were respectful of it, and their relationship with her moved onto a more adult footing.

> When Randy graduated from law school, his family expected him to go to a corporate law firm or to work in a financial institution as his father had done. Instead, he went to work for an international human rights agency as its executive director. By choosing a different career path than the one laid out for him by his family, Randy not only managed to separate from his family, but to fulfil his own ideals as well.

HOSTILITY

Hostility is the universal bond-breaker. It is a component of nearly every pre-adult's strategy for separating from his parents (and, not infrequently, of his parents' strategy for separating from him). And although this hostility doesn't always start out as a treatment for separation anxiety—it might start out, for example, as rivalry or frustration—it is, nevertheless, quickly put in the service of the need to separate.

Although hostility is often conscripted in the battle against separation anxiety, the person utilizing it for this special purpose is rarely conscious of doing so. He believes that his hostility is justified. The only clue he may get of his true motivation is the fact that his anger is out of proportion to the event that triggered it, or that it surfaced only when he was about to separate. He may blow up at his parents before boarding a plane, for example, just because they asked him to call them when he arrives home. The conflict that results from this trivial incident relieves both parties of their sadness about separating and replaces it with a feeling of anger. Rather than feeling the pain of being apart, they can feel the pain of being unfairly treated, which allows them to feel that the relationship is not only ongoing, but hot. They may even use the conflict to convince themselves that they're relieved to be apart—the exact opposite of the way they really feel, of course, but a relief to their sadness nonetheless.

One day in early September, Sally was preparing to go to France for her junior year of college, when her mother came into her room to give her a hand with the packing. Her mother began refolding some shirts that Sally had already put into her suitcase. Within minutes they were shouting at each other. Sally accused her mother of meddling, and in return her mother accused her of being sloppy.

"Your clothes will be all wrinkled when you get there," her mother told her. "How are you going to be able to look after *yourself*, if this is how you look after your things?"

A fight ensued, and within minutes they were both in tears.

"I can't wait to get out of this house!" Sally shouted.

"I can't wait either!" her mother answered back as she stomped out of Sally's room.

At supper that evening Sally was subdued. But when her mother came around the table and gave her a kiss, Sally burst into tears. "I'm really going to miss you," she said.

"I know, sweetheart," her mother replied. "I'm going to miss you too."

Sally and her mother tried to use hostility to make the pain of separation easier. Fortunately, they were able to get beyond the hostility to the love before they parted. In many cases, however, the hostility persists until after the separation. And in a few cases, it never goes away.

There are psychotherapies that make antipathy towards parents their goal. The problem with this approach is that hostility is only a way station en route to true autonomy. To be truly autonomous, you need to be able to resolve your hostility towards your parents or, at least, to put it behind you. It's hard to feel like a grownup until you've achieved psychological equality with your parents, and it's hard to achieve psychological equality with your parents until you've healed old wounds and let go of old grievances.

You can't feel both aggrieved and equal to the object of your grievance at the same time. Harbouring grievances keeps you in a subordinate position. Many young people, in fact, hold onto their grudges towards their parents *in order* to stay attached to them. They maintain a bond of antagonism, which both conceals and gratifies their dependence, and at the same time allows the dependence to continue.

There are situations, of course, in which hostility *is* appropriate—in which parents or other mentors have truly earned it. Here's a case that illustrates how hostility was used to break the grip of a therapist's smothering "concern." It also shows the disdain we sometimes feel for adults who don't act grown up.

Celine was a forty-one-year-old religious woman who consulted a counsellor at her church to deal with feelings of sadness and loneliness. The counsellor's therapeutic framework involved discovering and healing the client's "inner child." She had gone through a similar therapeutic regimen herself in trying to recover from certain of her own problems—problems that, in Celine's view, left the counsellor still quite vulnerable.

After a number of months of working together, her counsellor encouraged Celine to attend a workshop on the "inner child." When Celine arrived at the workshop, she was dismayed to see that the participants—all adults—had brought little Teddy bears or dolls with them to the group sessions.

Afterwards, Celine told her counsellor how outraged she'd felt that this sort of regressive behaviour had been encouraged at the workshop. "I don't need to behave like a child," she said. "I am aware of the child in me, but I am an adult now and I want to be an adult!"

As she expressed her anger, Celine noticed that her counsellor was becoming defensive. A wounded look spread across the counsellor's face, and she struck Celine as being intensely vulnerable, even pathetic. Normally, Celine would have backed off in a situation such as this and spared the counsellor any further humiliation. But this time, she didn't feel like pulling her punches. She plunged ahead with her criticism of the counsellor's "inner child" ideology even though she could see it was causing the counsellor great pain. In fact, as Celine later realized, she went ahead with her criticism because it caused the counsellor great pain.

More from insecurity than from wisdom, her counsellor made this reply: "That's how I do therapy. If you can't accept it, maybe we can't work together."

Immediately after her session, Celine decided to end her therapy. She realized that her counsellor's fragility had evoked a feeling of revulsion in her. She realized that she had even wanted to hurt her counsellor by insulting her therapeutic approach. The cruelty of this impulse made Celine feel sadistic and guilty.

Much later, Celine had a further insight about her precipitous termination: She realized that, because her counselor's ultimatum had stirred up ancient fears of abandonment, she had retaliated by quitting therapy pre-emptively.

The point of this discussion is not to consider the merits of

Celine's counselling, which in fact seemed to be helpful to her in many ways. The point to take note of is Celine's reaction to being threatened with separation, at being infantilized and at being confronted by her counsellor's vulnerability. Her reaction to all three of these stresses was to lash out at the counsellor. Her cruelty towards her counsellor made her feel stronger, more independent and better able to withstand the pain of threatened loss and disillusionment.

Celine felt profoundly cheated by her counsellor and ashamed of her. Her counsellor seemed to be trashing something of great value—the dignity and honour of adulthood. Celine's disillusionment wasn't the ordinary disillusionment that comes when you begin to notice your parents' shortcomings or actual failings—that kind of disillusionment is a healthy part of coming to grips with reality and of becoming your own person. Celine's disillusionment was the *extraordinary* disillusionment that is triggered when you're witness to the wilful abdication of maturity by someone from whom you have the right to expect better.

Extraordinary disillusionment does not result from having to witness another person's ordinary fear and vulnerability. Extraordinary disillusionment results from having to witness self-indulgent, contrived or manipulative—in short, phony—displays of emotion that are inappropriate or histrionic. The expression of genuine and profound feelings—feelings which are appropriate to the circumstances that have aroused them—rarely trigger disgust or disillusionment. They usually elicit sympathy and admiration.

The ability to make these distinctions accurately marks the beginning of a sense of justice. If we see people crying in court because their parents have recently been murdered, for example, we're inclined to feel sympathetic and respectful towards them. But if we see people crying in court because they've recently murdered their parents, we're inclined to feel a little sceptical.

It may not always be fair, but we tend to be sympathetic to those who bear their suffering with dignity and stoicism, and unsympathetic to those who bear their discomfort with ostentation and self-pity.

Necessary and Unnecessary Cruelty

Celine felt that she was being cruel to her pastoral counsellor by chastising her when she was so obviously wounded and by quitting therapy without giving her sufficient notice. Though minor and specific, Celine's cruelty does illustrate the structure of cruelty in general. There were two components to her cruelty: one necessary, the other unnecessary.

The necessary component of Celine's cruelty was the adaptive cruelty that she used to break free of her counsellor's benign oppression. Her counsellor's insistence on the dominance of her "inner child" offended Celine. She felt that it devalued and impeded her adult sense of self.

She later told me: "I believe that we're adults and that we must deal with things as adults. We can go back and look at our childhood, but we must do that as adults, not as children."

If she had succumbed to her counsellor's insistence that she exhibit her "inner child," Celine would have had to deny her own true (and hard-won) feelings of being strong and adult. She would have been forced to go along with a lie—the lie that she was helpless and weak. Yet this lie and the offer of support and warmth that lay behind it were very seductive to Celine. She had received very little love from her own mother during childhood, and any show of maternal attention could easily tempt her. Still, Celine was not prepared to sell her adult sense of self for a little love, and she knew that the temptation to return to a childlike self-image had to be strongly resisted. Cruelty was the only way she could see to break free of her counsellor's well-meaning but oppressive solicitousness.

The unnecessary and more mysterious component of Celine's cruelty was the little gratuitous dollop of venom that she added to the insults of her counsellor's therapeutic technique. It was this unnecessary cruelty that produced the wounded look on the counsellor's face and gave Celine the tiny drop of guilty pleasure that contributed to her decision to flee therapy. This little extra measure of cruelty was not required to free Celine from the sticky syrup of her counsellor's simplistic concern. It was gratuitous cruelty done for the pure, evil pleasure of it.

The person who uses necessary cruelty *needs* to use it to assert her independence and maintain her sense of self. It is a form of self-defence that we learn to use in childhood to protect ourselves against the threat of an infantilizing and smothering love. Because we know that this cruelty, though necessary, will cause pain to someone we care for, we use it reluctantly, with empathy and regret, and mainly as a last resort. We might decide not to return home for Christmas one year or to call home less frequently. We know that our parents will be hurt by these decisions, but we hope that they'll weaken the grip of the ties that bind us.

The person who uses unnecessary cruelty doesn't need to use it; she *wants* to use it. It gives her sadistic pleasure and stimulates her lust for blood. It evokes her pity too, just as necessary cruelty does, but with the opposite effect on her behaviour. Instead of lessening her cruelty, it actually increases it. Sadism, in these cases, seems almost to be an antidote to an intolerable pity, though it may merely be the gateway to an unquenchable lust. This is the form of cruelty that arises unalloyed from humankind's aggressive nature and is stoked by pity, not softened by it. Unnecessary cruelty prompts us to get angry at our elderly parents for being feeble. It may help to weaken the grip of our pity for them, but it's gratuitous and inappropriate and can lead to further acts of hostility.

Necessary cruelty can be used in the service of independence and growth, but as with Celine, it can also open the doorway to unnecessary cruelty. Unnecessary cruelty can be used for one thing and one thing only—the gratification of sadistic impulses.

A NEW CENTRE OF GRAVITY OUTSIDE THE FAMILY

The formation of a loving relationship outside the family helps the pre-adult to pull out of the old orbit around his parents and into a new orbit centred on his partner. The new attachment gives his emotional life a new centre of gravity and weakens his attachment to his parents. As the tug of the original parent-child bond weakens, it can be replaced by a new, more mature, parent-child bond, which takes into account the pre-adult's other attachments and his imminent adult status.

This is a tricky business. If the young person is not ready for a mature relationship, if he hasn't achieved some degree of autonomy already, then there is the danger that his new relationships outside the family will end up being carbon copies of the old ones inside it. If the groundwork has been adequately laid, however, then the new relationships will give added impetus to the process of achieving independence.

The classic case of this is when two young lovers move in together—sometimes without their parents' approval—and begin to establish their own household. If they're reasonably mature, this cohabitation will help them to become more independent of their parents. But if they're not mature, it will only help them to become dependent on each other.

THE PARENTS SHOULD RECIPROCATE

Here's a familiar refrain: "Every time I go home to visit my parents, we end up falling into the same old pattern. I feel like a kid, I act like a kid, and my parents start treating me like a kid." Is there anyone who hasn't heard it? For that matter, is there anyone who hasn't *lived* it?

Typically, people blame their parents for the deterioration in behaviour that takes place when they go home. And it's true that the parental home is a very regressive setting, filled with years of associations that are hard to break. We go home, unconsciously, to get our dependent needs met, yet when they actually do get met, we feel consciously surprised and dismayed. Since *consciously* we were hoping to impress our parents with how grown up we've become, we naturally get petulant when they respond to our *unconscious* needs instead and treat us as though we were still children.

When college students return home for Christmas during their first year away, for example, they want to feel very grown up and proud of their new knowledge and independence. They may conduct themselves with an unaccustomed dignity and composure on the outside, but chances are that on the inside they're feeling homesick and a little lost. They may protest when their mother does their laundry for them or asks them if they're taking their vitamins, but they probably feel wonderfully reassured by these touches as well.

Of course, our parents retain their old patterns and concerns too. They need time to change. But they also need to be given the *opportunity* to change. If we act childishly, they will feel the need to help us grow up. If we are antagonistic, they will feel rejected and may retaliate in kind. However, if they perceive us trying to behave in a truly adult fashion, then they may be able to "grant" us greater autonomy, replacing the old downward spiral with a new upward one.

If we're fortunate, the parent-child relationship can by a series of incremental gains eventually become one that is based on mutual respect and reciprocity. Then the adult child and her parents can all have their dependent needs met, without threatening anyone's autonomy.

Unfortunately, family concord isn't always easy to achieve. It takes only *one* side of the relationship to wreak havoc with the whole thing. And since each party in the parent-child relationship knows the Achilles heel of the other, havoc is easy to wreak.

As in all relationships, the limiting factor to its success is the emotional health and maturity of each of the participants. Some family and marital therapists believe that the blame for troubled relationships should be doled out equally, but clearly this doesn't always make sense. There *can* be rotten apples in a family or marriage who stir things up. And while it is probable that all parties will sooner or later be drawn into the fray, attributing responsibility to everyone equally is just sloppy thinking. Not only is it inaccurate, it is also unjust. It would be the equivalent of blaming a bully and his victim equally for a schoolyard fight. It's true that it takes two to tango, but it's not true that it takes two to tangle.

Insular Families

One type of family that can't reciprocate its children's efforts to become autonomous is the insular family. This is a family in which the parents (generally one more than the other) have a bitter, mistrustful, critical, antagonistic and competitive view of the outside world and instil this view in their children.

Parents who establish an insular family usually come from insular families themselves, but regardless, their insularity always has a rationale. Either they feel morally superior to other people and wish to insulate themselves from outside contamination, or they feel narcissistically bruised by other people and feel the need to "circle the wagons" in order to prevent further

injury. (Sometimes they feel both.) Like all people with a rationale, they're constantly digging up evidence that supports it but
only rarely discovering evidence that refutes it.

Insular parents love their children ferociously—and they
love *only* their children and no one else's. They revel in their
children's accomplishments on the one hand but deprecate their
shortcomings on the other. They are quick to defend them but
equally quick to be disappointed by them. They are both doting
and demanding, indulgent and critical. And because insular parents see their children as their only true allies in the world, they
demand complete loyalty from them. They are critical of their
children's friends, their children's friends' families and of anyone with a contradictory viewpoint or a different way of living.
They are wary of all outside influences on their children and
contemptuous of any conflicting methods of childrearing.

Insular parents both indoctrinate their children and make
them insecure. They teach their children either to fear and mistrust other people or to look down on them and treat them with
disdain. Either way, these parents make it almost impossible for
their children to care for or about other people. And not just the
people outside their families, but the people inside their families—their own sisters and brothers—as well. Insular families
are rife with sibling rivalry.

Needless to say, the children of insular families become
extremely dependent on their parents and have great difficulty
in escaping their influence. Because they are comfortable only
when they're with their families, they may appear to be antisocial when they're with other people. They are dismayed to
discover that other people don't feel as positively towards them
as their parents do. But they are also relieved to discover that
other people don't feel as negatively towards them as their parents do, either. And it is this very dismay and relief, in fact, that
severs the umbilical cord and allows these sheltered children to
finally escape their parents' malignant influence.

Because once they begin to challenge the rationale underlying their parents' insularity, they can begin to shed their own
insularity. And once they begin to discover that they need and
like other people, they can begin to renounce their destructive
and exclusive attachment to their possessive parents.

Authority and Power

By the time we reach the end of pre-adulthood, we should no longer be afraid of our parents or of their disapproval. We should not be afraid to pursue our own aims, to have relationships with the people we choose to, or to live a particular kind of life-style, just because our parents might have chosen differently or because they refuse to understand and endorse our choice. Many of us, however, are still afraid of our parents by the time we reach the end of pre-adulthood—and sometimes for what appear to be good reasons. For example, I treated one woman who was cut off by her mother merely for contacting a relative whom her mother hated, and another woman who was told by her father not to come home with her boyfriend until he'd proposed. It may be difficult to overcome the fear of our parents—to go against their wishes or their beliefs—but if we don't, we'll never be able to live our lives according to our own wishes and beliefs, and we'll never be able to feel adult.

Sometimes the disapproval we fear is largely in our own heads. Our parents may no longer feel the way they once did about certain matters, or they may not care strongly enough one way or the other to want to interfere. We may even be projecting *our* doubts and reservations onto them. It would be bad enough not to confront our parents with potentially unpleasant facts because we wished to spare their feelings, but it would be even worse not to do so because we wished to spare our own feelings. Respecting our parents' feelings and sensibilities—if we really know them—is certainly worthwhile, but it should never be used as an excuse for avoiding the important things we have to do.

The fear of our parents that we have in pre-adulthood is different from the fear of them that we have when we're younger and weaker. When we're younger we fear losing their love or even being physically punished by them. When we reach pre-adulthood, we primarily fear losing their approval and respect. This may be somewhat less threatening to us than the fear of being physically punished or the fear of losing their love, but it derives some of its potency from those earlier fears, and it is sufficiently threatening on its own to keep us from deviating too far from the party line.

So how do we overcome this fear? How do we gain the strength that we need to risk our parents' disapproval? One way is to form close, loving relationships with other people so that we're not dependent only on our parents for love and approval. This is very important, of course, but only if we avoid substituting the authority of these new people for the authority of our parents. Another way to overcome this fear is to become independent of our parents. If we don't need them, so we reason, then they won't have as much power over us. Sounds sensible, but it's rarely enough. Because, even though we don't need our parents, we still want them to love and respect us.

The real answer is for us to become our own authority—to fear the disapproval of our own conscience more than the disapproval of any other authority, and to feel gratified by the fulfilment of our own ideals more than by the fulfilment of any outside person's. In other words, to gain the strength and courage needed to overcome the fear of our parents' disapproval—and, by extension, the disapproval of any other person or institution—we have to develop a clear sense of what we consider to be morally right and wrong, we have to construct a well-thought-out set of values, beliefs and ideals, and we have to build a strong, fair and sophisticated conscience to encourage and enforce them. We can do this during childhood by developing our physical and social bravery, and during pre-adulthood by thinking carefully and independently about what we really feel and believe, and by doing what we determine to be right regardless of the opinions of other people.

The case of Joseph, a twenty-nine-year-old businessman who came to see me because he was feeling depressed, illustrates some of the issues involved in overcoming the fear of our parents and other authorities.

Joseph was having grave doubts about his work and was on the verge of quitting. Since graduating from business school three years earlier with an MBA, Joseph had been working as a financial analyst in the mergers and acquisitions department of a small but prestigious investment banking firm in Toronto. He was highly regarded and highly paid, but felt "stressed out," and was having a harder and harder time getting up for work. He had already missed many days of work before coming to see me, but soon after starting therapy, he took a medical leave of absence and stopped going into the office altogether.

Here's how he saw his predicament: "I'm the victim of my own early success. I was brilliant in school, and when I joined my current firm I just kept on being brilliant. The problem is that I've painted myself into a corner. In my business all the action is in deal making, but I'm so good at analysis, they won't let me do any deals."

As a result of his reputation for brilliance, Joseph had been assigned to assist Bob, the firm's senior partner. Bob was a well-connected, mediocre man in his late fifties, who'd charmed his way to the top of several organizations, including the Department of Finance, before quitting to set up his own investment banking firm. He was the consummate insider, a society schmoozer and front man who needed other people—bright tacticians like Joseph—to provide him with his ideas.

At the beginning of their relationship, Joseph admired Bob a great deal and worked like a dog to help him. It seemed like a satisfactory arrangement: Joseph came up with the ideas and strategies, and Bob made the decisions and handled the clients and investors. Joseph did the thinking, and Bob did the doing. Joseph went home after midnight to his one-room apartment, and Bob faxed in comments from his house in Muskoka. Joseph got praise from Bob and a huge Christmas bonus, and Bob got praise from the business press and a huge private fortune.

After a year or two of this arrangement, however, Joseph began to feel trapped. He had become Bob's creature. Bob was the commander-in-chief, the senior partner and the captain, while Joseph was the second-in-command, the junior partner and the first mate. He couldn't see a way to get out from under Bob's control without jeopardizing everything he'd worked so hard for. And because he couldn't see a way to take control of his own destiny, he started to feel oppressed, disillusioned and depressed.

These feelings were not new to Joseph. He'd had

them repeatedly throughout his life. He was forever standing in the shadow of a larger man—resentful of his subordinate status, yet afraid to step forward into the limelight.
He recited incident after incident: In university, a professor
he'd worked for published a paper based on his research;
in high school, a classmate he'd tutored was named vale-
dictorian; and in junior high school, a friend he'd intro-
duced to his girlfriend started going out with her.

   And each of these incidents reminded Joseph of his
relationship with his father—a man he both admired and
resented. Like Bob, Joseph's father was a doer, not a
thinker. He was a quiet, vigorous man who ran his own
insurance agency, played golf with a few close friends and
loved his wife deeply. He was an intelligent man, but unlike
his son, he was not an intellectual. He attended church every
Sunday, followed all the commandments and was deeply
ethical. He was also deeply judgmental. He disapproved of
divorce, showiness, frivolity and money-grubbing.

   Joseph's father was not particularly nurturing. He
believed in the value of discipline, hard work and thrift, and
was suspicious of intellectual speculation and artistic experimentation—forms of self-expression to which Joseph felt
drawn. When Joseph compared himself to his father, he felt
vaguely wimpy and inadequate. He had irrational phobias
and superstitions that, for fear of embarrassment, he was
afraid to divulge. And at times he could be painfully shy.

   After several months of therapy, Joseph recounted an
incident that occurred when he was twelve years old, but
which still made him blush to think about. Though the incident was minor, Joseph seemed to think it was emblematic
of his relationship with his father and that it coloured all
their subsequent dealings with each other.

   The event took place one pleasant summer evening
after Joseph and his father had played tennis together. For
the first time in his life, Joseph had given his father some
real competition on the courts, and he was feeling especially proud of himself and very happy to be chatting with his
father—almost as an equal—as they strolled lazily home
through the park. Suddenly, a large, threatening German

shepherd set upon them, barking furiously and foaming at the mouth. Joseph was generally fond of dogs, but when he saw this strange one snapping and growling at them, he froze in terror and involuntarily clutched his father's arm for protection.

Joseph's father, however, did not panic. He stood his ground until the dog stopped, then knelt down slowly and called to the animal, which sidled over to him quietly and cautiously and began to lick his hand.

"Dogs are like people," his father told him sternly, as he patted the animal. "If they sense fear, they'll try to take advantage of you. Never show them you're afraid."

After the dog bounded off in search of its negligent master, Joseph and his father resumed their walk home, but the bond between them had been broken, and Joseph could barely keep from crying. He felt deeply ashamed that he'd been so frightened, and he sensed that his father, who'd grown up with several dogs, felt ashamed of him too.

"Don't you think anybody might have been frightened in that situation?" I asked Joseph, after he'd finished his story.

"My father wasn't frightened," he answered.

"How do you know?" I asked.

"I *don't* know," he replied. "All I know is that I had nightmares about that dog for years afterwards. I still get them sometimes.

"You know," he continued, "I had just finished beating that bastard two sets to one. I think he was secretly pissed off that I'd got the better of him for once. He needed some way to prove he was still the top dog, and when that rabid-looking mutt showed up and attacked us, he had his chance to do it—literally! He knocked me back down to size."

By recalling this forgotten interaction with his father, Joseph realized why he was afraid to try for the top position. He had interpreted his father's actions that evening as a warning to him not to get too big for his britches—an interpretation that had persisted right up to the present time. After that incident, he made sure never to appear to be encroaching on the bigger man's turf—never to go head to head with someone who might be more powerful. Instead, he carved out a niche for himself as the bigger man's assistant—the brains behind the brawn—and learned to keep a low profile. Playing the talented, but unthreatening, protégé became his *modus operandi*. And whenever he got into a relationship with a man he admired, the pattern reasserted itself. What had begun as a conscious adaptation to his father's domination ended up as an unconscious reflex to all competition with a strong rival. It was triggered with his professor in university, with his classmate in high school, and even with his friend in junior high school.

"The same thing is happening with Bob," he realized. "I'm reacting to him just like I did with my father. And if I don't make some changes soon, I'll end up undermining myself this way my whole life."

So Joseph ended his leave of absence and went back to work with a renewed enthusiasm. He asked to be transferred to a different partner—one who worked more collaboratively—and he took the opportunity to manage deals from conception right through to completion.

Whenever he noticed that he was getting the urge to subordinate himself, he stopped and tried to figure out why. In every instance, it was because he was encroaching on another man's turf and was afraid he'd be put in his place and humiliated as he was by his father. He reminded himself, that if he took second place in order to pre-empt the humiliation he feared, he was taking himself out of the action before the action had even begun. So he faced his fear instead and forged ahead with his plans despite his fear. Sometimes he won, sometimes he lost, but he never took himself out of the game.

By understanding his fears, Joseph was able to overcome them. He realized that his father had fears too, and that his own fears were neither unique nor shameful. In short, Joseph became a man. But he didn't become a man like his father or like Bob. He became a man like himself—his own man.

He even got himself a dog.

The Capacity to Face the Deaths of Our Parents Without Fear or Guilt

How will we know that we've achieved a feeling of equality with our parents? One way we'll know is by seeing how we feel when we think about their deaths. If we feel sadness, but not fear or guilt, then we'll know we've achieved a feeling of equality. But if we feel fear or guilt in addition to sadness, we'll know we still have a distance to go. Because if we feel fear when we think about our parents dying, then it means we're still dependent on them for our sense of security and well-being, and if we feel guilt when we have those thoughts, it means we're still intimidated by their authority and power.

During pre-adulthood, we worry about how well we'll do when our parents finally die, and we feel guilty about even having such thoughts because we imagine that, if our parents knew about them, they'd find those thoughts offensive. But by the time we're ready to make the transition to adulthood, we no longer feel this way. We know that we'll be able to thrive without them, and we know that we won't feel guilty. This confidence doesn't spring from hard-heartedness or bravado; it springs from an awareness of our own strength and resilience, and from a sense of having given our parents no pain or offence, save the pain or offence of living our own lives.

Brit couldn't imagine living without her mother. She'd always been very close to her mother and used her as both confidante and whipping boy. When Brit turned thirty-one, however, her mother developed ovarian cancer and had to undergo surgery and chemotherapy. The relationship between them changed abruptly. Faced with the possibility of her mother's imminent death, Brit was forced to grow up and rely on herself. She came to grips with the fact that she'd eventually have to survive on her own, and she began to look after her mother instead of expecting her mother to look after her.

Harold's father owned several appliance stores and worked late every day but Sunday. He tended to be gruff and impatient when he got home after working all day, and as a result, Harold learned to steer clear of him.

By way of compensation, Harold became very close to his mother. She was not physically affectionate with him, but very interested in his intellectual and cultural development. They listened to the opera together on the radio, went to plays and concerts, and discussed political, religious, philosophical and literary ideas with great fervour. But when Harold's father got home, his mother would break off her discussion with Harold and attend to his father. Harold believed that his mother didn't really love his father, but that she didn't want to cross him either.

Harold and his mother had a mutual admiration society that left him very attached to her and very wary and resentful of his father. In fact, until Harold left home at the age of nineteen, he often wished that his father would just drop dead and leave his mother and him alone. Every time he had these fantasies, however, Harold would be overwhelmed with guilt and fear. He kept having the uncanny feeling that his father knew what he was thinking.

At nineteen, Harold went away to college and never returned to live in his parents' home again. Each time he returned for a visit, his feelings towards his parents changed a little. He began to see his mother in a more negative light, and his father in a more positive one. He began to see his mother as demanding and manipulative, and his father as stoical and hard-working.

By the time Harold was twenty-eight, his mother didn't captivate him anymore and his father didn't intimidate him. He felt equal to them. And when he thought about his father's death at that point, it was no longer with hatred and guilt; it was with sadness and regret.

DEATH-DENYING FEATS

Mind you, even when we get to the point where we can contemplate the deaths of our parents without fear or guilt, we're still not home free. Because we still have to deal with the sadness—and that's not easy to do. We may try to avoid dealing with the sadness by, for example, replacing it with anger. We unconsciously reason that, if our parents can still absorb a good blast of anger from us, then they can't really be aging and mortal, they must still be young and robust. Anger makes us feel, and makes our parents seem, less vulnerable.

One of my patients, a middle-aged woman with two adult children of her own, had never visited the graveyard in which both her parents were buried. In fact, from the way she continued to talk about them in therapy, you might not guess that they weren't still alive. A trip to the cemetery, I figured, might be just the thing to help her mourn her parents and move on with her life.

I advised her accordingly, and she made the recommended journey several weekends later.

"How did it go?" I asked her on her return.

"Very well," she answered. "I found the graves of my grandparents and great-grandparents and had a very nice cry."

"And at the graves of your parents?" I asked her.

"Oh, that wasn't too bad," she answered gaily. "I haven't had their names inscribed on their headstones yet. So it didn't even seem as if they were really there."

"Why didn't you have their names inscribed?" I asked.

"I just didn't feel like it!" she replied with irritation. "They were always telling me what to do, and this time I just decided not to do it! They gave me detailed directions of what they wanted on their gravestones after they died, but I'm sick and tired of doing what they want."

It finally dawned on me. This woman kept her dead parents alive in fantasy by continuing to fight with them. Her rebellion made it seem as if they were still looking after her. If she gave up the struggle, she would have to accept the fact that they were gone. And that would force her to confront not only her grief, but also her unresolved feelings of hostility and need.

Needless to say, if we can't face our grief about losing our parents, then we obviously haven't achieved equality with them.

THE CAPACITY TO CONFRONT OUR OWN DEATH

Confronting the end of our parents' lives leads naturally to contemplating the end of our own. We start to feel death's cold breath on the back of our necks, and it makes us want to stop and catch our own breath before we continue our headlong rush towards life's inevitable conclusion. It prompts us to take stock of where we've been and where we're going—to put things back into their proper perspective and to reset our priorities.

An awareness of our own mortality forces us to face facts and seize control of our own lives. On the one hand, it forces us to accept the fact that people and opportunities *can* be lost forever, and that they have to be cherished and valued. And on the other hand, it reminds us that we still have plenty of life left to live and that there is still a chance to make good on some of the promises we've made to ourselves. It cautions us not to wait for someone else to solve our own and the world's problems, and it renews our hope. It challenges us not to shirk our responsibility for what happens in the world, and it rekindles our desire to make every moment count.

An awareness of life's finitude produces both sadness and joy.

LEARNING THAT WE ARE PART OF CIVILIZATION

The initial resolution of the Oedipus complex in childhood changes our relationship with our parents and prepares us to achieve independence from them, and equality with them, during pre-adulthood. The final resolution of the Oedipus complex at the transition to adulthood changes our relationship with the world in general and prepares us to assume our social responsibilities and rights.

The Assumption of Our Social Responsibilities

At the moment we feel adult, it is our new status in the world that we become consciously aware of. We feel that we're finally equal to other adults, including our own parents, not necessarily in ability, rank, prestige, wealth, wisdom or achievement, but in having the same social rights and responsibilities as they do, and in possessing "adultness" *per se*.

This change in self-awareness is the result of, and further fosters, a massive restructuring of our psyche. After the transition to adulthood, our superego continues to act as our guide and judge, but rather than deriving all its authority from identifications with our parents and other individuals, it begins to derive its authority from identifications with civilization as a whole—not just from one government or state in particular, but from the principle of social existence in general. We accept—not merely with resignation but with the enthusiasm of participants and co-creators—that we are, of necessity, social beings, and that we have a stake in social life.

During pre-adulthood, we widen the scope of our interests and passions to include the world beyond our families. As a result, when we make the transition to adulthood, we expand the concern and love that we have for our parents onto the world at large and begin to take a mature interest in the world and assume our social obligations. In other words, the final resolution of the Oedipus complex inspires and empowers us to assume our social responsibilities.

The Assumption of Our Social Rights

When we resolved our Oedipus complex at the age of five, we killed two birds with one stone. By moderating the resentment and jealousy we felt towards our parents for preferring each other romantically, rather than us, we reduced the need to feel guilty or fearful of being punished. By identifying with our parents and by taking them as our models—especially the parent we perceived to be our rival—we found a new way to express our love for our parents and to earn their respect and love in return.

But what happens to this desire to be respected and loved by our parents during the transition to adulthood? As with the desire to give respect and love, the desire to receive respect and love is expanded beyond our families to the world at large. It produces the mature desire to be granted our social rights. In other words, the desire to be loved by our parents is transformed into the desire to be loved by humanity.[1]

What does "the desire to be loved by humanity" mean? It means the desire to be treated by other people with dignity, respect and compassion—as an adult. In other words, the final resolution of the Oedipus complex inspires and empowers us to assume our social rights.

The Transition to Adulthood

How does this massive restructuring of the psyche come about? How do we come to feel equal to our parents, and how does our superego become identified with the principles of social existence? We know what initiates the initial resolution of the Oedipus complex in early childhood: It's the fear of being punished by our parents for our improper passions, and the fear of losing their love. But what initiates the final resolution of the Oedipus complex in pre-adulthood? Is it still fear of our parents? That's a possibility, of course, but it's not likely, because as we've already noted, by the time we're ready to feel adult, we perceive our parents as less threatening and our superego has become more moderate.

Then is it the love of our mate that prompts the final resolution of the Oedipus complex? Do we identify with the ideals of society and assume our obligations because of our desire to protect and nurture the person we love? That too is a possibility, and it certainly makes some contribution, but I don't think it's universal enough or powerful enough to bring about such a massive restructuring of the psyche in every pre-adult.

I believe that the final resolution of the Oedipus complex is driven by the fear of social sanction or disapproval. Putting it in superego terms, the tension that prompts us to assume our social rights and responsibilities is the fear of being sanctioned by society and of losing humankind's love. Just as the fear of our parents' punishment and disapproval motivated us to identify with our parents' authority and values to form an Oedipal superego, the fear of social sanction and disapproval motivates us to identify with society's authority and values to form an adult superego. That's why we feel badly if we fail to live up to our social responsibilities or don't assert our rights. We feel unworthy of our own superego's love—we feel ashamed.

The "civilizing of the superego" is also the reason why feeling grownup is such an important watershed, and why it's so hard to reverse. It represents a change in the structure of the psyche so decisive that, after it has taken place, failure to behave like an adult produces intense feelings of guilt and shame.

It is important to note, however, that living up to the rules and ideals of our adult superego doesn't mean merely following the laws and norms of our *particular* society; it means upholding the *principles* of social behaviour. What we're conforming to is not convention, but the dictates of our own adult conscience.

This too is a parallel with what happens in the initial resolution of the Oedipus complex. As we gain adult experience in the world, our superego becomes increasingly liberated from simple, primitive identifications with social authority. Social norms continue to hold power over us, of course, but less power than our own increasingly moderate, abstract and personal principles. As adults, we certainly continue to fear society's power to punish us when we violate its particular laws and mores. But much more than that, we fear the punishment of our own shame when we violate our personal principles of civilized conduct.

Adulthood and Civilization

The act of becoming adult and the act of becoming civilized are identical. We become adult at the precise moment we decide to throw in our lot with civilization—not necessarily with any particular social arrangement, but with social order as the best fulfilment of human nature.

That's why feeling like a grownup is delayed for a number of years after we are physically mature and legally adult, and why the feeling of being an adult has to be conscious. It takes time to come to an understanding of our dependence on civilization and to accept it. It is only by virtue of our commitment to our work and to our family, out of economic necessity and an awareness of our own fragility, that we can eventually come to realize that we have become invested in civilization.

When we become adult, we accept that we will experience more pleasure (and less pain) if we restrict and channel our erotic and aggressive impulses in accordance with our own moral code. We realize that our own deepest and highest aims are not opposed to, but are congruent with, the aims of civilization—that we can't fulfil the one without fulfilling the other. We come to believe that real individuality and self-expression—the kind that fulfils the noblest ideals of human nature, not the kind that panders to the conventions and mores of a particular social arrangement or ideology, or rebels against them—are the true goals of civilization.

The act of becoming adult signifies that the balance has tipped away from narcissism and towards participation in social life. The process of feeling like an adult is congruent with the process of becoming civilized—the two terminate together—and, likewise, an awareness of the one is coincident with an acceptance of the other.

CIVILIZATION AND THE INDIVIDUAL

If "becoming adult" is the same as "becoming civilized," then what becomes of individuality? Being civilized and being individual would seem to imply different things: Being civilized implies belonging to a larger entity, whereas being individual implies the opposite. Is being an individual just another one of those pre-adult things you have to give up to grow up?

The answer, fortunately, is no. You don't have to give up your individuality in order to become a grownup. In fact, the two concepts seem to be in opposition only because we're used to framing their relationship in terms of the age-old conflict between the aims of the society and the aims of the individual—a conflict that often seems irreconcilable. But becoming civilized and becoming truly individual are actually part of the same process.

It is certainly true that becoming civilized involves participating in humankind's collective achievements—language, culture, law, technology, construction, art, science, ordered conduct and so forth—but so does becoming an individual. You can discover and define your individuality, in fact, only by using the resources of civilization. In becoming adult, you recognize your indebtedness to humanity's historic achievement, civilization, by internalizing it—by becoming civilized. You identify with civilization by becoming adult, and you enhance civilization by contributing to it.

Civilization and Its Deep Contentments

Two years ago, at the age of forty, Robert left the large, established architectural firm where he'd spent the last seven years, and set out on his own. It had been a risky decision. He had a four-year-old daughter and a newborn son at home, and, because his wife had given up her teaching job to stay home and raise the children, they had limited savings. But after two years of taking whatever jobs had come his way, Robert was awarded a plum commission—the design of a new primary school.

While driving home from work one warm, early spring evening, the radio started to play a song from his teens—early Stevie Wonder, very upbeat—and he thought about how far he'd come since first hearing it. He remembered driving his mother's Buick Skylark home from a dance at the high school, empty-handed, sweaty and exhausted from a night of dancing, but still full of adolescent excitement and hope. Things had come to him so easily back then, that it seemed those bitter-sweet days might just go on forever.

He remembered that, when he got home from the dance that night, his parents were just pulling into the driveway. They were dressed in tux and gown, having just returned from a gala at the country club, and he remembered how glamorous and happy and young they looked.

The adult world had seemed so exciting to him as a teenager, yet so forbidding and remote. He'd had no car in those days, no real income, no steady female companionship, and almost no responsibility. Today, he had all four. During the intervening two and a half decades his father had died, his mother had remarried and moved away, and he'd begun a career and a family of his own.

He glanced at himself in the rearview mirror. He was losing some hair, just like his dad, but he was handsomer than he'd been as a teenager. He no longer had that awkward, unformed appearance he'd had as a youth. His face was more lined. It had more character. He wasn't a kid any more.

I've made it, he thought. I'm finally a man.

A deep feeling of pride began to swell in his chest, a feeling of euphoria, but solid and grounded, that filled his chest and made him sit up taller. And, for the first time in his life, he felt like an adult, really like an adult.

Robert pulled into his driveway, closed the sun roof and locked the car. To avoid tracking mud into the house, he walked around the wet, uneven lawn and stooped to pick up some tattered flyers that had blown into the bushes. An image of his father, age forty, flashed through his mind. He remembered watching him through the living-room window when he came home at the end of the day. And he saw his father stoop and pick up bits of wind-strewn paper in just the same way he was doing at that very moment.

A question crossed his mind: I wonder if the old man was feeling then what I'm feeling now? And somehow he knew the answer was yes.

He felt a sudden kinship with his father that he'd never known before. He felt weightier, as though he'd taken on ballast, and, at the same time, he felt incredibly light and free.

"This is *my* lawn," he announced to no one but himself. "This is *my* house. This is *my* family. This is *my* life!"

And for the first time in his life, Robert felt he was truly the master of his own fate, the architect of his own destiny.

As he approached the front door, he could hear his wife talking to the baby. Somewhere farther off a nursery tape was playing. He stopped for a minute to listen to the intimate sounds of his own family going about their lives. Then, smiling inwardly, he dabbed his eyes with the back of one gloved hand and opened the door.

We can see in Robert's experience of starting to feel like an adult many of the elements of becoming civilized—the economic stake in society, the emotional stake in family life, the satisfaction of building something worthwhile and of contributing to the wider community, the awareness of generational continuity, and the quiet enjoyment of a life well lived.

CHAPTER NINE

THE ROLE OF PSYCHOTHERAPY IN BECOMING ADULT

> A child becomes an adult when he realizes that he has a right not only to be right but also to be wrong.
>
> *Thomas Szasz*

The more you understand about yourself, the easier it is to feel adult. All you need to do that, normally, are a few decades of life experience and a growing capacity to integrate and interpret those experiences. If you've given your life some thought, and tried to be honest with yourself, then by the time you're ready to make the transition to adulthood, you'll know what makes you tick. Specifically, you'll understand your desires, feelings, beliefs, principles, abilities, limitations, strengths and weaknesses, and the external and internal obstacles that stand in the way of your achieving happiness and fulfilment. Given the magnitude of the task, and contrary to popular belief that "we're too soon old and too late smart," it's fortunate that we do get smarter as fast as we get older, and that, barring psychological complications, life becomes generally more intelligible with age. Not that life loses its capacity to surprise us, of course, because it doesn't. But because we now *expect* life to surprise us, the surprises don't invariably throw us, and on occasion they even give us delight.

But what if there *are* psychological complications? What if you keep making the same mistakes over and over again? What if you can't seem to learn from your experiences or even understand them? What if you're stuck in a rut—emotionally, socially or professionally—or have a problem you're depressed or anxious about and can't figure out how to solve? What if you simply can't face growing up? At that point, clearly, you need to take a closer look at yourself. And these are precisely the situations for which psychotherapy was designed.

But there are other situations for which psychotherapy is helpful too. Not everyone who enters psychotherapy has hit a dead end in her own attempts to understand herself or is experiencing a crisis. Many people simply want to improve the quality of their lives. They want to deepen their self-understanding beyond the minimal level needed to feel adult, and they want to feel freer and more fulfilled.

The operative principle behind most types of psychotherapy is insight. But if insight is very good at providing understanding, it's not so good at providing motivation—the motivation has to come from you. And insight alone is not enough to make you freer and more fulfilled—you have to work at changing your behaviour too.

Fortunately, most people who enter therapy *are* motivated to make their lives better—that's why they're there. For those people who are motivated to explore their own thoughts and feelings, and who are prepared to act on what they learn, psychotherapy can be a rewarding and fruitful experience. It can change their lives.

SELF-ANALYSIS

The process of self-understanding—whether undertaken alone or in concert with a psychiatrist, psychologist or other therapist—requires self-analysis. And self-analysis is something you can do before, during, after, and sometimes even instead of a formal psychotherapy. In fact, after psychotherapy has ended, it's your mastery of self-analysis—more than the specific insights you've acquired while in therapy—that helps you in your ongoing life.

How do you perform self-analysis? Is there a specific technique? If so, can it be described or is it some kind of mystical process absorbed by osmosis while lying on an analyst's couch? There *is* a specific technique of self-analysis. It isn't mysterious. And although many therapists seem for some reason to be coy about doing so, the technique can be described.

In self-analysis, the basic idea is to catch hold of the thoughts, feelings and sensory experiences that flit through your mind while you're thinking about or describing a particular event. For example, while describing a discussion you had with your boss earlier that day, you might become aware of feeling anxious, or your mind might wander to a conversation you had with your brother, or you might remember a dream. Those associations are threads that connect the incident you're describing to some other central memory that is psychologically significant. As you trace those threads back to their starting point, one thread is dropped and another is taken up in a continual process of unravelling the source of your present conflicts. Over time, a map is built up from these interconnected threads that permits you to navigate back to the central memory or memories from which your conflicts spring.

It's important to have a starting point for your associations— an actual event, a recent interaction, a specific thought or feeling, or a puzzling dream—otherwise, they will tend to be random, inchoate and fugitive, and you'll end up chasing your own tail. Interpersonal interactions, memories and other experiences to which strong feelings (negative *or* positive) have become attached are particularly helpful in this regard.

It's conceivable, of course, that choosing a topic, instead of talking about the first thing that pops into your head, will cause you to avoid dealing with something important—to resist some uncomfortable insights—but then so will starting with a blank slate or a mind full of noise. Most people free-associate whenever they get a chance. They don't call it free association, of course—they call it daydreaming or thinking—but they do follow their own train of thought from one point to another, without trying too hard to structure it, very much as they would in psychotherapy. And when they're on their own, they begin to free-associate precisely because there is something specific they're trying to grapple with. It's only when people try to start a psychotherapy session with something "plucked from the air," instead of something they've had on their minds all day, that they seem to draw a blank, quickly run out of material or become detached and bored. The process of initiating associations in therapy is not radically different from the process of doing so when you're on your own. The main difference is that you do it out loud.

Once you have your starting point, you should try to describe the interaction, event, memory or dream in as much detail as possible. As the architect Mies van der Rohe said, "God is in the details." It's only by examining things minutely that patterns, trends and significant discrepancies can be recognized and genuinely fresh insights made. Without the details, all you're left with is a rehash of predigested material or a stale overview from which nothing new can be gleaned.

Free Association

Let's see how this kind of free association might occur in an everyday setting or be reported to a therapist.

You're sitting on the bus to work and notice that you can't get absorbed in the morning paper. It dawns on you that you're feeling vaguely distressed, a feeling you rarely have first thing in the morning.

Under normal circumstances, you would shake off the feeling and get your head back into work, but today you decide to follow your thoughts to see where they lead. This is where you begin to free-associate.

Glancing down at the paper, you notice there is an article in the Arts and Entertainment section about a famous television actor who died the day before. He had been a household name when you were a kid, and you can picture him in black and white on the TV screen.

Then you notice the old man sitting on the bench opposite you. He rides the bus every morning, but today, for some reason, he seems particularly frail and lonely. Why today? After all, you see solitary old people on the bus and walking on the street all the time and rarely give them a second thought.

After pondering this question for a moment, you realize

that you were feeling pensive and a little melancholy
before you got on the bus that morning. When did you
notice you were feeling that way? You cast your mind
back. Was it at breakfast...in the shower...? Then you realize: You felt melancholy the moment you woke up that
morning.

Did you have a dream last night that might explain it?
You recall having a dream, but not one that you can reconstruct just at the moment.

Perhaps this feeling began yesterday then? Aha! It
comes to you: You were *not* feeling this way until you
spoke to your father on the phone last night. He had called
you from your family home in Vancouver, which is unusual for him, because it's normally your mother who makes
the calls. *He* called this time, however, because your mother is in the hospital recovering from hip replacement
surgery. He told you that she came through the operation
nicely, though it's taking her a long time to recover from
the anaesthetic. Now the associations come more quickly.

You remember that during the phone call from your
father, you felt guilty that you hadn't flown back for your
mother's operation. True, she told you not to bother, but
you're sure she would've appreciated having you there.
And you expect your father would have appreciated it too.
He sounded so old and lonely on the phone last night that
you really felt sorry for him. You recall worrying that he
wouldn't be able to look after himself if your mother died.

For some reason this brings to mind the day your
grandfather—your father's father—died. You were ten and
your father was forty-six. It was the first time you saw
your father cry, and it frightened you. He had always been
such a pillar of strength, and you recalled wondering at the
time what would happen if *he* died? Then *you'd* have to
look after your mother. *You'd* be the man of the house.
What would that be like? Could you handle it?...

I could go on, but I think this illustrates how people go about
figuring out why they're having a particular feeling. If our fictional bus passenger were in therapy, this set of associations

might lead him to further memories of his father. He might discover that he had actually *enjoyed* the childhood fantasy of being the head of the family and felt guilty about eliminating his father from the imaginary picture. Or he might recall seeing his father being threatened by an irate driver and worrying that his father wasn't strong enough to protect the family in the event of violence. Perhaps, as a result of these conscious memories, he'll even recall the dream he had that night and recognize some connection to his melancholy mood.

The point is that he would have been unable to discover any of this had he simply shaken off his melancholy feeling that morning and gone about his business. And, normally, that's precisely what happens. We *do* shake off our feelings and go about our business. We ignore our feelings, or perhaps attribute them to fatigue. They get buried under the heap of other experiences that crowd our busy lives and are quickly forgotten.

Most of the time it doesn't matter very much that we've set aside our feelings. Doing so may even help us to be more efficient. Every now and then, however, our feelings can't be ignored. They haunt us and call out to be examined.

That's where the process of free association helps. Because, if we have the courage to stick with our feelings and follow them back to their sources, they will cease to be mysterious and become understandable. The confusion and distress of ignorance will then give way to the calm and mastery of knowledge.

Many people worry that just the opposite will happen to them if they delve into their feelings. They imagine they'll feel even more depressed. They want to believe that ignorance is bliss. But nothing could be further from the truth. In fact, facing a problem almost always alleviates a non-clinical depression—if not right away, then very soon. Alcoholics, for example, report feeling enormously relieved when they finally admit to themselves (what they've always known) that they're alcoholic, and manic-depressives say they feel comforted by the knowledge that their problem is biochemical.

When disturbing feelings are examined, they become less diffuse and vague. They stop sticking to everything they touch and are more easily handled. And, because they can now be explained, they become less disturbing.

PSYCHOTHERAPY

There are times, however, when self-analysis isn't enough—when you've reached the limits of your own capacity to gain further insight and need the help of someone with more training and objectivity in order to proceed. But how do you know when you've reached that point? How do you know when you need psychotherapy?

When Freud first invented "the talking cure" at the beginning of the twentieth century, his goal was to eliminate neurotic symptoms. He saw himself as a physician treating disease, not as a therapist treating problems of living. His early patients had symptoms that mimicked neurological conditions; some had weakness or paralysis or odd sensations in their limbs, and others had peculiar amnesias or troubling images in their minds. His later patients suffered from compulsions, phobias, paranoid ideas, depression, sexual disorders or other conditions with definite symptoms. They were not merely unhappy.

Freud didn't see psychoanalysis as a cure for all that ails us: he saw it as a cure only for symptom neuroses like hysteria. In *Studies On Hysteria*, he explained that he told his patients: "much will be gained if we succeed in transforming your hysterical misery into common unhappiness."

As it has turned out, Freud was right about the limits of psychoanalysis, but he was wrong about what it's good for. He had it backwards—psychoanalysis isn't particularly good for treating conditions with specific symptoms, but it's not bad for treating conditions *without* specific symptoms. In other words, psychoanalysis is good for treating problems of living, and not so good for treating serious depressions, obsessive-compulsive disorders and phobias.

Nowadays, however, we expect more from psychotherapy than mere relief of our hysterical misery; we expect relief from our common unhappiness as well. We no longer regard common unhappiness as evidence that we're alive and engaged in the struggles and triumphs of life; we now regard it as evidence of personal or social pathology. Here Freud was right: Psychotherapy can't eliminate common unhappiness. Nothing can. It can't cure disappointment, misfortune, illness, broken hearts, poverty or war, but it can help to reduce certain psychological barriers to fulfilment and growth.

It is worth noting that there are many therapeutic activities that are not formal therapies. Walking in the woods, reading a good book, falling in love, painting a picture, doing a job well, and talking to a friend are all potentially therapeutic activities. Indeed, because they build feelings of accomplishment, these activities are sometimes more therapeutic than formal therapy. There are, however, problems that self-help can't solve: deepseated and unrecognized barriers to satisfaction and accomplishment that block the path to adulthood and make it impossible for us to reach our potential. These problems require a more formal therapeutic intervention.

Symptomatic Disorders and Bad Habits

There are, roughly speaking, two types of mental impediments to fulfilment and growth: symptomatic disorders and bad habits. People with symptomatic disorders have specific symptoms— such as suicidality, weight change, apathy or the inability to experience pleasure—that are thought to have mostly biological causes. People with bad habits have maladaptive patterns of behaviour—such as marital conflicts, relationship or work problems, or identity confusion—that are thought to have mostly psychological causes. The two types of impediments are rarely separable in practice, of course, but for the sake of simplicity, I'll discuss them as if they were. Examples of symptomatic disorders are schizophrenia, major clinical depression, obsessive-compulsive disorder, psychosomatic disorders, anorexia and bulimia, and panic disorder. Examples of bad habits are personality disorders, many forms of substance abuse, lesser forms of anxiety and depression, academic and work failures, difficulties in establishing relationships, social and sexual inhibitions, problems of self-esteem and confidence, and difficulties in becoming adult.

Medical treatments are fairly good at controlling, if not curing, symptomatic disorders. Medications can ameliorate such physiologically based symptoms as depression, panic attacks, obsessions, hallucinations, delusions, agitation, suicidality, binge eating, compulsive rituals, sleep disorders, mania, hyperactivity, paranoia and a host of related symptoms that were once thought to be untreatable. And if these symptoms aren't concealing an unrecognized bad habit, then no other type of treatment may be needed.

But if the problem is a bad habit, then medication generally won't help. People with bad habits don't have discrete symptoms that can be eliminated to reveal an intact personality beneath. They have reflexive and irrational thoughts, feelings, perceptions and actions that are woven into their personalities in complex patterns and can't easily be untangled. Because most bad habits begin as rational adaptations to specific childhood difficulties, they are difficult to change. People with bad habits continue to be plagued by past events they've consciously forgotten. They react to the present as if it were the past, as if they were still living in the childhood situation in which these habits formed. If they want to be able to respond to their current reality instead of their repressed memories, people suffering from bad habits need to look afresh at their formative childhood experiences. They need to review the past from an adult perspective.

How is this fresh look accomplished in therapy? And how are bad habits changed?

The two separate tasks—*exploring* the sources of the bad habit, and *modifying* the behaviour associated with it—are handled differently in each of the two main types of therapy. In what I call "exhortatory therapy," the underlying causes of the bad habits are either ignored or explained simplistically, and the person's behaviour is changed by submission to the therapist's exhortations or coercion. In "exploratory therapy," the underlying causes of the bad habits are examined carefully and in detail, and the person's behaviour is changed by his or her own hard work.

Exhortatory Psychotherapy

Exhortatory psychotherapies aim to teach people good habits without necessarily examining the origins of their bad habits. The person is *exhorted*—bullied, persuaded, encouraged, cajoled and embarrassed—into trying to change his behaviour.

Behaviour therapists, for example, use learning techniques to condition new patterns of behaviour in their clients—rewarding desired behaviours and punishing undesirable ones. They don't provide any insight into the causes of a problem, but they can be very helpful in removing the symptoms. Behaviour therapy is especially helpful for overcoming phobias.

Charismatic therapists, by contrast, get their followers to change by making them submissive, and though their message may be embarrassingly simple, their marketing is highly sophisticated. There are two preferred formats: the marathon weekend "seminar," where they harangue a large, emotionally receptive audience for two days, and the TV infomercial, where they chat pleasantly with a celebrity interviewer.

The marathon weekend seminar is "hot." The leaders exploit group dynamics to wear the audience down and bring intense emotions to the surface. They humiliate the audience members to make them feel needy, then tell them they're special to make them feel lucky. They use intimidation, humour, scapegoating, catharsis, theatre and marketing techniques to sell the audience their own brand of scientific-sounding dogma.

The infomercial, by contrast, is "cool." It exploits the family-room familiarity of television to soft-sell the guru's books, tapes and weekend seminars. In a congenial setting designed to simulate the intimacy of a nice one-to-one chat, the guru is "interviewed" by a celebrity interviewer, who is actually a shill for the guru's program. This format implies not only that the guru is a celebrity in his own right, but one hell of a nice guy to boot. "Proof" of the program's efficacy is provided in two ways: first, by the rags-to-riches story of the guru himself (or herself), and second, by the "unsolicited" endorsements of celebrities and "ordinary people."

All these therapies are coercive—some, like behaviour therapy, for the good of the client, and others, like charismatic therapy, for the financial good of the "therapist." They are also quite limited. Exhortatory therapies may be able to provoke strong emotions, get people off their behinds, or modify certain discrete behaviours (some of which may be worthwhile accomplishments), but they can't help people to become adults.

Why can't exhortatory therapies facilitate the transition to adulthood? The reason is simple: In coercive therapies, the therapist is setting herself up as a parent to the person being treated, and from the vantage point of her superior wisdom, instructing him on how to live his life.

The person being treated, if he is compliant, may learn to conduct his life according to the therapist's notion of normalcy, but he can never achieve autonomy in this way. To the contrary, the exhortatory therapies impede the attainment of autonomy, and in so doing, actually postpone the person's transition to adulthood.

Exploratory Psychotherapy

Exploratory psychotherapies attempt to uncover the causes of a person's bad habits. They rely on an individual's own essential health and desire to change to steer him towards the acquisition of good habits. The uncovering psychotherapies (including psychoanalysis) depend for their success on the skill, knowledge and humanity of the therapist, and the motivation, flexibility and openness of the person being treated. They may provide some degree of support, encouragement, education, and even advice, but that is not their primary purpose, and they never, or very rarely, rely on coercion. Unlike exhortatory psychotherapy, exploratory psychotherapy *can* help the person being treated to become adult.

The exploratory therapies don't push the person being treated; they merely remove some of the debris impeding his forward progress. In contrast to the exhortatory therapies, they help increase his autonomy, thereby making him more adult. If, upon entering psychotherapy, the person is still pre-adult, then the process of exploring his bad habits will facilitate his transition to adulthood. If he's already adult, then exploratory psychotherapy will help him to extend his adult perspective into those areas that were excluded, by repression, from making the transition to adulthood. The bad habits that made sense to the person when they were initiated in childhood may no longer make sense to him when re-examined in adulthood. The exploratory psychotherapies thus help a person to adopt an adult perspective on his own habits and actions, and they allow him to consolidate an adult self-image.

Exploratory psychotherapy does, of course, have its limits.

For one thing, it's not particularly good at giving people motivation. If a person lacks the oomph to get going on his own, then exploration of his problems may not be of much use to him. In fact, when a person lacks drive, exhortation—by giving him a temporary shot in the arm—may be more helpful than insight. The therapist, in effect, lends her drive to the person being treated to help get him going. If the client then maintains his forward momentum, he will be in a much better position to make further changes on his own or with the help of exploratory psychotherapy.

TOWARDS A NEW DEFINITION OF OPTIMAL FUNCTIONING

Why is it important to know whether a particular psychotherapy has the potential to foster a person's transition to adulthood? Most people, after all, don't enter therapy explicitly wanting to become adult. They usually just want to be able to function optimally and without great distress.

The reason it's important is this: The primary and secondary traits of adulthood, taken together, constitute a pretty good definition of optimal functioning. Therefore, helping a pre-adult to become adult is really the same as helping her to function optimally. And since feeling like an adult is just the summation of most of the requisite traits of adulthood, we can use "feeling adult" as a proxy for "functioning optimally."

But if this is so—if feeling adult is equivalent to functioning optimally—then how do we account for those people who have made the transition to adulthood, but still have "bad habits"?

Let's say that the new tax partner at a law firm gets highly anxious each time she has to report to her senior partner. When she meets with clients, drafts briefs, or pleads cases before the tax courts, she is the picture of confidence. Yet whenever she has to meet with her old mentor to get his advice, she starts to stammer and breaks out in a rash.

Clearly, this lawyer is adult in almost all important respects. However, she has obviously retained one bad habit—the habit of seeing her senior partner as a critical parent—that undermines her feeling of being adult in that one situation.

If there are still bad habits left after the transition to adulthood has taken place, it means that the process itself has been incomplete. It means that some pre-adult components of the person's sense of self, quarantined by repression, have not participated in the process of becoming adult. These residual pre-adult self-images manifest themselves as bad habits. And because they are pre-adult, they conflict with the person's new adult sense of self. As a result, bad habits undermine the feeling of being adult.

The role of psychotherapy, in such a case, is to consolidate the transition to adulthood—to make sure that all the self-images that were left behind the first time round are subjected to scrutiny from an adult perspective and are integrated into an adult sense of self. More generally, therapy enables a person to stop being her parents' person and to start becoming her own person. By helping her to acquire, and then recognize in herself, a critical number of the primary and secondary traits of adulthood, therapy helps her form an adult identity. In most cases, once a person has undergone this transition to adulthood, she can move on from pursuing psychotherapy goals to achieving life goals, and from resolving inner conflicts to dealing with external reality.

HOW TO EVALUATE WHICH PSYCHO-THERAPIES ARE POTENTIALLY CURATIVE

If we accept that a "cure" in psychotherapy is the restoration of optimal functioning and that optimal functioning is the equivalent of feeling adult, then it ought to be possible to determine whether a particular kind of psychotherapy has the potential to be curative simply by figuring out whether it can foster the transition to adulthood. In other words, if it can help people to feel adult, then it can cure them of their bad habits. If it can't foster their transition to adulthood, then it's not even potentially curative. Therefore, on this basis, we ought to be able to eliminate all those therapies that are likely to be merely palliative or whose benefits would be ephemeral.

In general, treatments that help clear away obstacles to becoming adult are potentially curative. Those that don't, aren't. Therapies that encourage people to uncover past experiences and emotions, without fostering an adult perspective or interpretation, may be cathartic and emotionally satisfying, but they can't be curative. And therapies that teach people how to live, without allowing them to discover their own desires and aspirations, may be comforting and reassuring, but they can be of only limited benefit. In order to be considered curative, a therapy must promote the transition to adulthood.[1]

Clearly, the fact that a particular therapy has the potential to be curative doesn't mean that it will be curative. We can use our test only as a screening device to try to rule out therapies that are likely to thwart a person's maturation. To prove that a therapy is curative, we would have to test it out in a properly controlled clinical trial. But since most psychotherapies have not yet been subjected to rigorous clinical testing, and won't be any time soon, the following theoretical criteria and practical guidelines may have to suffice for narrowing the field or making a rational choice in the meantime.

Some of the Features Found in All Curative Psychotherapies

A therapy must have six critical features in order to be considered potentially curative.

1. RESPECT FOR REALITY

A curative therapy must be based on respect for reality. It can't foster illusions in the person—even flattering illusions, such as that he is brighter or more personable than he really is.

> One man tried to tell me, for example, that his two young children wouldn't be affected if he went abroad to study for two years. He was obviously kidding himself, and he wasn't going to be able to make the right decision about whether to go away to school until he faced this issue realistically. When he finally did so, he decided not to go away and tried to find a similar course locally.

2. RESPECT FOR THE TRUTH

A curative therapy must have respect for the truth. It must allow the person being treated to discover for herself which of her memories and perceptions are accurate, and which are not. It is incumbent on the therapist, therefore, to create an atmosphere in which the truth can emerge. He needs to be open-minded but not credulous, probing but not coercive, and respectful of the stories that people tell him, but respectful also of the principles of logic and reason. He should never pander to people's prejudices about themselves, their parents or the world; and he should never be lazy about confronting his own prejudices either.

Many people enter therapy with preconceptions about how their parents treated them when they were children. Sometimes these preconceptions are confirmed, but sometimes they aren't.

A young woman who was very angry at her mother told me that, one summer while she was away at camp, her mother had put the family dog to sleep because she didn't want the hassle of having to look after it. Although she never confronted her mother about this disturbing incident, it loomed large in her mind as evidence of her mother's cruelty.

One day while trying to convince her younger sister of her mother's cruelty, she decided to tell her the story.

"Don't you remember the summer I came home from camp, and mother had put Barney to sleep because he was peeing all over the carpets?" she asked.

"What are you talking about?" her sister replied. "I was home that summer. Barney was hit by a car, chasing a squirrel into the street. The vet told mother that he was badly hurt and had to be put out of his misery. Mother was heartbroken about it. She didn't tell you about it until after camp was over, because she didn't want it to ruin your summer."

3. RESPECT FOR EQUALITY

In a curative therapy, the therapist must respect the person she's treating as an equal, not in the sense of having equal psychological knowledge or skill, but in the sense of being another human being trying to deal with life's complexity. The relationship between therapist and patient or client should never be based on dominance and submission.

Therapy does not rely on a tacit agreement that the therapist is strong and omnipotent, and that the person being treated is weak or ignorant. The therapist must acknowledge the potential adultness of the people she treats. And in so doing, she must allow them not only to succeed in therapy, but to fail in therapy as well.

4. RESPECT FOR HEROISM

A curative therapy must recognize the person's capacity not just for health, but even, occasionally, for heroism. Heroism is never to be expected, of course, nor is it a therapeutic goal, but it must be permitted within a therapy. Occasionally a person will surpass his own expectations and accomplish something wonderful. He must be allowed to transcend not only his own limitations, but the therapist's limitations and the limitations of the therapy as well. Human potential should never be subordinated to therapeutic ideology. It is acceptable to analyze exceptional actions, but only if that analysis does not imply that the exceptional is pathological.

A nineteen-year-old student with severe diabetes was referred to me because he was having difficulties at school. He was very juvenile-looking and still played with children who were twelve and thirteen years of age. He had no real interest in school and spent most of his time reading comic books and watching television.

When he first came to see me, he was sullen and unwilling to talk. But when I asked him what he wanted to do after he graduated, he began to perk up. He told me that he wanted to be a cartoonist or possibly a comedian. His drawings, however, were crude and unimaginative, and I began to wonder whether he was incapable of being realistic about his limitations and whether he'd ever be able to make something of himself.

One day, as promised, he brought me a five-minute tape of himself performing his own routine on amateur night at a comedy club. He turned on the tape and I got myself prepared to laugh politely. But I didn't laugh politely—I laughed genuinely. His material and presentation were not only hilarious, they were clever and unusual. He totally surprised me, and I told him so.

This unremarkable-looking young man had failed at everything ordinary he'd ever tried. But at the one extraordinary thing he tried, he succeeded brilliantly.

Unfortunately, two weeks after this wonderful moment, he was discovered by his father dead of an insulin coma. This sad news made me glad that he'd had his moment in the sun and grateful that, despite my doubts, I had never discouraged him from pursuing his exceptional dream.

5. RESPECT FOR AUTONOMY

A curative therapy must permit autonomy in the person being treated, and preferably foster it. Many people, despite vociferous protests to the contrary, do not actually want to be autonomous of their therapist. This desire to be dependent must be analyzed as a resistance to growing up, not catered to or colluded with as a way of meeting the therapist's desire to feel needed or important. For example, if a patient or client wants to call her therapist regularly to discuss issues that could wait until the next therapy session, then she should be told to call only on urgent matters, and her desire to treat the therapist as her friend should be explored.

Because the goal of therapy ought to be the fulfilment of potential, not merely the attainment of normality, a curative therapy values autonomy more highly than normalcy. The therapist is not a god who can determine right from wrong as it applies to the person he's treating. The patient or client must learn to trust her own perceptions and judgments—even if they sometimes turn out to be mistaken—because there is no superior criterion on which she can base her actions. She can consult other people, but in making important decisions that affect her own life—such as whether to get married or quit a job—she must ultimately rely on her own gut feelings. The more important the decision, the more important is autonomy in making it.

The person must determine for herself what her true feelings are. Therapy should provide her with a forum in which she can explore her feelings, their origins and history, so that she can gain a greater conviction about them, but it should almost never advise her on how to act. As her self-knowledge and conviction grow, her feelings will become more reliable as guides to action. They will become less ambiguous and less fraught with conflict. And they will acquire greater authenticity and become more autonomous of undue influence.

> A man in his late twenties came to see me in a quandary because he couldn't fall in love with a woman he knew was perfect for him. She had everything he wanted in a mate, but she didn't excite him. He was sure that he was neurotic and wanted to be told to have a relationship with her for his own good. But I couldn't do that. I told him that his feelings about this wonderful woman might be "neurotic," but that, rather than trying to circumvent them, he had better respect them and try to understand them.
>
> He did eventually come to understand why this woman didn't excite him, but he still didn't feel anything for her other than affection, and he ended their relationship. Many months later, he met someone just as appropriate as the first woman, but someone who excited him and with whom he was able to fall in love.

6. RESPECT FOR LIMITS

A curative therapy must have limits. It must follow certain rules, and it must come to an end. Therapy is not an adjunct to living, or a substitute for it; therapy is a procedure for helping eliminate impediments to growth and the fulfilment of potential. If a therapy is not terminable, then it can't produce a grownup. It's not a therapy at all in that case, but a life-style.

This doesn't mean that there is a specific time limit on a good exploratory psychotherapy. It just means that therapy should endeavour to do only what Freud himself recommended—replace the patient's neurotic misery with common unhappiness. Any therapy that aims to cure common unhappiness is, by definition, interminable.

HOW DOES EXPLORATORY PSYCHOTHERAPY WORK?

We know that exploratory psychotherapy lowers the barrier to achieving an adult sense of self by correcting distortions and misapprehensions that developed when the person was not yet mature enough to recognize them. But how does therapy work? What are its underlying premises?

All psychotherapies take for granted two aspects of human nature: Our innate desire for psychological health, and our innate capacity to act rationally once we understand our options.

Exploratory psychotherapies assume two further premises: that behaviour is motivated, and that insight is therapeutic.

The first premise—that all behaviour is motivated by impulses originating within us—is surprisingly radical. It is the basis of our belief that people are capable of becoming autonomous, and it implies that almost nothing we do is done without a purpose. This view—that behaviour is motivated—is partly empirical and partly philosophical. We could as easily say that all actions are produced by God, or happen by accident, or are produced in direct reaction to something our parents did to us when we were very small. But the view that behaviour is motivated says that everything we do is initiated and mediated by us.

This means we have to take responsibility for the actions we are free to instigate. It doesn't mean we're responsible for our actions in the silly way implied by the statements, "Well, if that meteorite fell out of the sky and bopped you on the head, you must take responsibility for it," or "If you are paralyzed with fear about getting into an elevator, you're just not trying hard enough," or (to someone suffering from a serious clinical depression) "You should just stop feeling sorry for yourself and pull up your socks." Clearly, there are many behaviours that we really have no conscious control over. Nor do I think we are responsible for actions taken under duress or when we're ill. We are responsible for our actions precisely to the extent that they are *truly* motivated—that they have their origins in our own wishes, desires and fears.

The second premise underlying exploratory psychotherapy is that understanding our motives and limits enables us to choose how we wish to act. In other words, insight—self-understand-ing—allows us to make choices about how we want to live instead of reflexively repeating old patterns.

The liberating process of insight works something like this:

You become conscious of some emotion that you don't understand—for instance, that you get anxious each time you're about to go into a business meeting. Throughout the meeting your anxiety grows. By the time your boss finally gets around to calling on you, you fumble your presenta-tion and do less than your usual competent job of explain-ing things.

Later that week in therapy—by the process of self-analysis—you discover why you felt anxious in the meet-ing: It reminded you of a piano recital that you flubbed when you were nine years old. You recall that after the recital, your father couldn't look you straight in the eye. He didn't want to show his disappointment, but you knew how he felt anyway. You felt sorrier for him than you did for yourself. And now, in retrospect, you feel angry at him for making you responsible for fulfilling his dreams.

At the next meeting, you notice yourself starting to become anxious again, but this time you remind yourself that your anxiety has nothing to do with the present situa-tion—it has to do with your fear of your father's disap-pointment—and your presentation goes more smoothly. (You might not remember until afterwards, in the privacy of your own office, precisely what it was that made you anxious; you may only remember that it had nothing directly to do with the present situation and something to do with the past.)

Thereafter, each time this meeting anxiety occurs, you become aware of it a little bit earlier. Soon you can antici-pate getting anxious before the meeting has even taken place. By the time you have to make your presentation, you've already managed to calm yourself down. With each successive opportunity for self-analysis, you get closer to fully understanding the causes of your anxiety. Finally, it ceases to be an issue for you at all.

Exploratory Psychotherapy Is Both
Progressive and Regressive

Exploratory psychotherapy helps us to recognize patterns of reflexive behaviour that may have been appropriate historically, but that aren't appropriate now. Once we have some emotional distance from that experience—once we're no longer in its thrall—we're in a better position to distinguish between current reality and neurotic misperceptions of the past. And since most events can be anticipated, or at least occur over an extended period of time, we gradually learn to intervene with freer, less reflexive behaviour before the event takes place, or at least while it's still happening.

In other words, this kind of therapy is both *progressive* (in that it facilitates the process of growing up), and *regressive* (in that it seeks to look at the past—although this time from an adult perspective). Exploratory psychotherapy requires both components—the progressive and the regressive—to be complete.

When all is said and done, psychotherapy is a modest undertaking. The person being treated doesn't have to be especially smart; the therapist doesn't have to be especially charismatic or eloquent. The person being treated doesn't need to make a leap of faith; the therapist doesn't need to make a persuasive case. The only requirement is honesty—both intellectual and emotional.

The Ring of Truth

Psychotherapy isn't propaganda, it's interpretation. Therapists shouldn't try to indoctrinate the people they're treating; they should try to appeal to their understanding. The validity of an interpretation doesn't depend on how authoritative the therapist is; it depends on how well the insight resonates with the patient's or client's experience. A good interpretation will make sense to him, though not necessarily right away. It will make his experiences seem more coherent, integrated and sensible. It will ring true.

Does it matter then whether an insight is actually true, or is it enough that we believe it to be true? Does truth make a difference to outcome? For example, will you feel better merely by *believing* that your symptoms of meeting anxiety were caused by the piano recital débâcle, whether or not they really were, or does the explanation have to be true? Can a plausible fiction, in other words, be as therapeutic as a probable reality?

I would like to believe that discovering the "true" cause of a neurotic reflex is therapeutically important, but I'm not sure that it is—at least not at a superficial level. The reason for my doubt is this: In everyday clinical practice, truth is more elusive than symptomatic relief. People seem to *feel* better long before they really *know* better—which leads me to suspect that symptomatic improvement may be due, at least in part, to the degree of conviction the patient and therapist have about an insight. And, often, the degree of conviction they develop will depend on what's considered psychologically relevant according to the current *zeitgeist*.

In one era, working mothers will be denounced as the source of all social and psychological ills; in the next era, shaming parents or dysfunctional families or absent fathers or broken homes will be targeted. Sometimes mothers will be seen as the culprits, sometimes fathers, and sometimes social pressures. At one moment nurture will be in ascendence, and, in the next moment, nature. Both therapists and the people they're treating are inclined to pluck their interpretations from what's currently in the air. They are unconsciously pre-programmed to believe some things and to reject others—whether or not those things are "actually" true or relevant. And in any era, interpretations that blame other people for a problem are generally greeted with more enthusiasm and credence than interpretations that ascribe responsibility to the person with the complaint.

Everyone knows that objective truth and subjective truth aren't always the same. But does that excuse us from *trying* to discover the objective facts if we can? And will it make any difference to the outcome of a person's therapy if we *do* discover the objective truth? I believe that it will. For example, sorting out whether a person was actually kidnapped by aliens or only dreamt it, or whether he was fired from his job because he was short and overweight or because he was incompetent, will make a great deal of difference. Because if he ends up believing that he really was kidnapped by aliens or fired because of his physique, he will have to live his life in fear and outside the reality of other people. But if he comes to the conclusion that he only imagined that he was kidnapped by aliens or that he was fired because of incompetence, then he will be able to live his life without those fears and inside the reality of other people.

Luckily, the thing that saves most people from accepting false interpretations of their feelings and memories is the fact that most false interpretations ultimately feel false. In other words, they're able to detect a difference in comfort between the subjective beliefs that they hold based on objective facts, and the subjective beliefs that they hold based on misperceptions of objective facts or on outright falsehoods. The beliefs based on facts feel different from the beliefs based on misperceptions. A child's fear of the witch in Snow White, for example, feels different to him than the fear of real killers he hears about on TV, or the fear he has of bullies at school, or of his father when he's angry. And since insights that aren't grounded in some objective reality also lack the ring of truth, they don't ultimately find favour even with those who might initially want to believe them.

The reverse of this axiom, however—that interpretations that *feel* true *are* true—doesn't hold quite so firmly. Insights that feel true can very easily be false. In fact, people in therapy often receive bogus insights with great enthusiasm, in my experience, especially if those insights involve criticism of their parents. The reason for this love of the ersatz is that, even though the person in therapy consciously wants to change and will eventually do so, his unconscious psyche wants to perpetuate the status quo as long as it can. It wants to preserve all the old prejudices and inclinations just the way they were. By leading the patient or client away from anything really disturbing, false insights allow him to maintain his psychic arrangements essentially undisturbed. True insights, because they lead to the heart of his conflicts, threaten to overturn his psychic apple cart and upset the status quo. But since most people's apple carts contain one or more rotten apples, overturning it may be the only way to rid the psyche of its rotten fruit and preserve the health of the rest of it.

In most people, fortunately, the desire to get healthy is stronger than the desire to retain the status quo. Therefore, after they've been in therapy for a while, they lose their enthusiasm for false interpretations and want to hear the truth. If their therapist respects the truth, they're on their way. But if their therapist is wedded to some faddish theory or has some axe of her own to grind, then the person she's treating may never really understand himself. A gay man I know, for instance, stopped talking to his mother for several years because a therapist convinced him that homosexuality was the result of maternal domination. It was only when he was out of therapy—when he finally had the chance to examine his own memories honestly, free of his therapist's preconceptions—that he was able to arrive at the truth: that his sexual orientation had nothing to do with her.

What then can we conclude about the therapeutic importance of truth? Just this: Truth may not be important for merely feeling better, but it is important for actually *being* better.

The Therapeutic Relationship in Psychotherapy

The biggest psychological obstacle to becoming adult that a pre-adult usually has to overcome is her childish relationship with her parents. She insists on seeing them unrealistically, the way she wants to see them—endowed with magical powers to punish and redeem. She's afraid to adjust her perceptions, to reconstruct her tie to them, and to make her own way in the world.

When a person enters psychotherapy, she often transfers to the therapist the strong feelings she has towards her parents. This is called transference. She sees her therapist as like her parents in some ways, but unlike them in other ways. And it is this difference that permits her to examine her transference feelings with objectivity. It reassures her that her therapist is on her side and on the side of truth, and that he has no other agenda. If the therapist were actually like the person's parents, then it would be impossible for the person to step back and look at her old perceptions with fresh eyes, or to trust the therapist's interpretations of those perceptions.

So powerful are the re-enactments of these parent-child relationships within psychotherapy that, at times, the therapist may actually feel and act like the person's parents. These moments of "countertransference" can be the occasions for a startling therapeutic breakthrough, or, if unrecognized, the beginnings of a stifling therapeutic stalemate.

For example, some therapists find it so gratifying or threatening to be envied or idealized by the people they're treating, that they begin to take these feelings personally and forget the fact that these feelings have their origins in the person's own needs and prior relationships. Instead of helping the person to discover the roots of her transference, the therapist will deflate the person's opinion of him to avoid feeling guilty.

Martine was a first-time mother in her late twenties who was in psychotherapy with a well-trained psychiatric social worker in her middle forties. Martine had all the normal insecurities and questions that new mothers have about raising children, and she looked to her therapist for reassurance and expertise.

Because her therapist was warm and maternal, Martine naturally assumed that she was a great mother and would have a lot to teach her. What she couldn't know, of course, was that her therapist was having trouble at the time with her teenage daughter, and that she was in the middle of questioning her own ability as a parent. When Martine began to treat her therapist as a surrogate mother and child-care expert, it made her feel inadequate and ashamed.

At first the therapist tried to deflate Martine's idealization of her by pointing out that she wasn't an expert in child development and that Martine ought to consult her pediatrician. But when Martine continued to idealize her anyway, the therapist decided to examine the roots of her own discomfort as a mother so that it wouldn't interfere with the therapy. She rightly concluded that deflating Martine's idealization would be self-serving and anti-therapeutic.

Because the therapist wisely allowed Martine's idealizing transference to unfold undisturbed, they were both eventually able to understand it. They recognized that Martine was idealizing the therapist in order to provide herself with a role model to take the place of her disappointing mother.

The feelings that the person in therapy has towards her therapist have both subjective and objective components. The subjective component is made up of the feelings that she's transferred from her earlier relationship with her parents and other important people; the objective component is made up of the more realistic perceptions that she has of her parents, her therapist, and herself. The subjective perceptions are older in origin and more tinged with unresolved sentiments such as fear, longing, antagonism, idealization and scorn; the objective perceptions are more recent in origin and less tinged with conflict.

Therapy then is a microcosmic laboratory in which the person examines the subjective component of her relationships (with her parents, spouse, employer, therapist, etc.) in light of the objective component. As she performs this experiment in reality-testing—comparing as best she can her subjective beliefs about people to the objective reality about them—her understanding of the important people in her life (and of herself) becomes more realistic. In the process, she is liberated from her childish relationship with her parents and freed to make the psychological transition to adulthood.

Ashley, for example, had always had a hard time getting along with women bosses at work, so when she decided to enter therapy, she chose to do so with a woman. And, as expected, Ashley soon began to have trouble getting along with her as well. She accused her therapist of looking down on her and of being condescending, and she began to feel envious of her therapist's position, income and style.

The therapist was tempted to point out to Ashley that she didn't make as much money as Ashley imagined and to reassure her that she wasn't looking down at her at all, but she decided to ask Ashley what those feelings reminded her of instead.

"It reminds me of when I was eleven and I came downstairs to dinner wearing one of my mother's evening dresses, her jewellery and make-up, and my mother got absolutely furious at me," she replied after some thought. "I really wasn't expecting that reaction. I thought it was kind of funny, and so did my dad, but my mother was really upset that I'd taken her stuff without her permission. She had so few nice things."

This led to many sessions in which Ashley recalled various aspects of her relationship with her mother and father. She realized that she envied her mother and was jealous of her mother's relationship with her father. But she also felt sorry for her mother because her father put her mother down and sided with Ashley in their disputes. She eventually recognized that she was transferring many of the same feelings of envy, mistrust and pity onto the more senior women at work, as well as onto her therapist, and that those feelings were misplaced and inappropriate.

In order for a person in therapy to be able to transfer her feelings about her parents onto the therapist, she has to have the capacity to be vulnerable, to trust the therapist, and to be self-analytical. She also needs either enough objectivity at the outset of therapy to perceive the differences between her therapist and her parents, or enough trust in her parents to permit her to trust the therapist.

The success of exploratory psychotherapy depends to a considerable extent on the person being treated. Some people can't accept the frustration of not having their emotional demands met by their therapist. They get disappointed if the therapist gives them what they need—insight and objectivity—instead of what they want—admiration and love. There are even people who, when faced with this necessary frustration, will deliberately subvert their own therapy, wrecking their relationship with the therapist merely from spite.

But if their disappointment and spite can be analyzed and the therapy salvaged, they may be presented with a unique opportunity to make a breakthrough. They may gain fresh insight into their early frustrations with their parents and, by virtue of the fact that the therapist has handled these frustrations differently from their parents, be helped to accept the rewards and renunciations of adulthood.

Not everything that goes on in therapy is transference. Most of what goes on, especially when the therapy is not a pure psychoanalysis, has to do with the person's life as she is currently leading it. A forced preoccupation with the transference, whether instigated by the therapist or the person being treated, can actually be used as a defence against looking at the person's everyday life. In fact, it's only when she reports thoughts and feelings that are on the surface of her consciousness—thoughts and feelings that have been triggered by recent events—that fresh and emotionally meaningful connections with the past can be made. Forced attempts to recount past calamities are usually boring to the person being treated and reveal little about her that isn't already pre-digested and stale.

The same thing happens when a person enters therapy having already made up her mind about what caused her problems. Although her formulation—generally cobbled together from a grab-bag of pop-psych clichés—may contain a kernel of truth, it more often than not contains a silo full of self-deceit and rationalization. In order for the psychotherapeutic partnership to be successful, the therapist and the person he's treating must have respect for each other. And in order for the psychotherapy to be successful, both must have respect for the truth.

CHAPTER TEN

BECOMING ADULT IS AN ACT OF CREATION

This above all: to thine own self be true,
And it must follow, as the night the day,
Thou canst not then be false to any man.

Hamlet
Act I, Scene 3, 78–80
William Shakespeare

The transition to adulthood is a watershed. On the pre-adult side of it, you are your parents' child; on the adult side of it, you are your own person. It is just that simple. And just that complex too—because being your parents' child and being your own person are not simple opposites. Being your own person is not merely the negation of whatever you were before you became adult—being your own person is a declaration of faith in yourself. It is a positive achievement, a discovery and an act of creation.

The positive achievement is all the work you do and all the experiences you have during pre-adulthood that prepare you to handle being adult. It is the development of competence across a broad range of categories from work to sex to morality; it is the assumption of responsibility, first for yourself and then for other people; it is the development of a new relationship with your parents—and thus with all other adults—that is based on equality and mutual respect; and it is the recognition of your dependence on, and obligation to, the civilization you share with all other people—the sense of empowerment that permits you to undertake your social rights and responsibilities.

The discovery is the crisis you experience as you approach the summit that divides pre-adulthood from adulthood. It is the pain and disappointment you feel when you realize that, despite your many positive achievements, you won't be able to accomplish all of your fondest hopes and dreams. It is the crisis created by the collision of fantasy and reality, the moment of truth when you have to dig deep down within yourself to muster the strength and courage and faith you need to climb to the top of the great divide and face the transition to adulthood. It is tempting to stay on the pre-adult side of the watershed—to stay where you once felt comfortable and secure, and where you can still look up at the stars and dream impossible dreams—but you can't do that, because you no longer belong there. Staying pre-adult when you ought to be adult is too humiliating and painful to bear. There are generations below you scrambling to make the summit too. They crowd you and push you and remind you that you can never stop moving forward until the day you die. And there is also the sun peeking over the crest of the mountain you've been climbing, beckoning you towards the promise and pleasures of adulthood that lie on the other side.

So you shoulder your burdens, take stock of your opportunities, confront your limitations, and cross the watershed to the adult side. And that is where the act of creation begins. Because once you accept the fact that you have to grow up, once you stop dreaming of ultimate happiness and awaken to the possibility of real happiness, once you stop preparing for life and begin living it, and once you embrace all that adulthood has to offer— love, pain and the whole damn thing—then you can no longer rely on anyone else to show you the way. You have to rely on yourself.

Adulthood is the time when you actually fulfil your potential, when the accumulated energy of your mind—the mainspring that you've been winding up bit by bit throughout your childhood and adolescence—is finally released in concerted action. It is the time when you find your own voice and deserve to have it heard, produce things and reap the rewards, accomplish your goals and enjoy your life—but *really* enjoy your life, because you've earned it.

Most important, adulthood is the time when you truly become your own person. It is the time when you come to grips with who you really are, who you want to be, and who you can be—and then become it.

Once you've reached this point, there is only one other thing you need to become an adult.

A spark.

BIBLIOGRAPHY

Bowlby, J. 1973. *Separation Anxiety and Anger.* New York: Basic Books, Inc./Harper Colophon Books.

Erikson, Erik H. 1963. *Childhood and Society.* New York: W.W. Norton & Company, Inc.

Erikson, Erik H. 1968. *Identity Youth and Crisis.* New York: W.W. Norton & Company, Inc.

Freud, S. 1893-5. *Studies On Hysteria.* Standard Edition. II. London: The Hogarth Press.

Freud, S. 1916. *Some Character-types Met With in Psycho-analytic Work.* Standard Edition. XIV. London: The Hogarth Press.

Freud, S. 1930. *Civilization and Its Discontents.* Standard Edition. XXI. London: The Hogarth Press.

Fukuyama, Francis. 1992. *The End of History and the Last Man.* New York: The Free Press.

Kuhn, Thomas S. 1970. *The Structure of Scientific Revolutions.* Chicago: The University of Chicago Press.

Naipaul, V.S. 1984. *A House for Mr. Biswas.* New York: Vintage Books.

Roth, Philip. 1988. *The Facts: A Novelist's Autobiography.* New York: Farrar, Straus & Giroux.

Watson, T. J., Jr., and Petre, P. 1990. *Father Son & Co.: My Life at IBM and Beyond.* New York: Bantam Books.

ENDNOTES

Chapter Three: The Three Primary Traits of Adulthood

1 V. S. Naipaul, *A House For Mr. Biswas* (New York: Vintage Books, 1984), p. 2.

2 Ibid, p. 5.

3 T. J. Watson, Jr., and P. Petre, *Father Son & Co. My Life at IBM and Beyond* (New York: Bantam Books, 1990), p. viii.

4 For a full discussion of separation anxiety, see J. Bowlby, *Separation Anxiety and Anger* (New York: Basic Books, Inc./Harper Colophon Books, 1973).

Chapter Four: The Twelve Secondary Traits of Adulthood

1 In this section, I am using the feminine pronoun to refer to the parent and the masculine to refer to the child because the phenomenon of over-identification is more common among mothers than among fathers, especially when the child is very young. However, parents of either sex are capable of over-identifying with their children and of using them to meet their own unmet needs.

Chapter Five: What Do You Have to Give Up to Become an Adult?

1 Erik H. Erikson, *Identity Youth and Crisis* (New York: W.W. Norton & Company, Inc., 1968), p. 143.

2 S. Freud, *Some Character-types Met With in Psycho-analytic Work.* (I) The 'exceptions.' Standard Edition. (London: The Hogarth Press, 1916), pp. 311–315.

Chapter Seven: Becoming Adult by Word and Deed

1 James Watson, quoted by Stephen S. Hall from a speech given at Cold Spring Harbor Laboratory, March 1–3, 1993. *Science*, Vol. 259, March 12, 1993, p. 1533.

Chapter Eight: Becoming Adult in Heart and Mind

1 Paraphrasing Plato in *The Republic*, Francis Fukuyama labels this "desire to be desired by other [people]" as *thymos*. He says "human beings seek recognition of their own worth, or of the people, things, or principles that they invest with [value]." He believes it is *thymos* that drives people to demand their rights. Francis Fukuyama, *The End of History and the Last Man* (New York: The Free Press, 1992), p. xvii.

Perhaps *thymos*—"the desire to be desired by other [people]"—is a derivative of the love a child feels for the parent of the same sex—the negative Oedipus complex. In the same way the resolution of the positive Oedipus complex impels a person towards the seeking of a mate, the resolution of the negative Oedipus complex might impel him towards love for his fellow humans and the desire to be loved by them in return. This would be another mechanism by which the final resolution of the Oedipus complex promotes the shift to adulthood.

Chapter Nine: The Role of Psychotherapy in Becoming Adult

1 In psychoanalytic terms, promoting the transition to adulthood is the same thing as resolving the Oedipus complex once and for all. (See Chapter Eight, Becoming Adult in Heart and Mind, "The Transition to Adulthood," p. 253.) The ego and superego, which before the transition to adulthood were dominated by Oedipally determined images of the self and of other people, after the transition to adulthood become dominated by more realistic—in other words, more adult—images of the self and of the world. The final resolution of the Oedipus complex, therefore, is the psychoanalytic definition of cure.

INDEX